BETWEEN
GRASS AND
SKY

Environmental
Arts and Humanities Series
Series Editor / Scott Slovic

LINDA M. HASSELSTROM

BETWEEN GRASS AND SKY

WHERE I LIVE AND WORK

University of Nevada Press

Reno & Las Vegas

University of Nevada Press, Reno, Nevada 89557 USA
Copyright © 2002 by Linda M. Hasselstrom
Manufactured in the United States of America
Design by Omega Clay

Library of Congress Cataloging-in-Publication Data
Hasselstrom, Linda M.
  Between grass and sky : where I live and work / Linda M. Hasselstrom.
    p. cm. — (Environmental arts and humanities series)
  ISBN 0-87417-522-4 (hardcover: alk. paper)
  ISBN 0-87417-627-1 (pbk.: alk. paper)
  1. Hasselstrom, Linda M.—Homes and haunts—South Dakota. 2. Poets,
American—20th century—Biography. 3. Women ranchers—South Dakota—
Biography. 4. Natural history—South Dakota. 5. Ranch life—South Dakota.
6. South Dakota—Biography. I. Title. II. Series.
  PS3558.A7257 Z4636 2002
  818'.5409—dc21   2002004786

The paper used in this book meets the requirements of American National
Standard for Information Sciences—Permanence of Paper for Printed
Library Materials, ANSI Z39.48-1984. Binding materials were
selected for strength and durability.

University of Nevada Press Paperback Edition, 2005

14 13 12 11 10 09 08 07 06 05   5 4 3 2 1

Dedicated to my mother (1909–2001), who taught me to love reading, though she did not realize where it would lead me. She tried to appreciate my books in lieu of grandchildren, and I thank her for her efforts.

Contents

Acknowledgments

I thank Scott Slovic for suggesting this book, for believing it would be worthwhile, and for insightful suggestions; thanks to Trudy McMurrin for persisting in its acquisition, and to John Mulvihill for his precise work in helping me say what I meant. Thanks to Julie A. Johnson, and others before her, for directing me to the writings of Rainer Maria Rilke.

All previously published essays have been revised since first publication:

A short version of "From Rancher to Nature Writer" appeared in "The Rise of Nature Writing: America's Next Great Genre?" *Mānoa* 4, no. 2 (fall 1992): 84–86. Sources for quotations in this introductory essay are: John Murray, "The Rise of Nature Writing: America's Next Great Genre?" *Mānoa* 4, no. 2 (fall 1992): 73–74; Rainer Maria Rilke, *Rilke's Book of Hours: Love Poems to God,* translated by Anita Barrows and Joanna Macy (New York: Riverhead Books, 1996), I, 2, p. 48; Wendell Berry, *The Long-Legged House* (New York: Harcourt, Brace & World, 1969), 149. Tom Lyon, ed., *This Incomperable Lande: A Book of American Nature Writing* (Boston: Houghton Mifflin, 1989), 74; Joyce Carol Oates, "Against Nature," *Antaeus* 57 (autumn 1986): 236. Also in *(Woman) Writer: Occasions and Opportunities* (New York: Dutton, 1988), 66–76.

"Learning to See the Unseen." Published as "Finally Learning to See the Unseen" in "The Home Forum," *Christian Science Monitor,* 1 May 1995, p. 17.

"Whirlaway," *High Country News,* 23 December 1985: 16.

"Making Hay," *South Dakota Magazine,* July/August 1998: 70–76. "Haying: A Four-Part Definition." First published in *Caught By One Wing* (Holcomb, 1984; reprinted by Spoon River Poetry Press, 1990; reprinted in *Dakota Bones: The Collected Poems of Linda Hasselstrom* (Spoon River Poetry Press, 1993), 36–37.

"Out to Pasture," *South Dakota Magazine,* January/February 1996: 24–27.

"The Owl on the Fence," *Western American Literature* 30, no. 1 (May 1995): 29–36.

"The Pot of Hospitality Still Simmers." First published as "Brewing the Pot of Hospitality" in "The Home Forum," *Christian Science Monitor,* 18 October 1990, p. 16. Syndicated through *Christian Science Monitor,* reprinted as "There's More to Potluck than Just the Meal" in *Washington Post,* 3 January 1991, p. 11. Reprinted as "Prairie Potlucks: Our Idea of a Dinner Party," *South Dakota Magazine,* September/October 1995: 64–66.

"The Totally Integrated Crawly Kingdom," *New Letters* 58, no. 1 (fall 1991): 49–54. The quotation on "Lyme anxiety" comes from Gina Kolata, "Lyme Disease Is Hard to Catch and Easy to Halt, Study Finds," www.nytimes.com, 13 June 2001.

"The Duck in the Highway Department," *South Dakota Magazine,* May/June 1996: 73–76.

"Running with the Antelope" (published as "Antelope Hunt"), *Northern Lights* 11, no. 4 (May 1996): 23–28. An early version of "Antelope Hunt" appeared as fiction in *Free Passage,* no. 8 (August 1979).

"Sleeping with the Grizzly," *Mānoa* 8, no. 1 (summer 1996): 130–38.

"The Second Half of Life," *Northern Lights* 11, no. 3 (winter 1996): 17–18.

"Cattle Ranching in South Dakota." Parts of this essay were first published as "The Rancher-Environmentalist Feuding Should End" in *High Country News,* 9 July 1984: 15, and "Who Cares for the Land?" in *South Dakota Magazine,* September/October 1991: 33–35. The list of Green political goals in this essay originally appeared in *New Internationalist* in May 1987, and was excerpted in *Utne Reader,* September/October 1987: 32–33. Edmund Burke (1729–1797) was an Irish-born British Whig statesman and political philosopher. "Why Giving Up Meat Won't Save the Planet," syndicated by Writers on the Range as "Ranchers: America's Original Organic Farmers," published by the *(Moab, Utah) Times-Independent,* 2 October 1997, p. A8. Quotations are from "Meat from Diseased Animals Approved for Consumers," written by Lance Gay and circulated by Scripps Howard News Service, 14 July 2000.

"The Cow Is My Totem." Broadcast 7 and 21 April 1991, by *Facing West,* radio program for *Western Historical Quarterly.* First published in *Writers on the Range: West-*

ern Writers Exploring the Changing Face of the American West, ed. Karl Hess Jr. and John A. Baden (University Press of Colorado, 1998), 55–68. Additional information on the varied uses of cows can be found in Verlyn Klinkenborg's essay "Cow Parts," in *Discover,* August 2001: 57–62.

"Waddling over the Dam," *South Dakota Magazine,* January/February 1999: 45–50.

"Rising from the Condos." First published as "Rising from the Condos: Community Land Trust and Longtime Residents Team Up to Ensure Affordable Housing in Jackson, Wyoming" in *Chronicle of Community* 2, no. 3 (spring 1998): 5–16. Sources of information about preserving open space include the following: Institute for Community Economics, *The Community Land Trust Handbook* (Emmaus, Pa.: Rodale Press, 1982); Stephen J. Small, *Preserving Family Lands: Essential Tax Strategies for the Landowner* (Boston: Landowner Planning Center, 1992); *Conservation Options: A Landowner's Guide* (Washington, D.C.: Land Trust Alliance, 1993); *Protecting Land for Wildlife* (Washington, D.C.: Humane Society of the U.S.); Frederic O. Sargent et al., *Rural Environmental Planning for Sustainable Communities* (Covelo, Calif.: Island Press, 1991); and William H. Whyte, *Securing Open Space for Urban America: Conservation Easements* (Washington, D.C.: Urban Land Institute, 1959).

"Walking Burial Grounds," *South Dakota Review* 33, no. 1 (spring 1995): 114–20.

INTRODUCTION

FROM RANCHER TO NATURE WRITER

I

When I was nine years old, in 1952, my mother married a western South Dakota rancher. As a rancher's daughter, I immediately became a working cowhand, learning to spend each day outside, immersed in grasslands that showed little obvious evidence of human habitation. My labor became important, a contribution to my family's living.

Even as a child, I carried little notebooks in my pockets and noted down interesting things: how an antelope stamped his feet and whistled when my father and I rode by on our horses; how a meadowlark dragged her wing and whimpered when we got near her nest. In the evenings, I'd write in my journal about these events, and about the work we did. So, after helping to save a cow's life, I reflected in writing about the experience. By writing, I responded to, and tried to create order in, a new world, a childish version of trying to balance that cow's quality of life, and my own, with the rights of the wildlife sharing the range.

By the time I'd gotten an M.A. and returned to the ranch, I was describing myself as a Rancher/Slash/Writer. Feeding and caring for the cattle was my first priority. At night, I wrote poems and essays, trying to explain the theories and operations of ranching to people who sincerely believe cows are incompatible with wildlife on western grasslands.

When I read, both as relaxation and as study for my writing job, I began to realize that many writers and readers think of nature with a capital N. My first impulse, I am chagrined to admit, was laughter. What some folks call Nature is to me both home and office. Nature is my boss, manager of the branch office—or ranch office—where I toil to convert native grass into meat, neatly packaged in leather for sale to increasingly finicky consumers. I may grumble about the old gal over coffee, I may deplore her unfairness, but if I want to keep my job, as well as my home, I pay attention not only to Nature's orders, but also to her moods and whims.

When I first realized that most people see nature differently than I do, I looked on their definitions with narrow mistrust. An environmentalist, I suspected, must define nature as a sacred zoo, a collection of inert and untouchable plants and animals with no more reality than color close-ups on the wide screen in the living room. Conversely, people who enjoyed "four-wheeling" must see nature as a pile of rocks and dirt arranged as a test for roll bars and fat tires, or rocks and trees as a backdrop for target practice on cans and bottles they leave behind after blowing them to smithereens. To joggers, I guessed, the natural world is a smooth asphalt trail winding past nonthreatening critters and nontoxic plants. I relished folks with whom I could disagree when we both learned from the experience, but found it frustrating to read writers who seemed to hate ranchers, and who wanted nature tidy, with no dangerous fangs or messy droppings. I couldn't picture myself having a sensible conversation with any of them.

So when I first heard myself referred to as a "Nature Writer," I was astonished. In environmental circles, ranchers are routinely condemned as enemies. I'd worked hard in essays and speeches to change this easy and belittling depiction, but most of the work I submitted to publications outside my region had been rejected, and I'd had no idea anyone but other westerners had noticed the work in print.

I'd been reading books described as "nature writing"; they have multiplied in American bookstores and libraries the way prairie dogs multiply in my pastures when the neighbors have been shooting coyotes again. I was happier to find my books in that company than in some of the other places I'd found them, under "fiction," for example. But I wondered how writing about nature could be separated from writing about work or love. Would the act of naming ever-smaller parts of life become simply another aspect of the specialization rampant in our culture?

Most of the time, though, I was too busy doing ranch chores during the daytime and writing at night to worry about the world of nature writing. Then in 1992, John A. Murray, editor of numerous books including those in the prestigious Sierra Club series, asked me to participate in a nature-writing symposium to be published in *Mānoa* magazine. Among the writers asked to respond were Rick Bass, John Daniel, Gavan Daws, Pamela Frierson, John Haines, John Hildebrand, Edward Hoagland, William Kittredge, Barry Lopez, Nancy Lord, Christopher Merrill, Dan O'Brien, David Rains Wallace, and Peter Wild. I knew most of the names only from the spines of books in my library, and I was awed and honored to be counted among them.

The invitation furnished an opportunity to consider more carefully my role as a nature writer, and to air my views in the company of writers better known than I ever expect to be. Some of these writers actually get paid to travel to exotic regions specifically to observe and record their impressions of Nature. I also saw the request as a challenge and responsibility. So far as I know, I was the only working rancher in the group. Twelve men, three women—as a feminist, I found the division disturbing but not unusual. And being one of only three women was humbling when I considered the dozens of women whose fine writing on nature I regularly read.

Introducing the published symposium, Murray noted that nature writing had grown in popularity since the first Earth Day, April 22, 1970. He asked each writer to respond to two questions: Is nature writing the next major genre in American literature, or is it already? Will nature writing cross-fertilize other genres, and is such cross-fertilization needed, or desirable? Those questions are no less relevant now, nearly a decade later.

In 1992, Murray contended, nature writing was "arguably *the* major genre in American literature." I agreed then, and still think American writers and readers will be responding for decades to the writing on nature and wilderness produced by innovative thinkers during the thirty years following that first joyous Earth Day.

The first reason for the literary "Green Revolution," said Murray, was that readers caught in the "continued urbanization and mechanization of American life" and landscape have demonstrated their "deep concern for the environment" by buying books about nature. That observation rang true then, and still does, but other, more disturbing, forces are at work. Sales of books on nature continue to be brisk, though a large percentage of them are giant collections of lush photographs, too expensive for the average reader and intended only for display on polished coffee tables as a symbol of wealth.

Meanwhile, sales of nature gimmicks are also vigorous. I have never been a good target for such advertising ploys since I have little money beyond my daily needs, no regular salary, and thus enjoy none of the institutional benefits many Americans take for granted, such as life insurance or a retirement plan. I make vigorous attempts to remove my name from mailing lists. I use postage-paid envelopes to return flyers to organizations I don't support, often with a note pointing out that they are wasting paper by their repeated attempts to get money out of me.

Despite my efforts, I receive dozens of catalogs, including several in which nature is a major selling point. Furniture, clothing, tableware, stationery, posters, and anything else you can think of are decorated with pleasant pictures of exotic animals, and even with animal antlers or fur. The ad copy says buying all this stuff helps the world, and adjective-laden paragraphs assure me the rustic furniture is made from trees that died of natural causes (no doubt surrounded by grieving relatives).

Besides these examples of the hucksters' trade, I receive catalogs selling stuff that purports to be natural, including herb-impregnated oils guaranteed to invigorate the body and mind, all presumably made from herbs that chose to sacrifice themselves for my sake. (I don't need them because I make scented oils in my own kitchen from herbs I grow.) These catalogs assert that buyers traveled deep into jungles to search out primitive philosophers—naturally closer to nature than modern Americans—and persuaded them to give up amulets, charms, and potions guaranteed to bring the purchaser into harmony with the world. On any day, I could sign up for a vision quest with a "genuine medicine man," or take a cruise to Greek isles to meet the Goddess, twirl a Tibetan prayer wheel, or deck myself with ancient symbols. Only a few paltry dollars separate me from enlightenment. I am not persuaded, suspecting more fantasy than nature in the pitch.

No matter how it is created or marketed, nothing referred to as a "product" can substitute for the reality of nature. Put the books and catalogs aside. Go outdoors. Experience nature, in whatever form you find it, for yourself.

Then if you read the books and catalogs, your personal reality will help you assess the various claims. The proliferation of such catalogs *might* indicate the public's real interest in nature. Or this might all be a brief and specific fad.

A greater danger, I think, is that consumers may think they are accomplishing several tasks at once: not simply buying gifts, but helping the natural world and expressing their political views. They don't have to bother with all that awkward marching, or take time to write letters to congresspersons, to vote or discuss the issues with colleagues, or to separate the recyclables. Just buy a wolf T-shirt and assume you've done your civic duty to the environment.

Perhaps, I reflect uneasily, the people who buy books on nature are looking for the same affirmation these catalogs seem to offer: all you have to do to save wilderness is buy this stuff.

One catalog offers a product that suggests an entirely new relationship to nature. Wear the device around the neck, says the ad, and create "your own personal climate-control system." Escape nasty nature entirely, it implies, avoid the real chills and humidity most humans endure. Another product provides a "personal air supply," sucking in pollutants, allergens, and viruses, and blowing a stream of "pure air" to the wearer's eyes, mouth, and nose at 1,000 feet per minute, effectively separating the wearer from the emissions created by her own air-conditioned car. Buy these devices, and you won't have to be concerned about either actuality or whether anyone else can breathe.

All these sales bulletins, I believe, lead us away from responsible, personal action on behalf of a community, and toward selfish indulgence—overlaid with assurance that it's all OK. I'm afraid a lot more people buy the goods offered in the catalogs than buy the books written by all the aforementioned nature writers. And I wonder how many of them spend time in the outdoors doing anything, or spend time working to aid the environment.

Among book buyers, does the same logic prevail: do readers believe they have done their part for nature by buying a book? Do purchases of gadgets or books indicate a real concern for the environment? Perhaps readers are simply looking for affordable, soothing assurance that nature is lovely and unspoiled. Further, writers who study their own sales figures may be tempted to remain popular by sticking with reassuring topics, allowing the readers to believe all is well in nature. Do readers who think they are making a contribution to conservation by their purchases become smug and comfortable? Asked to contribute to an organization that promises to save the rain forest, a customer may think she's done enough by buying curios made by rain forest natives from dead wood. I'm tempted to conclude that the popularity of natural products, and nature writers, proves only that Nature is "in."

Murray said in the published symposium that nature writing has become popular because interest in the environment has become general, even "politically institutionalized." He noted that national leaders like George Bush (senior), Margaret Thatcher, and even Mikhail Gorbachev "suddenly found it expedient to identify themselves as environmentalists." Since 1992, we have watched more leaders emerge on the world scene expressing similar sentiments about the importance of the environment. Very few have dared to propose any action that is new or astonishing, and, as former secretary of the interior Bruce Babbitt would testify, the response was not especially indicative of a new age of environmental enlightenment. As Murray suggested, it seems clear that a particular administration's interest in protecting the environment may fade or be reversed if vocal and energetic voters express other concerns. It's still true that jobless, hungry people of any nation tend to accept jobs at any cost to the environment.

One significant change in the last decade, however, may focus more intense attention on the environment: the world is in considerably worse shape. As we run out of clean air, water, and food, not to mention fuel, each of us has a greater stake in environmental reform. The attitude of the George W. Bush administration suggests that folks seriously interested in improving their environment face an invigorating challenge.

Murray's second question for writers in the 1992 symposium was whether cross-fertilization between nature writing and other kinds of writing is possible, needed, and desirable. Asserting his belief that nature writing would seep into, and influence, other kinds of writing, he named a couple of dozen writers he called the best in America. All, he noted, were writing either partially or exclusively about nature. Nature writing, with its emphasis on concrete reality and its use of lyrical language, was popular, said Murray, because it's livelier and more engaging than traditional poetry and fiction, both in decline since the 1960s.

I agree, and see an example Murray might not accept: "cowboy poetry gatherings." Folks in new hats and worn boots have begun reciting rhymed verse filled with authentic rangeland experiences, collecting audiences of thousands all over the nation. Academic poets, in contrast, are lucky if their own colleagues attend their readings.

I feel comfortable among the cowboy poets because I've always considered nature just another part of my writing and my ranch work. We hustle back and forth between poetry and fixing fence, trying to express ideas, emotions, and observations from a daily life that is exotic or mythical to most Americans today. I doubt the average reader with an interest in nature has explored cowboy poetry. Yet the genre's primary subject is how people interact with the natural world. Nature, in the form of bucking horses, unruly cows, wily predators, and weather, receives no more respect from the average nature writer than it does from a cowboy poet. Maybe readers and critics alike need to expand their definition of nature writing.

In this regard, I believe it is significant that Thomas Jefferson is often celebrated at cowboy poetry gatherings. Participants respect his vision of democracy, casting farmers and ranchers in a leading role, as husbandmen in the original sense of the word: prudent and thrifty managers. These pioneers were charged with feeding the rest of us, preserving the actual dirt on which "the land of the free and the home of the brave" was founded. Agriculture was hailed for its achievements, and considered the economic anchor of the new democracy. Farm and ranch families were once loyal Americans, supporting their government with their bodies in war, and with their votes in peacetime. Jefferson foresaw a nation of such upstanding individuals owning small private estates on which each family could be self-sufficient, with enough leisure to obtain a decent education and participate in the politics to keep the nation running smoothly.

But the picture has changed, and politicians who do not in any way resemble statesmen are only part of the reason. Today, writers whose arguments are based on misinformation automatically receive widespread acclaim for bashing land-based professions. With enough promotion, readers accept colorful sham as fact without looking behind the facade. A hack writer who perches at a computer in an air-conditioned office may be invited to appear on talk shows, taunting workers who have no notion of how to fight back, no avenue of response. The opinions expressed in the most poorly researched anti-agriculture tirade have a greater chance of reaching policy-makers than the comments of living farmers and ranchers, or of loggers and sheep-raisers, waitresses and gas station attendants. Sadly, many ordinary citizens are credulous, accepting misinformation as fact because we have moved so far from the soil most of our ancestors worked that we no longer remember how food should be produced. Our leaders call this "progress."

Today's economic principles include slogans like "Bigger is better," and "Ya gotta spend money to make money." Many of today's ranchers and farmers are struggling to find a way to live in a modern world increasingly urbanized, increasingly ignorant about their lives—and unknowingly de-pendent on the products of their work. The gap between their lives and the lives of the majority of Americans in urban centers has fostered cynicism and distrust of the government. Few people who work in agriculture can or will spare the time to write about their work or their beliefs, so the truth of their profession is not available to readers.

Many popular nature writers no longer share Jefferson's view, often dis-missing everyone who works outdoors under an all-purpose, negative term like "land-rapers." In the environmental magazines I read, ranchers are of-ten lumped with miners and loggers as folks whose only purpose and joy in life is exploiting and abusing land and wildlife. Even the most cursory thought reveals the fallacy of the generalization: Mining companies remove resources from the land permanently. Logging companies remove old-growth forests and "replace" them with rows of immature seedlings planted by underpaid laborers on hillsides bare of other vegetation. Both spend mil-lions of dollars advertising their profit-making as conservation. Conversely, a ranch-er's livelihood depends on harvesting some of the native herbage on his land in a way that keeps it healthy and growing, renewable and con-stantly renewed. Profit margins are too low for self-congratulatory promo-tion. These realities seldom appear in the popular press.

In my opinion, nature writing, including mine, is enjoying popularity in large part because Americans sense, and are worried about, their growing de-tachment from reality. People who spend most of their lives in air-con-ditioned offices crave physical action. They long for greater challenges than getting home without a dinged fender. Readers might go directly to nature for their instruction, skipping our books, but they're trained to read the instruc-tions first, watch the how-to video. Beset by a consumer society devouring itself, assaulted by flashing lights and screaming voices, breathing chemically treated air, and reading gibberish masquerading as wisdom, they haven't the energy or time for nature in the raw. If they read modern poetry or fiction for solace, they find more jargon, more despair, precious little of the natural.

By contrast, the nature writer can be seductive. Humanity is proud of its ability to level forests, cover meadows with asphalt, and poison air and water, but we all know a higher moral law than we practice, and with the right ad campaign, we can be persuaded to change our ways. Nature herself doesn't bother with persuasion. In a world of change, nature is reliably unpredictable, and predictably more powerful than any human agency. Writers who learn from her can provide audiences with considerable hope and confidence, as we draw her lessons into poetry, politics, and, eventually, posterity.

Once nature writing became a genre, it quickly became a teachable course, with lesson plans and approved reading lists. By now perhaps some universities devote an entire department to it. I don't spend much time in universities these days. Neither reading lists nor polemics will alter nature herself, or the quiet truths she imparts to those willing to listen.

Let's get those students out of their desks and into the country. Send nature writing classes to talk with people who work in any kind of agriculture available in the immediate neighborhood. Visit ranchers, but also visit the packing plants where the cattle raised by the ranchers are killed for your table. How about an apprenticeship? Perhaps students could learn while they act to preserve wildlife by helping a rancher fence cattle away from a riparian area. Accompany a hunter, whether of deer or mushrooms, to learn their methods firsthand before venturing to assumption or criticism. For the more timid, a visit to an urban garden might be in order: What pests threaten the tomatoes? What chemicals does your blue-haired neighbor lady consider acceptable in her salad?

I've noticed two categories among nature writers. A few consider themselves primarily laborers; they write to communicate insights they've gleaned from labor. The majority consider their primary job to be writing, a self-created vocation still mocked by many working people. When my writing students say they want to be nature writers, I tell them their approach is backward; first they have to learn something about nature by getting deeply involved in it. I have always found myself straddling these two camps, since I believe that physical labor may be essential to certain important insights about land use, and that people who work with their hands may possess, in their muscles and sinews as well as mentally, an awareness unavailable to writers who spend most of their time thinking about nature in front of a computer or typewriter.

I think we all ought to spend half our work hours at physical labor. Jogging or lifting weights doesn't count. This is not a simplistic equation:

$$Outside + muscles = Good$$
$$Inside + scholarship = Bad.$$

My own ideal life would comprise some combination of physical and mental labor. But that is not my primary point.

I envy the few popular nature writers who have received enough recognition (translation: made enough money and publishing contacts) so they are free to simply wander the earth, frequently observing new landscapes, and writing about fresh topics. They don't live in the neighborhoods they write about, so they are free to speculate, to adopt lofty philosophies. I suspect some of them are delighted when their work creates controversy—after they have moved on and found a fresh topic to stir up a new conflict. But if a writer does not delve deeply into a particular locality, he or she may miss an important fact, or fail to ask a question that would alter the whole premise. Conversely, a writer who makes a living outdoors, writing about real actions and observations, dares not be overly theoretical.

Some of the best modern nature writers have worked at jobs that later inspired their writing; they took nature as a topic because of what they knew from arduous experience. Wendell Berry is a farmer. Sue Hubbell kept bees. Loren Eiseley was an anthropologist. Aldo Leopold managed forests and game. John Wesley Powell explored wild lands and rivers. For those writers, the work was foremost. The writing grew from a need to record what they were learning from their labor, and perhaps a desire to spread that knowledge to others. I suggest aspiring nature writers emulate these models. But working nature writers may be a vanishing species if we have made it impossible for the voices of laborers to be heard.

Wendell Berry's reflections on darkness, conceived while he walked a dark night on his own land, made me watch and listen more closely as I walked among my pregnant heifers. Paying attention taught me that a mountain lion hunts the same draw; one night she may have heard me reciting Wendell Berry poems as my way of "making noise" to let her know I was not prey. Knowing she's there helps me protect the domestic animals as well as the wild one. Sue Hubbell deepened my appreciation of bees, but I still called my bee-keeping neighbor for help when a swarm converged on the elm by the corral. Aldo Leopold's comment about listening to geese overhead reminded me to pay more attention to their gabbling passage and to consider education in a new light: by its direct relationship to survival. His struggle to dig up a Silphium plant so he could study why it disappears from grazed areas caused me to walk my pastures, eyes turned to the ground. Finding native plants like sego lily and Indian turnip helped me to understand their place in the community of forage that my cattle use, and was part of my inspiration to establish in my pastures a botanic garden of species native to the Great Plains. Each of these writers helped me understand my place in the plains community, and their views on subjugating writing to one's other work echoed and strengthened my own convictions—and led me to concrete action to support those beliefs.

From Leopold's farming experience came an ethical judgment so blinding it caused me to examine and ultimately adjust my opinions on ranching, the basis of my life. "A thing is right when it tends to preserve the integrity, stability, and beauty of the biotic community," said Leopold. "It is wrong when it tends otherwise." That simple truth gave me the courage to protest when my father poisoned prairie dogs or sprayed his alfalfa fields to kill grasshoppers. Nothing else in my experience had prepared me to clash so strongly with my father and the traditions of my ranching community. Every question that arose from my reading, every discussion, prompted me both to examine the practical aspects of the idea and to write.

The labor that preceded the writing seems to me an essential element, a condition without which the writing would not have occurred. Can I trust someone who sits in an air-conditioned room, reading Leopold's land ethic as black type on a white page, to apply it wisely to a particular landscape? Always, I feel compelled to rephrase philosophical questions on a practical level, to understand them on my own terms, to try to understand what they mean specifically to me. So I must ask, "If you rarely walk anywhere but a shopping mall, are you capable of making a wise judgment about the use of my land?" Our democratic system of voting, combined with the power of the media and public opinion, means that large numbers of people might answer that question without regard for my opinion, without reading my words. People who have never walked the prairie, who have never met a rancher, may decide the fate of my ranch and my community.

Modern Americans seem intent on specialization, on dividing all aspects of life into smaller and smaller elements. Yet American writers have always shown a broader awareness of nature in their poetry, fiction, and nonfiction. Before our mechanized age, when most people lived in the country, nature was simply the outdoors, a place of labor rather than recreation. Writers and readers both, even those in cities, spent most of their lives immersed in nature, but they were working to feed their families. How many other laborers learned important lessons lost to us because they didn't have time to write them down, because they lacked the skill or the patience required to get their lessons into print? Or because they could not reach or impress an editor? Yet for my work to remain available to readers, I must satisfy the requirements of publishers' marketing departments, who view books as just another product.

In a fat anthology of American nature writing, *This Incomperable Lande,* Tom Lyon remarked, "to write precisely about nature now simply takes more study than it did a century ago." Nature writers who do not live in the place they write about may see nature the way any tourist does, as a pleasing picture to be preserved only for its beauty. Without long-term residence, the writer may lack information that would alter a seemingly logical conclusion. Without the intimacy gained in working on the land, the author may omit a fact that interrupts the flow of a paragraph, may misinterpret a scene. Poetic language may enhance my enjoyment of learning, capture and focus my attention, but accurate information is more important. Pretty language should not be allowed to obscure inaccuracies and fallacies.

When I was working every day to raise cattle on an arid prairie ranch, writing in time stolen from sleep, I was not thinking about Nature or book buyers. Like most responsible ranchers, though, I considered how my life and work would affect my immediate surroundings, as well as the larger world. Fully understanding that my actions might be insignificant, I went on recycling political circulars into shopping lists, and reusing envelopes, just so I could say I'd accomplished something on a day when I had no time to write.

Now that I live in a city all winter, I pay more attention to the interests of the urban population. Freed from much of the physical labor of the ranch, I can concentrate on its future beyond my life. My primary motivation for writing remains the same: to understand my ranching background as a means of explaining the principles and practices of cattle ranching to citizens who do not appreciate the importance of native grasslands to their own welfare. These days, I meet more people, and collect more discouraging information on the disappearance of family ranches and the paving of prairie. But I also meet ranchers and farmers who are working with environmentalists, hunters, and wildlife lovers to find workable compromises that will result in the most good for the greatest number of citizens—and many of these folks count animals and plants as citizens. Yet I'm certain that if Americans continue to buy, develop, and pave and drive at their current rate, we are all in for a major shock as food prices rise, and options dwindle.

Certainly we cannot all live in wilderness, so I suggest that we may need to search out, even recruit, more "nature writers" who labor on the land. The writers whose work I read, and read again, are those who teach me something new about the place where I live, or who cause me to review my role in the life of the land. It's neither possible nor desirable to separate our ideas about nature from our ideas about the lives of the people who live closest to the piece of land under discussion.

Still, in the nationwide debates on whether farmers and ranchers should be displaced by subdivisions and shopping malls, the voices of farmers and ranchers are often missing from the public forums and magazine articles that help shape public opinion, and from the textbooks and anthologies from which our children learn to develop their views. Environmentalists need to open the door. No, just opening the door isn't enough. Environmentalists need to get out in the country we all care about, track down people who work in agriculture, and hold give-and-take conversations. We need to understand one another's positions, and find ways to become allies in our conservation efforts, and not only because desperate people are dangerous.

Nature writing, like all creative endeavors, is a chaotic mixture of ideas, constantly being modified and transformed. We're all part of a population being revolutionized with every immigrant, every new house in the country. To do their civic duty, writers must accept their role as leaders, reexamine their own assumptions and priorities, and demonstrate how to make the hard choices society must face in the next decade or so.

II

Since 1987, I've received nearly 800 letters about my first published book, *Windbreak,* a diary of a year on the ranch. In one, a young woman gushed that she wanted a marriage just like mine. Reading the book had convinced her that George and I spent twenty-four hours a day together, working, living, sleeping, and never had a fight.

I laughed a little, and then cried. George was dead by then, and I wished I could hear his response to her cheery ignorance. Of course we disagreed— over my role in raising his son, over who did the dishes or how much mud we tracked into the house; we clashed over all the silly and serious things most couples fight about. I didn't consciously lie in my writing, nor did I intend to give a false impression. Our squabbles were no one's business but ours, and the book was not about marriage or relationships. Since I couldn't revise the book to include a little marital bickering, I wrote to the woman, telling her the truth, and suggesting that if she ended every relationship at the first argument, she'd spend a long, dull life alone. Arguments, I counseled, are a chance to reassess the relationship, an opportunity for both parties to revise their ideas and behavior, so living together can become more satisfying, if not always harmonious. I'd like to see arguments between environmentalists and ranchers conducted with the same awareness.

That letter made me consider whether discussions on ranching could be enhanced if readers knew more about ranchers. Does a writer owe readers more information than usually accompanies a published piece? I've heard Edward Abbey fans express dismay and anger on discovering that when he wrote *Desert Solitaire,* he had a wife and child. Omitting mention of his family was, say some, a betrayal of trust; even the book's title was a lie. I doubt Abbey had any intention of misleading his rabid followers; as successful novelists know, it's simpler to write about any experience if you reduce the cast of characters.

Still, this book grows in part from such considerations. This collection of essays should fill some gaps for readers, provide a clearer view of my mind, and by extension demonstrate something about the way other ranchers think. My writing seeps or dribbles, but rarely gushes from my experiences; the essays that follow are varied because I'm interested in many subjects. The most significant event of my life, to date, was moving to a South Dakota ranch at the age of nine, and most of my writing centers on that place.

As I grew up, attended college, taught at various levels, and married twice, my viewpoints changed. Similarly, these essays spiral outward from the ranch in both locale and time. German poet Rainer Maria Rilke once wrote, "I live my life in widening circles," a comment that reverberated as I sorted through these essays. Some are set entirely on the ranch, while in others I viewed my ranch experiences from new territory, taking a broader view. Each time I wrote about a new idea, I learned more, so I agree with Leopold, who quoted Cicero in saying, "It is doubtful whether a man ever brings his faculties to bear with their full force on a subject until he writes upon it." From thinking writers, and from attentive readers, will come the slogans of survival for this new century—if we survive long enough to need slogans.

Few writers spend all their time sitting around in nature gazing at the beauty of a wolf or a blossom, and the rest of us who have to make a living working outdoors in all weather may resent folks who enjoy that luxury. Novelist Joyce Carol Oates once titled an essay "Against Nature," describing nature writing as exhibiting "a painfully limited set of responses," which she reported in capital letters (to emphasize, perhaps, as Tom Lyons says in quoting her, their headlinelike simplicity): REVERENCE, AWE, PIETY, MYSTICAL ONENESS. For once, I agree with Oates. In order to evaluate nature writing, perhaps readers need to know what nature writers do when they aren't writing about nature. We may know—even if we would prefer not to—how a writer disposes of personal wastes in a national forest. But in most cases readers have no idea what else the writer does, or of his or her views on other important issues. When I read an essay that makes me want to revolutionize my life, I also want to know if the writer lives as he or she advocates.

I do not believe in making full disclosure. But the following essays should allow careful readers to round out their picture of a woman who is still a little surprised to be considered a "nature writer." I have welcomed and responded to an assortment of friendly responses from readers—books, letters, flower seeds, advice on the warmest long underwear and the most healing soaps and hand lotions, even an odd device designed to enable a woman to urinate standing up. (Yes, it works.) But I won't disclose matters I consider personal, or my unlisted telephone number. Even readers who like my books have no right to drop in unannounced, or to tell me how to eat.

Shocking revelations about public figures have made careful readers picky about details, and who can blame them? We live in an era when our highest officials apparently tell lies, considering them business as usual. Some writers go beyond omission to deceive. Annie Dillard, one of my own role models since *Pilgrim at Tinker Creek,* admits she never had a cat; she borrowed some-one else's experience to create an effective anecdote in that book. I find her tale less moving if the cat didn't leave bloody pawprints on *her* chest. Learning of such deceptions prompted me to examine the truths in my own writing.

I've always thought the distinction between truth and lies was clear, but during the past few years I've collected examples of differing views on the is-sue of how much truth a reader can expect in a book labeled "nonfiction." While writers' renditions of truth vary widely, most readers feel betrayed to discover that an event did not happen as written.

Therefore, I find it necessary to note that the following stories are true, with certain irregularities I'll explain shortly. I consider the most important part of my job to be telling the truth about grasslands ranching as I see it. Readers who trust my word, who have confidence in my judgment as shown in my writing, may be more willing to listen to my viewpoints, to vote, or to take other significant action to preserve ranching on the plains. How can I expect a reader to trust my opinion if I say I received a kaleidoscope as a birthday gift when I really didn't?

My writing springs from my labor, and I have chosen to live primarily in one region, the arid High Plains, for the past forty years. Gradually, I have de-fined my primary job as writing about one topic, grasslands ranching. In forty years of labor in a single ecosystem, I've learned a great deal, though I've never made time to take technical courses about nature. When I vote, I do so with an awareness that those who see the issues as I do may be too few to sway political leaders who respond to numbers, to cash contributions, to glitz and dazzle and power. So besides writing to understand, I write to help spread my interpretation.

But I did not set out to be what I have become, a nature writer and a some-time spokesperson for ranching. I settled on writing as a way to remain a rancher and still be a Great American Novelist; that plan lasted until I returned to the ranch, older, wiser, and divorced, in my middle thirties. While I was trying to discover if my writing would offer me anything besides a private way to record my thoughts, I lived through the experience narrated in the essay "Running with the Antelope." Later I fictionalized the story for its first publication, changing the names of the men and combining two men into one composite character. None of this would be of concern if I had not decided my talent lay in nonfiction that uses the events and viewpoints of my ranching life as material. Because I persisted in writing nonfiction about grasslands ranching, I have come to be regarded as a nature writer. Now, with some reluctance, I must consider myself partially answerable to people with concerns about both nature writing and ranching.

As I explored nonfiction, both as a writer and as a reader, I developed strong opinions about the amount of fiction allowable in my own writing. If I were writing about the antelope hunt for the first time today, I would still change the names of the men, as I have done in other essays, to protect the privacy of people who did not choose to be my subjects. But I would not combine two real men into one composite character; that decision was made for the fictional version of the essay, and I have found it easier than not to retain it in the present narrative, which is otherwise true. I believe this essay has merit besides as a lesson in how not to hunt pronghorn, and I trust that no one will conclude from my participation in the events that I don't deserve to be called a nature writer.

In writing, I try to reveal what the reader needs to know, without becoming addicted to narrating my life. Each writing project presents a new challenge. Publication of these essays may help a reader appreciate the origins of my work, but may not persuade you to agree with me.

I was thoroughly engrossed in raising cattle with my mother, father, and husband when my life changed; the deaths of my husband and father forced me to leave the ranch and settle in a city. The shift broadened my horizons, taught me more tolerance, threw me into new situations requiring new approaches to my writing. My job is self-defined. My idea of fun is writing about something I don't understand, often a topic that infuriates or entertains me. Not every essay leads the reader to a deep philosophical analysis, but each one emerges from my somewhat anomalous positions as a woman, a rancher, and a lover of prairie.

Indeed, perhaps certain of these essays remained unpublished until now because some editors have accepted the description of me as either a "nature" or "ranching" writer and refused to look at writing that didn't fit preconceived notions. A few years ago, a rejection from a major magazine mentioned the editor's belief that I was attempting to deceive him and the readers, since I did not disclose until the second page that I am a rancher. Responding, politely as I was taught, I noted the biographical information accompanying the submission, and added that the essay's subject, cows, might have been a major clue; few nature lovers write about cows.

In retrospect, I learned several things from that rejection. Why did the magazine's editor think it possible that someone writing about cattle and ranching might try to conceal her profession? Perhaps the editor was responding to previous experience. Apparently he had not read my biographical information, and had no idea that ranching is my primary interest in writing. Further, perhaps he'd had experience with folks—environmental writers?—who think that if they can't honestly persuade readers, it's OK to fool them into agreement, or force them into certain behavior "for their own good."

Since that time, I've been careful to announce myself as a rancher who also writes. Though I live in a city and have no cattle, I am a rancher because I own and make decisions about the operation of a working cattle ranch. I'm proud of my ranching heritage. I wince when either ranchers or environmentalists make ill-informed remarks for the media.

In the spirit of revelation, then, I include several essays with themes that don't concern ranching, centered around my time as a buckskinner. My husband George and I often camped with other folks who replicate the historical period of beaver trapping and black powder rifles. My memories of these events are among my favorite, though I haven't attended a rendezvous in so long my tipi poles have dry rot.

But none of the essays in this volume are included simply for their value as nostalgic glimpses of my past. Each, I believe, illustrates my attitudes about the environment belonging to all of us. Each conveys an idea; perhaps it is not too strong to say each carries a message. I enjoyed buckskinning nearly as much as I enjoy riding a horse or writing, and admired buckskinners' tolerance for differences.

Other essays show experiments with a different tone or style; I wrote some for enjoyment, as I might tell a joke to friends with no need to explain or apologize. In thirty years of environmental activism, I have often thought that the movement's greatest need is humor. Many discussions and debates are so serious, so politically correct, that they bore even the most committed activist, and humor can sometimes persuade as statistics cannot. I trust readers will recognize the humorous intent, and relish my approaching incarnation as a true curmudgeon.

So this volume is more than an argument for ranching, its focus wider than my ranch or my bio-region. I am usually writing about several different ideas at a time, and my writing has always been intermingled with my responsibilities for making a living. Most of the essays here were published in periodicals, but either didn't fit the themes of my previous books, or were deleted to make a book shorter, and thus more "marketable."

Read this book, and others about nature. But remember to go outside, to experience and study the place nearest your home where you are closest to the earth, whether it's a patch of weeds amid concrete, or an estate. Visit the wilderness if you can, but attend to your home first. Do what you can to save the earth: write letters; be as responsible for your own wastes as possible. And if you come to the grasslands, don't aspire to build a big house and stay. Don't knock on my door. Just enjoy the experience, and know that this writer, flesh and blood created of grass-fed beef, is somewhere on the prairie, between grass and sky.

PART · I

LEARNING
TO SEE

LEARNING TO SEE
THE UNSEEN

• • •

For years I was haunted by invisible birds. In summer, riding my horse, I heard nearby twittering, as though dozens of birds were singing on my shoulder. Quickly, I'd look overhead; nothing. I'd look down, toward the buffalo grass that our cows turn into beef; even a very small bird ought to be visible in grass that is six inches tall. If I couldn't see them, I couldn't identify or write about them.

Finally, I wrote about them anyway, and a bird-watcher told me they are horned larks, *Eremophila alpestris*. I grabbed my bird book—so naive I only had one before I realized that even a casual observer needs at least three—and examined photographs showing another of the brownish-gray birds whose camouflage suits them so well to the prairie. This one dresses for success with a black necktie and eye mask; another black patch marks the "horns," feathers on the head that can stand erect. In flight, said the experts, its song is a high-pitched tinkling that sounds "brittle in the frozen air," and it is related to the Eurasian skylark.

I closed the book, and drove out to a stock dam to feed the cattle, thinking about feed supplies and the weather. I didn't expect to encounter horned larks until spring. I scattered hay, then drove to the dam to chop a hole in the ice so the cattle could drink.

As I shut off the motor, a bird alighted on a rock beside the truck, and tinkled at me. A horned lark. Tiny black feather "horns" stood up on his—or her—head; around its neck was a black crescent. The bird might as well have been carrying a sign.

I believe it is important to know about the natural world, but this demonstrated a corollary theory: knowing the bird's name made it visible to me after thirty years of blindness. The bird pirouetted on the rock several times, making sure I got a good look at its markings. Suddenly I heard the high tinkling notes that had followed me for so many years. I stepped out of the truck and looked up; a flock of larks swooped and darted, playing with the winds. They landed among the cattle, in a fluttering chaos of brown wings, and darted among the huge hoofs pecking seeds.

I explained to the birds that if they'd hopped around on the ground under my feet thirty years ago, I would have identified them immediately. My accusations didn't keep them from snatching hayseeds while twittering cheerily.

After I saw the horned larks once, I saw them often, and wondered how I could ever have missed them. Perhaps, I reasoned, they resemble the fairies I believed in as a child: as soon as I could name and believe in them, they could not stay hidden from me: horned larks, the shape-changers of the plains.

During recent years when an unusual amount of rain fell, however, I realized I wasn't seeing or hearing the larks. I consulted one of the many reference works I've accumulated while trying to gain a clearer understanding of my neighborhood. "This species," says the National Audubon Society guide *Grasslands,* "favors the most barren habitats; as soon as thick grass begins to grow in an area, the birds abandon it." So I must conclude that the birds are now puzzling and entertaining folks in a drier climate. Like my father before me, I have been careful to limit the number of cattle in our pastures to what the grass could support without damage. In addition, we have enjoyed several years when rainfall was above average, so the pastures have benefited both from human management and from natural conditions. Our gain is clearly also a loss. I will miss the horned larks, but they have become a symbol: every action has an effect, and it's important to understand, as fully as we are able, the consequences of our actions.

WHIRLAWAY

· · ·

We'd named the old black white-faced cow for a famous racehorse, because she was fast on the straightaway and tricky on the curves. Besides speed, Whirlaway possessed intelligence, or instinct if you prefer, that alerted her when humans were going to do something she wouldn't like. She preferred not to cooperate with them.

Whenever we moved the cattle anywhere, she ran the opposite direction. If she had a calf, it galloped along in her wake, eyeballs rolling white, tail straight in the air just like mama's, genetically programmed to cause trouble.

We knew she'd be difficult to handle when we gathered cows that fall, culling out the old ones for sale. We'd already discussed the alternatives: it was time to sell her because she was fifteen years old, and dry. That is, she was not carrying a calf, so she would not contribute the next year to the crop we rely on to pay the bills. Had she been younger, we'd have kept her, giving her a year's vacation, and relying on her good breeding to pay us back in better health and future calves. But at fifteen, she was nearly at the end of her productive life. We can't afford to run a nursing home for elderly cows, feed them while they stand around the pasture waiting to die. Best to sell her this fall, rather than risk her teeth going bad during the coming winter, causing her to starve and suffer.

Furthermore, she was pastured three miles from the corrals, the only place where we had plank fences tall and strong enough to guide her into a truck to haul her away. My father, having spent fifteen years handling the cow quietly in the hope she'd calm down, suggested half in jest that we just shoot her in the pasture and consider it our donation to the coyotes and vultures. "Might be the most sensible thing we could do," he pointed out. "Because she's going to tear down fences and run you around, and we'll be lucky if you or the horse doesn't break a leg before we get her outta there."

Foolishly optimistic, I convinced my husband, George, that I could drive her to the corrals with the rest of the cattle. I rode to the pasture with George following in the pickup, and eased the horse along behind the little bunch of cattle, paying no attention to Whirlaway. If all the other cattle moved ahead of the horse, maybe she'd follow them out the gate and down the trail home.

My horse that day was Oliver, a beautiful gray part-Arab with a wonderfully easy gait. But he was lazy, willing to get along with as little work as possible. Only when he was really angry, hot, and tired did he turn into the cutting horse his sainted mother was. Then he spun and pivoted on his hind hooves, slashing back and forth behind a cow, anticipating every move she made, crowding her with his chest, biting when he could, until she had no choice but to go in the direction we chose. Whenever you see a "cowboy" yelling and swinging his rope as he thunders along behind a herd of cows, he's either in a movie, or he doesn't own the cows and he'll soon be unemployed. In real life, running cattle causes them to lose weight on a hot day, poundage that translates into hard-earned money lost because of haste or ignorance.

When I'm handling cattle, I don't care if my horse is fast, but it must be nimble and alert, be smart enough to anticipate a cow's moves, and turn with her to block her escape before she breaks into a run.

The rest of the cattle were quiet as they reached the gate George had opened. Ostentatiously relaxed for Whirlaway's benefit, he leaned against the pickup nearby with his young son, Mike, a summer visitor. I'd slowed the horse so much a few cows began stopping every few steps to graze. Quietly, I maneuvered among them, gently separating the ones to be sold. Each time one or more ambled into a direct line with the gate, I'd speak to the horse, maybe trot a little as I eased them through.

Finally, every cow we wanted to sell was outside the gate. Except Whirlaway. While the others grazed quietly, she stood beside the fence, head up, ears erect, snorting.

I turned the horse and ambled her way. She threw her head higher, raised her tail, and trotted around me to join the cows we planned to leave in the pasture. I reconsidered, then gathered the whole bunch and aimed them all at the gate, waving at George. He nodded and drove the pickup away through the gate, encouraging the cows already cut out for sale to move on down the road. If Whirlaway followed the second bunch quietly through the gate, putting the rest of them back into the pasture would still be less trouble than we usually had cutting her out of a crowd.

Nope. The other cows trotted between the posts in a neat line. When Whirlaway was four steps from the gate with me close behind her, she seemed to turn inside out and vanish. I spun the horse and whipped around her again. Again she ducked aside at the last instant.

The third time we got close to the gate, Oliver shoved Whirlaway with his shoulder while I yelled and hit her with the reins. She raised her tail and shot out a stream of used grass, splashing green chunks all over his chest and side, over my leg and the saddle.

Annoyed, Oliver opened his mouth to bite the cow on the hip. She raised her tail. He reconsidered, snapping his mouth shut so hard his teeth clattered. The cow ran off. I eased one foot out of the stirrup to rest a moment. George drove back, shut the gate, and handed me the water jug while I explained Plan Number 3: I'd tire the cow into giving up.

Trotting the horse, I simply followed her wherever she went, back and forth on the flat. I was grateful that prairie dogs had not invaded this spot, for I was watching the cow and the horse's ears so I could lean with his quick turns and avoid falling out of the saddle. Each time the cow got close to the gate, George and Mike would move out from the opening so she'd have a clear view of the rest of the cows grazing outside.

Half an hour of trotting made my horse mad enough to get serious about his job. The tall autumn grass was slick and treacherous. Each time he made a turn so tight his body was nearly horizontal to the ground, I feared he'd fall, but he never even slipped. He trotted closer and closer to her, snapping his teeth.

Then Whirlaway kicked him in the chest. He gasped, snorted, and bit her

tail. Unlike horses, cows rarely kick with both hind legs at once, but Whirlaway kicked again just as the horse turned, connecting with my knee with one
back hoof, my ankle with the other. The shock was so intense I was absolutely sure the ankle was broken. Then the pain hit and I reined the horse
in, mumbling that I'd have to let the damn cow go so we could get to the
damn hospital before the damn ankle swelled so much they had to cut the
damn boot off. Then my whole leg went numb, and I kicked the horse into a
gallop to catch up to the cow.

Whirlaway made a wide circle down into a gully and up the side, with
Oliver right behind her. When she reached the top, she spun, lowered her
head, and roared back down the hill. Her head struck Oliver's chest and
lifted his front feet off the ground. I was yelling words I hoped Mike didn't
know, picturing myself with the horse on top of me, but Oliver slid sideways
as the cow hurtled past. I've seen lots of bovine escape maneuvers, but
Whirlaway was the only cow who ever tried to tip my horse over.

George, realizing the cow was working us away from the gate, had put the
cows we weren't going to sell back into the pasture. Now he shut the gate and
came racing toward us in the pickup, trying to get ahead of the cow before
she headed into rough ground. With no seat belt or handhold, Mike bounced
beside him, grinning with excitement. Faster, Whirlaway ran straight down a
ten-foot bluff. George veered off with the pickup, but the horse and I slid
down in an avalanche of rocks. By the time George caught up, we'd covered
nearly a mile and the cow was outrunning the horse. George drove up beside
her and forced her to turn. I kept the horse right on her heels while the
pickup detoured around another gully.

For a while, we alternated following the cow. Whenever George took a detour, I'd see posts, baling wire, fence stretchers, and all the other essential
junk in our pickup hanging suspended in a cloud of dust as the truck ricocheted from rock to rock, billowing black exhaust. Whirlaway kicked the
pickup bumper. She swung her head and smashed a door panel. Once, she
dashed straight into a tight four-strand barbed wire fence. The recoil knocked
her back on her haunches. The next time she swung her head against the
truck door, she smeared blood over it from a dozen small cuts.

Finally, she trotted down the final slope into the most distant corner of the
pasture. Her head swung as she looked at the cross fence and at the other
corner of the pasture a half mile away. I mumbled a prayer that she wouldn't

jump into the railroad right-of-way, since we have no gates into it, and the mess of old ties and cable left by the railroad crews makes it almost impossible to ride a horse there. She might have tried to climb or jump any of the fences. Instead, without pausing to rest, she turned and began to plod toward the gate, two miles back. Running with sweat, all of us followed her back. Beaten, she never once looked around as we all trudged through the gate.

Later that week, she destroyed several sections of 2 by 8 planks six feet high, broke several ropes, and dealt bruises and scrapes to all of us before we got her in the truck, but that's another story. When we finally got her loaded in the truck and headed for the sale barn, she looked fat and healthy. We could see no cuts on her head, no visible evidence of her last epic struggle. My ankle and knee turned purple and green and remained swollen for a couple of weeks.

Most range cows aren't as hard to corral as Whirlaway, but it wasn't especially unusual for us to spend a hard half-day's work getting a wild cow out of the pasture. Whenever a city friend envies us the ranching life and says, "All you have to do is sit around and watch those cows get fat," I just nod and raise my glass of iced tea in a salute to Whirlaway.

MAKING HAY

...

Whenever I glanced toward the highway, the glare nearly blinded me. The drivers were silhouettes in stone behind winking windshields, rushing past without turning their heads. I wanted to scream in their ears. Or perhaps a whisper would startle them more. I wanted to make just one driver jam his right foot hard on the brakes, jerk his sunglasses off, look out over the dusty alfalfa fields, and understand what he was seeing.

There I was in the hayfield, forty-seven years old, bouncing along eating dust on a little John Deere 420 tractor my father had bought on my twelfth birthday. The 420 was our newest tractor; equipment salesmen called it an antique, which may explain why they hadn't called us lately. Conditions weren't conducive to reasoned discourse, but to pass time, I imagined what I'd say if someone actually stopped to talk.

I tried to keep the fictitious conversation restrained and rational, but every few minutes I'd realize I was ranting again. *Pay attention!* I'd bellow over the tractor's clatter. *I'm doing this so you can eat!* I'd try to remember and calmly quote the statistics on how many family farms and ranches disappear each year under housing developments and strip malls. And then thirty years of writing explanatory essays, with footnotes, about the business of ranching would be swept aside in another burst of fury. This is why I am a writer, and not a politician.

Watch out for folks like me as you drive the highways. Look for the man, woman, or child on a tractor, hat pulled low, back bowed to the blazing sun. We really do want to be logical and mannerly in telling others about our lives, but sometimes we rave, and sometimes we plead, finding it hard to stay coherently abstract when our livelihood is at stake. We're making hay to fill the bellies of those calves on the hillside, to fatten them through the winter. Next fall, we'll sell them to a multinational corporation for too little money to compensate for our labor and expense. They'll be crowded into a feedlot owned by the same corporation, and some members of the public will say ranchers are responsible for polluting the river. Is it any wonder we get a little crazy sometimes?

Talking things over with myself on the tractor, my voice would rise, my throat tighten, and I'd be angry at the passersby again. *Why don't you care?* I'd bellow. When the blizzards arrive, we'll be out here, in bone-biting cold, riding the same Popping Johns to load the hay we're cutting now.

Sorry—slipped out of my moderate tone again. I mean, we'll load the hay and feed it to our cows no matter what the weather. We'll raise healthy calves, manufacturing beef. Even today, when I've spent ten hours on this tractor, with the thermometer registering 104 degrees and the wind blowing gritty dust into my teeth, I can feel the cold of the coming winter. During the long, dark evenings, I'll read environmental magazines; many of them will say ranchers are ruining the West. I'll grit my teeth.

Because ranchers work as I have worked today, you can choose a fine cut of steak, juicy and red, at the supermarket. Or you can stand at your grill, shaping hamburger, mouth watering as the grease pops in the pan. Think of us as you prepare to eat. Remember we who created it from blazing noons and freezing midnights. If you can't see us as you drive by, wave anyway. And when you see us in town and notice how our faces are carved like leather by the wind and sun, smile. We don't mean to be grouchy, honest.

I began driving the mower tractor the year I turned twelve, proud to replace, with my skinny body, a series of unreliable and expensive hired men. Each year I relearn intricate steps to start the motor because the generator didn't last past my sixteenth birthday. I tighten bolts like the one that whizzed past my ear last summer, check connections, hydraulic fluid, mower parts. Sweat runs out from under my hat, stings my eyes, makes me think there's a wasp in my pant leg.

Making hay in summer is mental and physical torture, as traditional as any religious rite, and essential to our ranch operation. My father spent his entire eighty-three years on this land, raising cattle on a small family ranch in western South Dakota, with help from my husband and me for the final ten years. My father, whose father left the shoemaking profession in Sweden to homestead this land in the late 1800s, was conservative politically and economically. His primary rule of ranch management was "Never Spend Any Money." Translated into practicality, that meant we never spent a dime for anything we could possibly do ourselves.

Making hay with old equipment meant we were using outdated methods. We were never typical representatives of modern, high-tech "agribusiness," a terrible word for an evil trend. None of us owed anyone money. We paid our taxes on time. Both couples took vacations yearly. Many of our neighbors with shiny new air-conditioned tractors could not make those claims. Still, most of them have done less labor as they moved into the modern age of debt and dependence.

First they bought a side delivery rake, a long implement with rotating toothed wheels that sweeps the hay into queues the length of the field, making big, even hay bundles. Meanwhile, we drove an old tractor towing a short dump rake. This model of tractor, designed with its two front wheels close together, was known for its ability to kill its drivers. When I hit the throttle, it leapt in the air. I always thought it was looking around for a hole to drop its front wheels into so it could tip over and break my neck. I never flipped it, but the summer a neighbor used it to put up our hay when I was occupied elsewhere, he rolled it twice on flat ground and survived. Later models have front wheels set nearly as far apart as car wheels for greater stability, but we could not afford to buy one.

To use our old dump rake, I sat sideways on the rusty metal seat, steering with my left hand while I looked over my right shoulder to gauge when the rake teeth filled with hay. At that moment—just before the rake began to slide over the loose hay on the ground—my right hand yanked hard on a rope that pulled a lever and dumped the hay. After an hour, my neck and shoulders hurt from twisting to watch the rake behind and the tractor's path ahead.

Hitting a boulder or two tied extra knots in my muscles. My hand was blistered and my arm aching from pulling the dump rope.

A few years after I started haying, the neighbors traded their side delivery rake for a windrower, a top-heavy machine that mowed hay in swaths twelve feet wide, gathering it in the same operation, and leaving neat rows around the field. The operator sat high on the machine where he could look down on me as I tightened bolts and greased zerks on my old nine-foot mower. I'd climb on the tractor and mow around and around the field for three hours, unless I broke a sickle tooth or mower guard and stopped to fix the problem. After mowing, I'd unhook the mower, attach the rake, and drive around in circles for another couple of hours to windrow my hay. During one of those summers, I wrote a poem about the work, working out each line aloud and repeating each new line over and over until I could write it down when I finished work for the day, shortly after dark.

While I was still mowing, the neighbor would have started piling hay, unless he was smart enough to mow another field and let the crop dry out a day before stacking. If he wasn't, his hay stacks sometimes burst into flames, spontaneously combusting, because they were stacked too green. In fairness, he might have admitted that I didn't break down any more often than he did. To be really fair, he might have admitted that buying advanced machinery used up a lot more of his cash than we spent repairing our old equipment.

Once hay is mowed and raked, a variety of machinery exists for making the big loaf-shaped piles common to the arid Great Plains. In our case, when I'd half-raked a field, I'd see a glint of light through the dust as my father drove the massive old John Deere carrying the hydraulic stacker into the field. A stacker is really a giant fork with wheels and a driver. The teeth operate hydraulically to raise the load to the height of a stack; another set of pressurized hoses and gadgets pushes the hay off the fork.

My father would drive to a far corner of the field and drop the teeth flat against the ground, then drive toward the spot where he intended to place the first stack. As he drove, trying not to stick the metal teeth in a badger hole that would slam him to a stop, and bend the teeth, the hay collected against a barrier at the back of the fork. When he got to the stack site, he'd stop and back up, working another lever to push the hay off.

Stacking my father's way was much more complex than simply shoving hay into a pile. His progress around the field on the noisy stacker was more like a ballet. He never drove a foot more than necessary to collect and pile the hay. He delivered hay from alternating directions, dumping each load so the end crossed a previous load, weaving strips of fodder together at the corners. Integrating the bundles this way made the finished stack firmer. Every three or four loads, he'd lift the teeth enough to dump hay into the center, building it high to shed water. A depression in the middle of a stack would collect rain and snow, rotting the hay from the core outward. His finished stacks looked smooth, but were shingled like a roof, bundles overlapping one another so the pile would shed water for years. When we were ready to feed the hay to cows, tearing that thatch apart with a pitchfork required great arm and shoulder strength, and a lot of patience.

Finally, as his strength failed, my father got a grapple fork he used in winter to load hay on the hayrack. Visualize a hand raised to catch a ball: the driver opens the curved fingers as the tractor is driven straight into the stack. Then, as the driver operates levers connected to the hydraulic system, the fingers close, holding the hay firmly against the bottom row of bars: just as you might pick up a handful of spaghetti. At the hayrack, the driver operates the same levers in reverse to open the hand and drop the load. For a while, because my father didn't like to "waste" gas, he kept the tractor beside the stacks to load the hay, but refused to drive it to where we fed, so one of us pitched it off by hand.

The neighbors' next innovation was a device I never envied: a four-paneled fence set up on the site of each stack. Using a stacking fork, they simply dumped hay casually over the fence until it made an untidy pile my father refused to dignify with the term "stack." Then they unhooked the fence connections and dragged the panels to the next site. The uneven little jumble of hay was not layered, nor were the haphazard corners woven together to resist wind, snow, and water. One good windstorm scattered the little heaps all over the countryside.

The neighbors defended this technique by saying they'd feed the hay that winter anyway, so it didn't have to last long. The same philosophy has created an entire throwaway economy. If we had a wet summer and fall, their hay was already rotting when the cows ate it in January, sometimes poisonous enough to make them sick, or kill them. If we didn't feed our stacks during the first winter after they were built, we knew they'd last a while. One winter when I was forty, we tore into a stack built the summer I turned fifteen. The outside of the twenty-five-year-old stack was weathered gray, a pile of leafless sticks that still shed water like a palm-thatched roof in the tropics. Inside, the hay was green and leafy, a little dusty, but with a freshly cut smell. I wouldn't have believed it either, if I hadn't stood on the hayrack and pitched it off to cows that ate it eagerly.

Making hay in summer was only one part of our year-round cycle of turning grass and hay into meat. All winter, either with a tractor, or with a pitchfork and his pickup, my father fed to his cows the hay we put up during the summer. Driving in the country on some March morning, watch for pickups with miniature haystacks in the back moving slowly through pastures along the highway. Look again; the pickup has no driver: ranchers who don't have kids at home, or who have working wives, are often standing in the pickup bed pitching hay. Some folks tie the steering wheel to avoid surprising lurches, but most of us just start out on level ground and aim the truck away from fences and deep gullies.

One of my ranching friends told me that one day when she was feeding from the pickup bed, she left her dog in the cab. Bouncing around in excitement as usual, he managed to lock both doors. As the pickup headed down a steep hill, she jogged alongside trying to pry open the wing window to get at the steering wheel, and hoping no neighbors were driving by. The dog barked encouragement. She was considering jumping into the back to smash the rear window when she ran out of time: the pickup hit a rock big enough to stop it, whereupon she broke the side window and resumed control. She tried to teach the dog to unlock doors and turn off the ignition, but he was old, and he never learned those new tricks.

When a rancher feeds, cows stream toward the pickup from all corners of the pasture. New calves, confused by all the action, run back and forth, bawling. When they find their mothers, they curl up to sleep on a tuft of hay, until a cow eats it out from under them.

A rancher likes to say, with a lopsided grin, that he's a gambler. One of his skills is figuring out in the fall how long the hay and winter will last before pasture grasses grow green and tall enough in spring to support the herd. If his ranch hasn't produced enough hay, the rancher has to decide if he has, or can borrow, enough money to buy it. Ranchers who don't keep surplus hay in case they guess wrong can be ambushed by spring blizzards. Entire cattle herds have died when the rancher miscalculated the time winter would be finished with him.

In fall, ranchers sell calves six to nine months old. Most are bought by feedlot operators who will maintain them through another winter, usually on grain, to produce the fat meat sold to supermarket chains. Some ranchers keep half their calves through another winter, hoping prices will be higher next spring. Meanwhile, each cow protects another calf in her womb.

The meat a rancher eats is nothing more than grass and hay, conveniently packed inside cowhide. By the time meat appears wrapped in cellophane at the grocery store, additional processes have raised the price far above the rancher's costs or profits. Large companies own the feedlots where steers, injected with hormones to increase weight gain, eat expensive, chemical-laden grain. Cattle that spend months crammed together in a feedlot that may be wet and muddy also receive medication to help them withstand disease. Besides the costs of these processes—in health and in cash—the supermarket customer also pays for trucking, butchering, and wrapping.

Increased concern about what we eat has brought about some changes. A customer who looks hard enough may be able to buy grass-fed beef from the family raising it. Some young ranchers are using some of my father's "old-fashioned" ways to accommodate the natural needs of their cattle. Cows are ruminants, after all, and, like elk, moose, and deer, they prefer to wander wide grasslands, selecting their own meals. On our ranch, hay was only a winter supplement when natural feed was covered by snow, and unavailable. I refuse to eat supermarket beef. Grass-fed meat is healthier. And while chewing a steak, I recall the poem I wrote that summer, picturing the hours of haying from which this firm, tasty flesh is made.

Haying: A Four-Part Definition

I.

When I was fourteen, my father bought a new John Deere 420
for me to drive. I'm thirty-four
                Some summers I've missed:
away at other jobs, married, teaching.

But I'm home for now.
For the twentieth spring he hitches up the mower,
mows the big yard, stops to sharpen the sickles, straighten
sections, grease zerks.
        Impatient, he begins before he's ready,
plunges in. When he's made the first land
he stops the tractor, grins, says, "I usually drive it in third"
(so do I, I growl for the twentieth year)
        Pours himself some coffee.
I mow around the field in diminishing concentric squares
trying to write a poem about haying.

II.

On the first round: alfalfa's purple smell.
On the third: redwing blackbirds fly up, screeching.
On the fourth: the cupped nest swings
from three plants; *on the fifth:* four chicks,
openmouthed, ride the nest down to die.
On the sixth: I remember the first time. They cheeped
while I carried the nest off the field. Two redwings
fluttered where it had stood. They never went near it;
a buzzard did. *On the tenth:* damp heat induces sleep.
On the twelfth: I watch the sickle slashing.
On the thirteenth: remember a story. A neighbor caught
his pants leg in the power takeoff. When his sons saw
the circling tractor he was a bloody lump, baseball-size.
On the fourteenth: calculate the temperature at
one hundred ten. The first hour ends.
On the twenty-eighth round: an eagle circles up the grove,
pursued by blackbirds. I think of the poem again:
seeking words for the heat, the pain between my shoulder blades,
the sweat bee stinging under my arm. For fierce hot time.
On the fortieth: I think of water. *On the forty-second:*
the sickle hits a fawn; his bleat pierces the tractor's chug
like cold water on a dusty throat. He lurches off.
There's no way to see them in the deep grass,

no way to miss. Still, we never tell my mother.
I begin to lose track, listening for loose bolts,
but around sixty my father finishes hitching up the rake,
waves me in for coffee. The second hour ends.

III.

Hay 1. n. Grass or other plants such as clover or alfalfa,
cut and dried for fodder. Slang. A trifling amount of money.
Used only in negative phrases, especially in "that ain't hay."

IV.

Today I mowed ten acres of hay, laid
twenty tons of alfalfa down, raked
it into windrows for my father to stack
this afternoon. Tomorrow he'll gesture
to the two stacks and say, "Well,
we've started haying." In a month
the two of us will put up eighty tons;
by August perhaps one hundred ten.
Hay for the cattle against winter, pitched
out in the snow for their slow chewing, snow
blowing among the stems, drifting on their backs.

OUT TO PASTURE

...

During my first winter at the ranch, when I was ten, I soon learned to help my new father feed cattle on weekends. I also learned that when, in his opinion, the snow was too deep for his 1950 Chevrolet pickup to get to the highway, I would be obliged to help him feed on school days as well. I looked forward to windy days with deep snow.

Muffled to the eyes in wool sweaters and scarves, I stumbled behind my father to the barn. Stamping my feet, I'd watch while he wove the harnesses onto the Belgian work team, a blue roan mare named Beauty, and Bud, the sorrel gelding. The team's size enthralled me. I wanted to learn to drive them, but my father said, "They're not pets. They're work horses."

Fastening straps, he always turned his back just as I held a cube of cake, an enticing mixture of grains and molasses, under Beauty's nose. Keeping my hand steady, I'd look into her eyes, except when I glanced at my feet to be sure they were far away from her hooves. Her downy lips warmed my fingers through my mitten as her massive teeth closed over the cube. A tongue bigger than my hand folded it inside her mouth. The *crunch!* sounded like a bone snapping.

When the horses were harnessed, my father would stand behind them, holding the reins, and holler, "Open the doors!" I'd struggle to lift the bar out of the metal braces, gasping, "I can get it!" I'd heave first one door, then

39

the other over the inevitable snowdrift outside. Then Father would cluck to the horses, shaking the lines. Bud would bow his neck and shake his mane, and they'd trot outside, hooves spraying arcs of snow.

"Gee, Bud!" Father would call, or "Haw, Beauty!" I could never remember which mean "turn left" or "turn right." When they reached the hayrack, Bud stepped carefully over the tongue, and both horses backed up in rhythm with Father's voice, "So, Beauty. Steady, Bud."

Then he'd boost me up and I'd burrow into the hay. Standing, he'd gather up the lines, and holler, "Giddyup." I saw his legs stiffen as the horses snorted and leaned into their collars. They'd toss their heads, blowing great steaming clouds. The joints of the wooden hayrack squealed as it moved forward. Wheels creaked against the drifted snow. Lifting their legs high, the horses trotted down the lane. Deep in the hay, I could feel the rack rise and hesitate at big drifts until Father shook the lines, and the big haunches—all I could see—bunched with effort. If the drift covered only part of the road, he guided the team around it to save their strength. I could lean forward from my hay nest and see the bill of his red corduroy cap bobbing in rhythm to the jingling harness. A clear drop of moisture trembled on the end of his sharp nose.

At gates, he'd loop the lines around an upright board at the front of the rack and slowly climb down. Sometimes I joined him to try my strength against the wire gates, but usually he'd wade through the snow, wrap his arm around the gate stick, and squeeze until he could lift the wire loop and carry the gate out of the way. Then he'd climb back up and drive the wagon through. If there were cows on the other side, I climbed down with him and shooed them away until he shut the gate.

Then he'd drive up the slope, the horses breathing deep and pulling hard, to a place where the wind had cleared the snow away. Handing the lines to me, he'd stick his fork deep in the hay. With one foot on a side board, he'd scramble to the top of the slippery pile.

"Ready," he'd say, and I'd glance back to see him standing with his feet spread, lifting a forkful. I'd shake the lines as he did, and try to deepen my voice. "Hup, Beauty! Hup, Bud!" Each horse would cock one ear back, and they'd take the first step together.

As the horses pulled the rack around in a wide circle, the cows ran toward us, bags swinging and snow showering from their hooves. They'd snatch big mouthfuls of hay, throwing their heads to jerk it loose from the pile. More heads appeared in silhouette against the skyline, and soon a line of dark forms would dribble down the slope.

Talking to the big team the way Father did, murmuring "Soooo, Beauty, Soooo Bud," I soon realized I wasn't really driving, just holding the lines as the horses did their job. I kept watch over my shoulder, afraid my father would fall off when the hayrack lurched over a rock. Eventually, I convinced myself I could probably drag him into the low hayrack, and the team would take us back to the house. At least I'd try. I was sure that if Mother were driving, she'd just cry and some man would probably come along to help her.

Despite the cold, I breathed deeply, loving the dry green scent, remembering the hayfield's glare and how Beauty and Bud shone with sweat as we cut hay. Concentrating, I'd think hard of heat, but my feet eventually chilled until I couldn't even wiggle my toes. When I stamped my feet, the horses flicked their ears back at me. The only other sounds were their deep snorting breaths, and thin squeaks from the hayrack's oak joints.

When the rack was empty, I'd lean back with the lines in my hands, and try to holler "Whoa up there" in a deep voice before Beauty and Bud stopped on their own. Father would drop the pitchfork and walk back across the empty boards, breathing hard, to take the lines. I'd stand beside him, hanging onto the plank across the front of the rack. Peering sideways at me from under his steamy glasses, he'd pull a ragged blue handkerchief out of his coveralls to blow his nose. He'd take off his glasses and rub them with the soggy cloth. Later he'd ask me to wash off the smears. Then, his head tilted so he could look through some spot on the glass that wasn't blurry, he'd shake the reins.

Bud raised his head, his red-spotted neck shining wet under the creamy mane, and lunged into the collar. Beauty, hide turned indigo with sweat, worked the bit with her teeth and kept pace with him. Like a sled, the hayrack flew over the snow to the jingle of harness and the pitchfork's tenor rattle.

When we rolled into the yard, I'd jump down, feeling as if I had tree stumps attached to my knees, and stagger to the barn door. Father unharnessed the horses and I arranged the straps on the right hooks. While he hung the collars, I'd slip a few pieces of cake to the horses. He usually sent me to the house to warm up, so it was a while before I realized he dumped buckets of cake and oats into their mangers after I left.

In spring, I rarely saw Bud and Beauty. If we came near them in the pasture, they'd shake their great heads, stomp a couple of times, and run away. As the hay ripened, they relaxed on the hilltop south of the house. One evening my father would say, "Well, I think it's about time we cut some of that hay." The next morning, Bud and Beauty would be standing beside the gate. He'd harness them in the barn and walk them to the mower. Each noon, he'd drive them to the water tank across a broad swath of mown hay.

The summer I turned twelve and became a woman, my father came home with a John Deere 420 tractor he said was my birthday present. Years later, I learned my folks had paid for it with a savings bond my grandmother had given me. Father taught me how to drive the tractor, so I could mow alfalfa and we could put up the hay faster. My Uncle Bud, Mother's brother, welded a hitch on the back for the rake. At the county fair that fall, my father said, "She can mow as much hay as a man." At the time I accepted this as lavish praise; I hadn't been a woman long enough to suspect the dangers of such comparisons.

All that summer I mowed and raked hay at the same time, wrestling the little tractor around corners, and turning to watch the bundles the rake gathered so I could dump the load at the right time. I loved the work, though all night my back and arms ached, and my ears rang. Only years later did my father say with a kind of astonishment, "I should have made you wear earplugs—I never thought what that racket might do to your hearing." While I worked, I could see Beauty and Bud standing on the hillside above the hayfields, head to tail, swishing flies.

My father also bought an old John Deere "A" tractor with a hydraulic lift, and while I mowed and raked, he'd move along behind me, arranging bundles of hay in complex patterns that became huge stacks. That winter, instead of pitching hay by hand from the wagon, he put a hydraulic grapple fork on the big tractor. Grabbing huge chunks, he could fill the hayrack in a half hour. Then he'd hitch it to the hayrack and tow the load out to feed the cows. I'd ride in back, jumping down to open the gates.

Then I'd wander among the cattle, looking for swollen teats or sick calves while Father unhitched the belching tractor and scattered hay with the grapple fork. I'd hear snorts as the work team pranced close, waiting for their share. Hides glistening, they'd trot easily through the drifts to share a pile of hay away from the cows. I could never get close enough to pet their noses, even if I remembered to bring a few cubes of cake in my pocket.

Bud and Beauty stayed in the pasture from then on unless my father drove the tractor into a deep drift or mudhole and got it stuck. Then he'd harness the team to heave it free.

After I went away to college, I helped feed the cattle only when I came home on vacations. By then conversations with my father had dwindled to his questions about my studies, or lectures on the expense of luxuries like my phone calls home. At the end of a visit, he'd usually disappear while I was loading the car, so I seldom got to tell him good-bye. The day I left for college after Easter break during my freshman year, I embraced my sobbing mother, reminding her I'd be home all summer. Then I noticed Father leaning on the corral gate and joined him.

"Bud and Beauty are gone," he said. "Went out one morning in February, that cold spell we had. Forty below. I was thinking I might have to hitch 'em up to feed, but the tractor started."

His voice sounded choked. Glancing sideways, I saw tears on his cheeks. "Neither of them came to feed, so I walked up to the top of the hill." He nodded at the big ridge south of the ranch. "I could see Bud standing down there. I had that handy little glass you gave me in my pocket, so I looked at him through that."

He shrugged. "Looked like Beauty just got tired and laid down. As soon as enough snow melted so I could get the pickup out of the yard, I loaded old Bud in the pickup and took him to the sale ring. They'd been together twenty years. I didn't like to think of him standing out there alone."

Redwing blackbirds whistled in the silence. I never saw my father cry again, though after his oldest sister died, he went off in the pickup alone, and when he came back there were streaks in the dust on his lined cheeks.

THE OWL ON
THE FENCE
...

I was probably eleven years old when I first saw a great horned owl. On my mare Rebel, I was learning how my father gathered cattle to move them into another pasture. While I rode around clusters of cows and calves, urging them down off sunny hillsides, my father drove his pickup to their favorite hiding places, parked the pickup, and walked among them waving his whip— but never hitting them—to start them moving toward the others.

I'd already learned not to rush while gathering. The cows stood and stretched when they saw me. Then they'd belch, a growl that brought cud up from their stomachs. Chewing slowly, they'd watch my horse walk up the slope until I yelled at them or got too close. Then they'd swallow, bawl to their calves, and begin pacing downhill. I'd ride back and forth above each bunch, whistling and hollering. Every few minutes, two or three pairs would emerge from a hidden glen, or pop out of a pocket in a limestone outcrop, and I might glimpse my father waving his whip behind them. When the cattle were bunched in the bottom of the gully, he'd count to be sure we had them all. Then he'd drive the pickup ahead of them, to keep them pointed the right direction and moving slowly, and I'd follow on my horse. My jobs were to keep the calves close to the cows, so they wouldn't panic and run back to the last place they'd sucked, and to stop any cow who decided to run another direction.

That day we were headed for the pasture we leased from "the government" a mile east of the land we called "the Lester pasture" for its first homesteader. The Bureau of Land Management specified the day in mid-July we could turn cattle into the adjacent grass, as well as the day we had to remove them. Once, when some emergency kept us from getting to the pasture and the cows stayed in an extra day, we got a nasty note from officials. After that, my father always grumbled that "they spend my tax money to fly over and count the cows." We were always anxious to move the cows into the pasture as soon as possible. When the government repossessed the land from failed homesteaders during the Dirty Thirties, agricultural experts dictated the bare ground be seeded to crested wheat grass, an introduced crop that grows fast and greens up early. The experts didn't know until much later that the grass forms huge clumps of soil around the roots, allowing all the soil between plants to blow away, resulting in erosion. And the seed heads are bristly and tough; in dry weather cows may not eat the grass at all, or if they do it may lodge in the linings of their throats and form a mass that can choke them. We wanted to make what use we could of the grass, before the seed heads grew so dry they were a danger.

I was recalling all my father had told me about crested wheat grass when I rode under a big cottonwood and felt the back of my neck prickle as if someone was watching me from the branches. I stared up into the thick leaves, trying to see through the shimmering patterns.

An owl dropped straight out of sunlight and shadow into open air, great wings snapping open a few inches above my face, wingspan greater than my outflung arms could reach. The owl glided down the draw and floated into the next cottonwood. Rebel snorted at the flying shadow in front of her hooves and reared. I grabbed the saddle horn and hung on. When I looked again, the owl was gone.

By nearly flying down my throat, the great horned owl became one of the first wild creatures I studied. I reacted like the writer I wanted to be: I described the incident in my journal while we ate lunch. Later I looked in my parents' books for more information on owls. I felt I had discovered a secret, as if I'd learned the Lone Ranger was my big brother, and I wanted to share my excitement. Shy and nocturnal, owls are such efficient predators that they're near the top of the food chain, but most people never see one. After that first glimpse, I saw them everywhere on the prairie.

My wildlife lessons had begun on trips with my father over east to the summer pasture to check the cattle. On nearly every trip, in those years before hunters found the public property mixed with our deeded land, we saw coyotes, antelope, and feral horses. I learned by experience to turn my head slowly, watching for movement out of the corner of my eye. The more carefully I looked, the more I saw. Now I believe there is a connection between knowing what you might see, and seeing it.

Around my parents' house stand cottonwood trees sixty to eighty feet tall, mixed with cedars and elms. Lilac and plum bushes, with a few willows, line the dry bed of a nearby creek. Fall winds pile tumbleweeds into thickets about the time skunks and mice move in for the winter. Above this pantry, the great horned owls nest—but I had never noticed them until I came face to beak with one in the isolation of the east pasture.

Riding alone over east before I was comfortable in the prairie's size and emptiness, carrying my diary, I sometimes thought an invisible danger was stalking me. Now I believe most children are more aware than adults, and that my senses were trying to tell me about animals I never saw. Fear kept me alert, but years passed before I learned to respect the anxiety, to realize that it heightened my awareness, and thus to recognize it as a useful survival tactic rather than a paralyzing force. Fear made me see more clearly, and gradually I realized what a busy and engrossing place the prairie is, and began consciously looking for its inhabitants. My jitters helped me see the great horned owl, and learn the particular perception necessary to one who writes about nature—and humans.

I was lucky. Owls sometimes viciously assault people who climb near owl nests to count owlets or study eating habits. When the bird strikes prey, the legs contract toward the bird's chest. The tendons at the base of the toes tighten, so the hooked claws curl inward like a fist—and lock.

When I saw that first owl, I wasn't climbing, but I was close to the nesting territory. Later, I rode down the draw and picked out the owl's sturdy outline among the branches of another tree. Her feather cloak, including the erect head feathers called "horns," resembled a brown and gray tweed crossed by thick brown shadows. Staring down at me from the treetop, the owl puffed her feathers and succeeded in looking broad and intimidating, though she probably weighed less than five pounds.

Neither the horse nor I heard a sound when the owl dropped out of her tree. If I hadn't been looking up, I might not have known she'd flown a foot over my head. By the time the horse shied at her shadow and I regained my seat in the saddle, she was again invisible. Having watched owls around the ranch for years, I now recognize nesting trees by the white splashes of excrement down the trunks, a sign, say experts, the owls feel secure. Nervous owls fly away from the nest before voiding, and protect their nests even if that means fighting an intruder. I must have startled her badly to make her fly.

In that summer pasture, at that time, only seven cottonwoods grew, all in a single branching valley; I nearly always saw an owl in one of them. In the forty years since that first shock, I've often seen one sitting on the untidy nest that grows larger every year. When I look up, the owl slowly opens one yellow eye, then the other, and tilts her great square head. Composed, she inspects me. She rarely flies if I'm alone. One of the cottonwoods is now dead, killed by standing in water during a rare five-year wet spell.

We leave cattle in the summer pasture, six miles from the ranch house, until snow gets so deep as to make our trips difficult, or until ice on the water tank becomes too thick to chop. Once, in early December, cows broke a fence around the tank on the shoulder of a steep hill covered with slick snow. We had to park a hundred yards away and carry the tools to the fence. After several trips, my father noticed a great horned owl perched slightly above eye level about thirty feet off the trail. He gestured and we both stared. Back to us, looking over one shoulder, the owl sat with one clawed foot extended to hold a vole.

I watched it while we worked, fascinated by the uncanny way its head swiveled. Pivoting and reversing, the owl's head whirled back and forth each time I walked by, but otherwise it remained still until we finished our work. While we sat in the truck warming our hands on cups of hot coffee, the owl began to eat, tearing chunks of flesh and fur from the vole and gulping them down. Superstitious people once believed demons could spin their heads in a full circle, so they thought the owl was a disguised demon and—following unfortunate human nature—began to fear what they did not understand.

One spring twenty years later, I spent a week teaching writing at a juvenile detention center for boys in northwestern South Dakota. On my last day, two Lakota boys bleeding from a hundred scratches on their faces and arms brought a plastic milk crate to class. Inside was a young great horned owl still covered in thick down, broad wings fluffy but sparse. When we gathered around, he puffed his feathers, inhaled, and hissed sharply. The circle of boys jumped back.

The two captors explained they'd been walking by the sluggish river when they saw the nest high in a cottonwood. They wanted it for their science project, a plan no doubt conceived on the spot. First they tried to climb the tree, but couldn't reach the bottom limb. So they threw rocks until they knocked it down. The young owl bumbled out from a muddle of fur and gnawed bones. When Robert picked him up, the black beak fastened on his finger. Thinking they might return the owl to a safe high branch, they tried again to climb the tree, but failed.

Did they see any adult owls while they were near the tree? I asked. No. I wasn't surprised. Whenever one of the boys escapes from the school, local ranchers turn out with loaded rifles in their pickups. Likely they use those rifles to kill owls and other animals they consider predators.

One boy reached inside the crate to touch the soft feathers. When the owl slashed his hand with its beak, the boy backhanded the bird into the corner of the box.

Filled with a reformer's zeal, I sent the boys to the school's meager library to learn about owls. Then I told them about the Rapid City flood in 1972, on the creek where Crazy Horse was born. A Lakota friend said she'd heard owls hooting for a week before. "They always hoot when somebody's going to die," she said. "But it sounded like thousands of owls, and they hooted all night for a week." More than two hundred people died in the flood.

The class was divided over what should be done with the bird. A few boys pitied the owl's prey, and wanted to kill him to save mice and rabbits. Others thought killing with talons is cruel. We skirmished over the owl's fate until the group decided keeping a wild animal caged was wrong—they understood being in jail. But they were afraid that if we put it on the ground beside the tree, some predator would kill it. I was equally afraid of what the boys might do to the owl if I left it in its classroom crate.

A dozen pairs of brown eyes turned to me. Felix, who had run away from the school several times and was always found at home caring for his younger brothers and sisters, spoke. "You know a lot about owls," he said.

"You take it." The boys cheered. When I left, the owl sat silent in his box on the seat of my pickup, trapped again by my tongue.

I didn't know any wildlife experts then, and balked at taking the bird to a government agency anyway. Jerry, a friend who lived on his grandfather Rudolph's farm while he attended the college where I taught, volunteered to return the owl to the wild. He installed it in an old icehouse, and then told Rudolph. A traditionalist who shot anything threatening his chickens, Rudolph was not pleased.

Jerry knew the owl should not be trained to expect food from humans. So each day he spent hours crawling through the windbreak trees, catching snakes. He'd tie each one by a string around its neck to a stake on the shed's floor, then watch through a crack as the owl stalked and killed it. Each time, the owl ate everything but the slice of snake under the string Jerry had touched. Working around the ranch, Jerry occasionally shot a prairie dog or rabbit and tossed the carcass into the shed. At first, the owl wouldn't touch them. After a while, Jerry says, he had a hard time finding snakes, and as fall approached they went into hibernation. So he started shooting rodents again, tossing them on the shed floor. Perhaps the owl's appetite had grown, or he'd gotten less picky. He'd snatch each small mammal from the floor and fly back to his perch on a ceiling joist.

One day in late fall, Jerry brought a prairie dog into the shed and found a regurgitated owl pellet filled with squirrel bones. He knew then that the owl had learned to kill; he hadn't delivered any squirrels.

By that time the owl was fully fledged. With his friend George (whom I later married), Jerry took the bird in his crate to an isolated meadow in the Black Hills. They opened the crate and hid at the edge of the woods. The owl stayed inside, peering through the cage bars. Jerry crept back to the cage, and used a stick to push the bird outside. The owl looked around briefly, then stalked back into the cage. Jerry pushed him out again, and shut the cage door. The owl turned his head back and forth while the men shivered in the chilly wind, then hopped to the top of the crate. Again, he looked carefully around, then flew to the top of the pickup. He hesitated, then leaped straight up and soared into the trees.

Our winter pasture is six miles north of the ranch, along Battle Creek. The land was first homesteaded by James Hartgering, a pioneering surveyor. His daughter first leased, then sold it to us. Hartgering's house once stood on a slight rise of land surrounded by apple trees. Some still bear fruit after sixty years of neglect. Cottonwoods now a hundred feet tall seeded themselves along the irrigation ditches he dug. During the 1972 Rapid City flood, water raged out of the Black Hills down Battle Creek, miles away from the most severe flooding, leaving dead animals and debris scattered over our hayfields. The only spot that stayed dry was the cellar Hartgering dug, on the little knoll where he'd placed his house. That man looked to the future. He'd have scoffed at experts who said we didn't have to worry about future floods because that deluge was an event likely to happen only once in a hundred years.

Most of our hay comes from this land we still call the "Hartgering place." The ditches are blocked with silt because my father wouldn't spend the money to maintain them for the one year in twenty the creek overflows. I suspect he believed, as I do, that irrigation is morally wrong in this arid country, unless a flood makes excess water available. After I turned twelve and began helping him make hay, my father and I spent most of every summer harvesting tall alfalfa at the Hartgering place. In winter, our pregnant cows grazed there until about the middle of March when we drove them—very slowly, big bellies swaying—home to bear their calves.

One February, a pair of owls must have borrowed a nest at the edge of the heron rookery, while the herons were still enjoying a winter vacation down south. In July, watching alfalfa fall in lush ranks over the sickle bar, I saw both great horned owls and herons gliding out of sloppy treetop nests to the creek. Lugging frogs to their young, the ungainly herons flew detours around the owls.

"Don't mention the owls to anybody," my father said. "Or somebody will want to get rid of them for us. One of those fellas that shoots anything that moves."

Each spring when my father drove to the creek place to check the cows on the evening before we trailed them home, he'd hear boisterous hoots. He'd walk in the back door saying, "Well, it's spring. The owls are back."

Once we began to mow hay in June, I watched the owls as much as I could. Every five feet, though, the mower would lurch, clogged with dirt from voles' earth mounds, invisible in the deep greenery and just high enough to catch the mower knives. After I mowed through them, mud began to cake the blades, making them work harder and harder as they grew sticky with juice from the alfalfa until the sickle finally clogged. If I didn't stop to tear the mess out, I'd strip bolts or break mower teeth. At first, I thought voles were cute. After I'd cleaned the blades a few times, I began to beg the owls, "Eat them all." But if the owls ran out of wild prey, they could always fly to the farm a half-mile north for mice and cats.

One chill fall day, I was fixing fence along the creek. Straightening up, I saw what looked like a dirty gray rag hung on the fence. I blinked and realized it was a great horned owl. For a long time, I fought for breath before moving closer.

The killer had blown an immense hole in the owl's breast, then hung his trophy where we couldn't miss it. Gently untangling the great wings from the top wire, I realized the delicate bones were shattered. I laid the owl on the floor of the pickup cab and went back to stapling wire. Insignificant data flowed into my brain: our word "owl" came from the Latin word *ululare*, "to howl." Their calls echo in the darkness of our ignorance, and the owls speak in our language as well. Or perhaps, these days, they are howling in fury and frustration.

Driving across a highway bridge on the way home, I looked closely at a bundle of trash I'd seen on my trip to the pasture, and realized it was brown and gray feathers. I stopped and walked back, not surprised to find the other great horned owl with a huge bullet wound torn in her shoulder. She probably flew low along the creek bed as long as her strength lasted, dropping defeated on the bridge. Trucks whizzed by, gears grinding, as I stood holding the corpse. This owl lay nearly three miles across country from the fence where her mate hung. If I took the body, it wouldn't be flattened by trucks and the hunter might never know he killed them both. Maybe he would wonder out loud, and I would hear him.

When I got home, I put both bodies on a table. The pointed blade of my pocketknife sliced easily into the first owl's breast, slitting the skin straight up to the hooked beak. I peeled it back on each side, scraping away pink flesh. The skin was fragile. If I tried to hurry, it tore. I slowed my breathing, recalling everything I knew about skinning deer, rabbits, and grouse. I'd always viewed those animals as legitimate prey, intended for meat. Skinning the owl felt like violating something sacred. Night mysteries were not meant for dissection.

I cut each wing off close to the body. I severed the feet and head, cutting carefully around the eye sockets and beak. A live owl's eyes glow like lanterns, but these eyes looked dusty. I salted and rolled the skins and stored them in a paper bag to dry. The skinny bodies looked weak and silly, like old ranchers in hospital gowns. I tucked them into the branches of a tall cedar tree near my parents' house. Time and small scavengers cleaned the bones, launched them into the wind again.

I scraped most of the flesh from the two skulls, then put them in an old aluminum pot. An artist friend once recommended boiling small animal skulls as the only practical way to remove all the bits of flesh. He left out a detail or two. With all the windows open, the stench was still so smothering I found urgent work to do outside. Once dry, the whitened skulls retained no odor, but I kept water and herbs simmering on the stove for a week before the stench stopped intruding on every meal.

The owls' wings, nearly fleshless, dried quickly with no scent. The feet shriveled and clenched as they dried, shiny black talons interlocking. I wove the feathers into dream wheels and hung them over my bed and typewriter. Raising my eyes from this page, I can see one clean, white skull. The other is in an artist's studio.

Keeping the skulls is a risk. It's illegal to shoot a raptor, and I have no proof of innocence. But their solidity reminds me of the living owls, and of the ugly reality of their deaths. Writing words and phrases, I recall their tranquil flight, the accuracy of their killing strike. An owl feather is the softest thing I've ever touched.

Once, I threatened to find and shoot the owl killer, to hang him on the same fence to dry in the sun. I'm sure he stood in our hayfield, using a telescopic sight to bring the owls so close he saw only a blurred shape he could not miss. Two bullets ruptured sixty million years of evolution—considerably more than the killer displayed.

A year after my husband George died, on a winter night when the mercury hung at forty below zero, I stepped out on the deck. A loud crunching surrounded me, as if an army were stomping through the snow crust, about to appear from the darkness. Startled, I snapped on the porch and garage lights—nothing in sight. The marching continued. Heavy breathing engulfed me. An invisible army. I backed against the outside wall of the house, trying to think, trying not to run inside and start loading guns.

Finally I remembered how cold magnifies sound. Below me, twenty yearling calves were stumbling through the old, crusty snow, searching for grass.

Back inside, I turned on the television set. For weeks, the screen had been filled with images of brash young men and women brandishing rifles as they talked vaguely about serving their country, about democracy, about freedom. Now, a few minutes after midnight, I watched a newsman announce that U.S. planes had begun bombing Iraqi territory.

I began to cry, and, startled at my reaction, instinctively stumbled out to the moonlit, icy deck. From the darkness came an immortal voice, an owl in the trees around my parents' dark house. By counting the hoots, I realized that a female great horned owl was announcing her arrival. She was ready to begin another spring, another family. Her sonorous song was a warning to her prey as well as a serenade of rebirth.

A MOUTHFUL

OF MICE

. . .

When my cat's muffled meow sounded outside the basement window above the bed at 3 A.M., I stumbled naked upstairs to open the door, afraid she'd been hurt by a wild barn cat or a visiting tomcat.

As she padded inside, I saw why she couldn't communicate properly: her mouth was full of a limp mouse.

"I wish you'd eat out, Blue," I mumbled. Dining at home, she usually left the tail, hind feet, and one kidney neatly arranged on the rug—not an enjoyable discovery with my bare toes at dawn.

Blue dropped the mouse and began to groom her whiskers; she always washed before eating. The mouse shook itself, ran into the corner, and dived under a trunk.

"Dammit!" I grabbed the yardstick and slid it under the trunk to scare the mouse out into the open. "Get it!" I whispered to Blue, hoping not to wake my sleeping husband. She hopped onto the trunk, curled her tail over her paws, and looked at me, purring.

"I thought you gave up on teaching me to hunt." I reached for the broom; maybe I could sweep the mouse outside. It darted toward the open door into the bedroom connecting our small apartment to my parents' ranch house. I sprinted, but the mouse was faster. I shut the second door, which led to my parents' bedroom and the hall. The mouse skittered under a sliding door into

54

the closet. Blue leaped to the single bed and stared at the closet door.

Behind me, George stood blinking in the doorway, mumbling, "Whatsa matter?" Now Blue had maneuvered two naked humans into a 3 A.M. mouse hunt.

"Blue brought in a live mouse. It's in the closet."

"Umgh. Want me to get the gun?"

"Very funny." I opened one closet door. On the floor were boxes of clothes my mother always meant to mend, beside an old doll trunk containing her childhood toys and boxes of my dolls she'd saved for hypothetical grandchildren. I shoved the trunk hard against the wall, hoping to squash the mouse. When I pulled the trunk out to look behind it, the mouse leapt from the top and scurried behind a box. Leaning forward, I knocked down a hanger holding three sack dresses and two miniskirts Mother was sure I could alter and wear if I didn't waste time writing.

While I untangled myself, George opened the other closet door a crack, and shook a box. When the mouse ran toward my end of the closet, I enveloped it in a wool suit I'd made in 1959. "Got him!" I said, standing on the hem while I tried to gather the cloth around the rodent. Blue minced to the end of the bed and stretched to look over our shoulders. Bent over, backs to the door, we both fumbled at the package. I heard my parents' bedroom door open, and my mother say, "What's going on?"

I looked over my shoulder—over the expanse of our naked backs and four jiggling buttocks—and saw Mother's blue eyes widen as she gasped. For a delicate woman, she commands remarkable vocal volume. Plumbers, cowboys, construction workers, and inquisitive neighbors who have made the mistake of startling her once never do it again. We never lock our doors, and one day a salesman walked into the living room while Mother was vacuuming. He fled after hearing her shriek, and rumor says he joined an order of monks sworn to perpetual silence.

At 3 A.M., she was too sleepy to utter one of her glass-shattering squawks. But she hollered loud enough to startle George, who dived forward, hitting his head on the pipe that served as a closet rod, and bit his tongue. He usually didn't swear in front of ladies, but he bellowed an expletive of ancient lineage. Mother slammed the door. The mouse escaped from the suit and raced under the bed toward our apartment.

Blue sighed—I heard her—leapt on the mouse, and bit through his neck until his slack legs stopped scrambling. George and I went back to bed. The mouse's tail and hind feet were symmetrically arranged on the rug in the morning; apparently Blue ate the lone kidney to restore her strength.

Mother divorced my father and fled north from Texas when I was four years old, bringing with her a collection of stories about the horrors of cockroaches, spiders, and rats. Before marrying my rancher stepfather, she worked as a secretary and lived in a tiny house owned by a widow who shared her views. A single tiny spider on the windowsill sent both of them into frenzies. They sprayed chemicals like mortar fire, and scrubbed everything—including me—with disinfectant. When we moved to the ranch, Mother demanded and got a new house, though while it was being built we lived in the old one, up on blocks in the alfalfa field. She shuddered, describing all the pests that must live in its cracks and joints, screamed a dozen times a day, and bought big spray cans of every poison available. She also believed that cleanliness could eradicate vermin and misfortune. Watching homeless people on television, she'd mutter, "They'd be OK if they'd only wash."

Once while I was attending college in the eastern part of South Dakota, I drove home for a holiday, arriving around 2 A.M. I dragged my suitcase inside and went to bed. When I woke and reached for clean clothes, the suitcase was gone. I thought I'd dreamed bringing it inside, and stepped out on the porch. My clothes lay everywhere in the front yard around the open suitcase. Dresses, bras, panties, lipstick, bead necklaces, underwear, shirts, and jeans—it looked as if the suitcase had exploded. Two cats slept on my favorite sweater and Mother's dog was gnawing a shoe.

Swearing, I grabbed the broom and swished cats in all directions. Mother came around the corner of the house as I gathered clothes. "Leave that stuff right there," she snapped. "I don't want you bringing mice and cockroaches into my house."

"There aren't any cockroaches in my underwear. Look what the cats did to this sweater!"

"Cockroaches can hide in very small cracks. Leave that suitcase in the sun for a couple of days. I shook it good and put some mothballs in it, but give them time to crawl away. I'm sure I saw a mouse in the kitchen this morning, and I certainly didn't have any in this house yesterday! Didn't you read that article on brown recluse spiders I sent?" When I sold the suitcase fifteen years later, it still smelled like mothballs.

Eventually, my husband George and I built a house nestled into the top leeward side of a hill in one of the pastures. During the years I spent there, both while he was living and after his death, I learned more about mice. During the long, snowy winters, most of the prairie's larger, more colorful wildlife were tucked into dens or snoring in the shelter of a tree. So I watched mice, gaining greater respect for their kind. I also began to believe there's something perverse in the way humans focus only on large predators when they speak of "saving nature." Few of us seem to consider nature as embodied by the critters in the dark corners of our houses, and yet they are as natural as grizzlies, and perhaps more deeply affected by our behavior.

Each winter, as snow deepened around the house, I'd see a tangled array of tunnels bulge up through the drifts. When the snow began to settle in spring, I attended a daily open house at mouse condominiums. Apparently, the winter dwelling was mostly underground with a few aboveground hallways and caves carved from snow. In spring, the tunnels appeared as sagging lines in a drift, becoming clearer every day.

I found passages from the woodpile to my compost pit and flower bed, and followed a trail from the propane tank to the railroad tie fence and on down the hill into the thick grass in the windbreak of juniper and buffaloberry. One led from the woodpile to George's canoe tipped over beside the garage. Frodo, my West Highland white terrier, spent many hours with his head under the aluminum craft, barking at a mouse he couldn't dislodge. When he gave up, he'd stumble out from under the canoe shaking his head, as if deafened by his own echo.

As the sun uncovered tunnels, I felt like a grownup peeking into a dollhouse. Patiently, I'd trace the interwoven trails to waste rooms and to food caches filled with grass seeds. Sometimes the tracks in a roofless passage reached to the edge of a snowdrift, as though the residents dug the tunnel simply so they could stick their heads outside and check the weather.

In summer, riding a tractor or horse, I've watched meadow jumping mice sway gently in the breeze halfway up a grass stalk. Later, I'd find grass stems gnawed into short lengths, until the head dropped low enough for a mouse to reach from the ground. A miniature haystack of chopped stems marked the harvest area. A mouse chewed through each stem a dozen times before it could haul one bundle of seeds away to the larder.

In winter, snowdrifts aided meadow jumping mice; a stem carrying late seed stood firm in snow until a mouse digging a tunnel encountered it. Gnawing, the mouse pulled the straw down into the tunnel section by section, leaving tiny holes in the snow. I wonder if the reaper sometimes discovered only after a head dropped that the birds had eaten all the seeds. After the tunnel roof melted, I'd find golden shards of chewed stems, like hay on a barn floor.

Some tunnels made me believe mice were intent on advancing the frontiers of their known world. From a tangle of passageways, a tunnel might lead straight a long way until it reached a rock, or my railroad tie fence. Gently using naked fingers to explore the tunnel's end, I sometimes found an escape hatch into a hole in the ground. At other times, the tunnel simply ended beside a rock, or level with the point where one railroad tie crossed another. Perhaps on sunny days or quiet nights a mouse sat there, acting as lookout or basking in the sun, unseen as Frodo and I slogged past to check the propane or gather wood.

Often, I found a walnut-sized hole lined with grass under an alfalfa plant, only a few mouse steps from several entrances to underground burrows. Do mice establish bachelor pads? Private napping spots? Lookouts? Do renegades or soldier mice sleep aboveground, even though their buried homes are sturdier and safer?

Occasionally, a tunnel end was enlarged and stuffed with grass and leaves, perhaps as a birth chamber. In several of these tiny refuges, I found grasshopper and insect wings, proving they can serve as dining rooms for the western harvest mouse. If I looked or felt carefully, I might discover vertical holes, a back door to the mouse basement. On still, sleepless nights when the only sound was the crunch of my footsteps on crisp snow, I imagined furry families frisking in warm tunnels.

Because I seldom saw the inhabitants of these quarters in winter, I was not always sure what kind of mice created these marvels of engineering, though one glimpse sent me to my reference books. I've seen both western harvest mice and big-eared prairie deer mice scurrying through the grass as I walked in the fields. From horseback, I once watched a ranch cat creep up on a western jumping mouse. As the cat leapt, the mouse did too—nearly four feet. Then it froze; the befuddled cat ran a tight circle, then sniffed more carefully where the mouse had begun its jump, but never discovered the trick.

As soon as the first snow fell, my mother began feeding the ranch cats dry dog food—so much of it that most of them spent the day snoozing in the barn. A mouse fattened on cattle feed could run over their paws without waking them. Every year, when my parents left to spend three months in an apartment in Texas—taking a good supply of insecticide and mouse poison— I instituted a program designed to save our winter feed from rodents and improve the health of our cat menagerie: Linda's Diet and Exercise Plan for Flabby Felines.

First, I lured the cats into the mouse-infested shed where we stored cattle cake and grain. Then I shut the door and forgot to open it for a day or two. The problem with this strategy was that few of our buildings were "cat tight." A full-grown badger could, and did, walk through some of the holes in the foundation. On the first day, a few clever kitties escaped; they spent the night mewing piteously on the back steps, where they were joined the second day by the slower, heavier cats.

After a week during which I fed them their scanty rations in the shed, however, they began to slink through the grass around the barns, lean bellies low and ears pricked, relearning how to hunt. After another week, they'd hardly visit the back steps at all, but lie around the granary belching and licking their paws. I felt as if I should send an announcement to People for the Ethical Treatment of Animals, noting my achievement in recalling domesticated cats to something resembling their wild instincts.

Each winter when it was time for me to begin feeding hay to the cows, I'd discover the surviving mice, or those who preferred rural life, in tunnels in the haystacks. Every cold morning, I'd start the truck, load supplies, and then park beside the barn with the windows open. I'd call cats, snatch them up, and shove them in the windows until they started to overflow and the truck was warm. Then I'd open the door a crack, slither in, roll up the windows, and drive toward the stack yard. The cats weren't used to motorized travel, so they ricocheted off the windshield and sprinted across the dashboard, yowling. I drove with my eyes shut half the time. After parking next to the stack of hay bales, I'd crawl out the door closest to the stack and start lifting bales. The cats leapt from the pickup window into gastronomic bliss.

After a few days of this, the felines would follow the pickup ruts like a line of tiny cows when I headed for the bales, trotting daintily to avoid the mud. A neighbor who happened by when I was leading the cats to feed laughed so hard I was afraid he'd require mouth-to-mouth resuscitation. Once I explained the system, and he saw the efficient way the cats burrowed into the stack, slaughtering mice, he grew thoughtful.

Throwing bales into the pickup bed one morning, I heard a pathetic meow. I turned to see the reigning female, Big Mama, sprawled like a cat rug with a mouse under each front paw, and three more—I counted—in her mouth. A sixth mouse sat trembling in front of her, but she had nothing left to catch it with—unless she could wrap her tail around it. She had six kittens to feed, so I stabbed that one with my pitchfork. She chomped the three in her mouth and dropped them in a tidy row beside the first, then dispatched the ones under her paws. Then without a glance at me, she sprang into a crack between two bales. Later that spring, I saw her dragging home a dead jackrabbit, its ears held firmly in her teeth and long legs dragging behind her. Jacks were getting rare in our neighborhood even then, but I could hardly fault such a hunter for snagging the biggest meal she could catch.

One spring, after my parents returned to South Dakota from their winter vacation in Texas, I helped my father clean out the trunk of his car. One of his rules for life was to throw nothing away. A corollary was to carefully examine any object headed for the garbage, because he habitually stuffed money in hiding places he thought no thief would find. After he died, I found money stuffed inside a paper bag of candy wrappers, and several times I found a fifty-dollar bill in the bottom of an old coffee can clanking with wrenches.

As we bent over the open car trunk, he picked up a pair of my mother's overshoes and reached inside. He pulled out an inner sole, grunted, and pushed it back. Then he straightened up and looked at me. "That inner sole had an *eye!*" He dragged it out again: a mouse, flattened and desiccated.

As I spent more time watching mice in winter, I became more aware of the actions of their predators as well. When I'd notice a peculiar darkness under a snow-covered patch of grass surrounded by mouse tracks, I looked for a secret door into the world beneath the drift. Often, a red-tailed hawk perched on the electric pole at sunrise stayed most of the short winter day near such a retreat, waiting for mice who emerged to romp in the sunshine without looking up.

I admired the hawk's teardrop silhouette on the light pole, its patient wait until it sensed the perfect time to plummet, to rise with a twitching mouse in its honed talons. I applauded the hawk's reflexes, and the removal of a slow or unwary mouse from the gene pool. While feeding a new generation of hawks, the red-tail was also endowing the remaining mice with reasons to be more alert.

Making coffee one morning, I glanced out the north window at the electric pole by reflex, then blinked and looked again. The heart-shaped silhouette that morning was huge, a full-grown golden eagle, feathers ruffled against the north wind. I grabbed the camera and gently eased out the front door in the shelter of the windbreak wall. Slowly, I extended the camera lens around the edge of the wall. Through the viewfinder, I saw the eagle crane his neck, leaning far to the side, peering down as if sighting prey.

Just then, Frodo moseyed around the corner of the house, up to his belly fringe in snow, snorting ice as he inspected tracks and marked his territory.

The eagle tilted his head and stared; Frodo rolled over on his back, wiggling ecstatically. The eagle spread his wings and rose a little.

I firmly believe in the natural order. Adhering to that tough code, I rarely interfere with a wild predator busy surviving. But surely it's not natural for an eagle to prey on pudgy terriers. I snapped the picture and flung myself off the deck toward Frodo.

The eagle's wings exploded outward, air popping and smoking as he broke off his stoop and flapped for altitude. He circled the house once, eyeing me, and then went elsewhere to dine.

THE POT OF
HOSPITALITY STILL
SIMMERS

...

I was stunned to read a popular columnist's opinion that inviting friends for a potluck meal, with each guest bringing a contribution of food, is impolite. Without potluck, we who live in the West would hardly have a social life.

Our potluck gatherings have impeccable lineage and an unusually long history. The expression "take potluck" was first recorded in 1592 when peasants worked the land for rich aristocrats. The laborers lived in chilly hovels and kept their hearth fires smoldering continually. After each meal, they tossed leftovers into an iron pot hanging over the flames, constantly simmering so the mixture was safe to eat. Servants in rich folks' great houses regularly tucked scraps of high-quality food into their pockets to eat, or to add to the pot at home. At dinnertime, everyone dipped a cup or bowl into the pot and ate whatever appeared.

At a later date, visitors invited to "take potluck" understood the expression to mean, "It's nothing fancy, just what we usually have," or in another commonly accepted shorthand, "plain fare." Later, the French called the ordinary family dinner *pot-au-feu,* the "fire pot," and raised it to a high culinary art with spices and herbs. In Ireland, a guest invited to partake of the "pot of hospitality" was always ready; most travelers kept a cup tied to their belts, or a bowl in a belt pouch, ready to dip into any meal offered. Few people could afford extra plates and bowls for company.

These days, people who live in the country don't necessarily keep a pot bubbling on the stove all day, though some of us use meat and vegetable scraps to make our own soup stock. Raised to "waste not, want not," I toss in washed vegetable peelings as well, creating nourishment out of what might be waste or compost in other households. Stored in the freezer, a stock can be thawed and enhanced with garden extras or leftover roast to become a hot supper in minutes—my version of "instant" soup.

Country people don't entertain the way city people do, anyway. Asking folks to drop in for a cocktail before the play when you live forty miles from the nearest theater is impractical. We might meet city friends in town for a drink or dinner before a movie or other entertainment, but expense and late hours often cause us to decline such invitations. If we go, we might be tempted to consume too much alcohol, so that the drive home becomes hazardous.

When planning parties in the country, we need to consider not only driving time, but weather. I learned not to invite guests from town to the ranch between November and June. If heavy snow falls on the day before they plan to come, I'll have to call them to explain that my road is impassable, even with a four-wheel-drive vehicle. Too often, the persistent or cocky ones won't listen. Usually, they'll get thoroughly stuck on the ranch road, requiring me to get out my truck, towrope, and shovels to help them dig out. After dinner, I'll have to repeat the process with a full stomach and a strong desire to sit still and visit. Sensible or native-born guests might call an hour or a day ahead to cancel. I appreciate their wisdom and experience, but I am still stuck with a large meal to store in the freezer and consume for weeks ahead. These are not inspiring memories as one ponders dinner invitations.

Parties planned for summer months usually suffer fewer interruptions, if you can schedule them at all between branding, moving cattle to summer pasture, and haying, though a lightning storm can change the timing of the event as half the men and women in the community fight prairie fires. Still, a hard rain that eliminates the fire danger also soaks into the entrance road. If visitors get in, their vehicles leave deep ruts. Months later, as we smack our heads bouncing over the hardened tracks, we reminisce, "Remember that rain, when the Larsons slid off here and got stuck? Now that was a good party!"

For all these reasons, we like to entertain large groups without much planning, wiping the slate clear of social obligations once or twice a year. To avoid spending a week at the stove, a busy woman usually calls friends to come and bring something. The nervous hostess cooks the main menu item and asks specific guests to bring their specialties, knowing Martha's baked beans will complement the roast in the oven. The three-bean salad Sandra brings will appeal to some guests, while others will prefer Diane's traditional Jello with canned fruit. Those concerned about health may actually eat some of Milly's broccoli with cheese sauce, but most will skip it to leave room for Polly's pumpkin pie, or Mavis's mince, or Sally's fresh strawberry.

A potluck dinner is my favorite entertainment, whether I'm the hostess or a guest. Some guests bring their food ready to serve. Others join me in the kitchen to chop, slice, warm, or frost their dinner offerings and participate in congenial kitchen discussions. Any guest, man or woman, who has prowled through my utensil drawer looking for a serving spoon has already broken through several social barriers that might have kept us from speaking honestly to each other. Conversations about current political matters are a lot more lively at a potluck dinner.

People of different backgrounds and cooking habits contribute to any pot-luck meal. If conversation drags, asking for a recipe is a sure way to start it again. Some of my friends are vegetarians, who season our talk with views on my profession of cattle raising. They always bring tasty dishes, often com-posed of ingredients new to me. Putting warning labels on meat dishes for these folks is a small price to pay for the recipe for tabouli I have come to love. Gay male guests, besides demonstrating to my conventional ranching neighbors that not all families are the same, taught me about sorrel and wal-nuts as green salad ingredients and gave me slips of sorrel, lovage, anise, and lemon thyme for my herb garden.

We westerners have another potluck custom that polite society might not approve. When guests begin to get restless, the hostess rises too. The com-pany doesn't simply grab their coats, mutter polite inanities, and leave. They take their serving dishes with them, neatly moving half the dishwashing job to other kitchens than mine. Usually, by the time they leave the house, their dishes are no longer empty: I've given each guest some of that huge roast.

One such exchange inspires another, and soon guests are happily trading leftovers. Milly may have divided her broccoli surprise among several dishes, and Mavis distributes the pie as well, explaining that she left a whole pie at home because it was as easy to make two as one. Guests who discover that "only a spoonful" of their dish is left may leave it in my refrigerator instead of taking it home to mold in theirs. While bustling in the kitchen, visitors usually whisk trash into the garbage, or rinse and stack the plates by the sink. When I finally face my kitchen alone, usually a party's worst moment, I find it much neater than it has any right to be after forty people have come for dinner.

With luck, I can also nibble for several days on food I have not cooked. At the same time, I know my hospitality has extended beyond the single meal—everyone has taken home something cooked by someone else.

In my opinion, potluck entertaining is a useful social tool particularly fitting for today's busy, often nontraditional families. Time is so precious many families no longer sit down to eat together. Snarling at one another over boxed fast food gobbled in an overheated car is no substitute for the benison of mealtime. A potluck allows entertainment to be a pleasure, rather than a time-consuming social ordeal testing a hostess's culinary skills. Each guest bears only a little responsibility for an evening's entertainment. Breaking bread together is a ritual sanctified by time. Today, guests may be brought together by interests rather than proximity, creating the kind of communities our ancestors knew. Gathering to share a potluck meal encourages something we all need: friendship.

THE

TOTALLY INTEGRATED

CRAWLY KINGDOM

...

At the rate U.S. wilderness regions are being logged, mined, turned into garbage dumps, and invaded by motorized campers piled with screaming children, there will soon be nowhere a large mammal, especially one with pointed teeth, can relax. You remember relaxation: when a beast can gnaw on a femur, kick back, produce a few offspring, and generally live the kind of life most of us envy.

A lot of folks realized this before I did, because my favorite mammals are appearing in zoos. Elk and buffalo (OK, OK, *bison*) stand around looking bored in cages in city parks, *Felis concolor* paces the concrete behind bars in St. Louis. I'm glad they will survive, but once caged, many animals are—at best—uncomfortable. At worst, they are dying slowly. They mutate before our eyes from fierce, dangerous, wild creatures to a new species called "zoo animals." Such critters are paraded on leashes before TV cameras in front of an audience cooing over how cute they are, or appear in movies as "trained" animals.

We have grown used to thinking of cats and dogs as domestic, though they don't deserve the fate most of them get, since they, too, are descended from wild predators. We are well on our way to domesticating panthers, cheetahs, wolves, grizzlies, and even whales if anyone can figure out how to make the leash stay on. I've rationalized and accepted my reasons for living with dogs, but I'm still uneasy with caging wild predators, though I under-

stand the usual defense: accessible animals teach people about the wildlife
with which we share our world. I suppose it's better than having no tigers
left, but that's not what I really want to talk about.

The conflict between folks who want wildlife to remain wild in a reason-
able facsimile of their natural habitat, and those who think dirt isn't attractive until it's been shaped by a bulldozer, is intense, and will get livelier as
parks disappear, or are turned into imitations of Disneyland. I can see it
now: "GRIZZLYLAND! SEE! The dancing bears! SEE! A wild grizzly dip a
salmon out of a rushing river! TAKE! Your kids' (only on the sign it will be
spelled "kid's") pictures! With a REAL bear! All our bears are guaranteed
toothless, clawless, and toilet-trained!"

I'm a peace-loving person, though I am flexible on that point. I'd like to
propose a compromise that might defuse some of the anger between warring
groups. Perhaps I'll call this the Japanese concept of park building. Many
Americans now think of the Japanese when they are replaced by small, efficient machines that can operate without stress under crowded conditions.
Efficiency could be the cutting edge of park philosophy, revolutionizing our
ideas about wilderness to fit our age of technology. The concept I propose
could be the most amazing park concept to emerge from the Stress Age.

I propose a series of Mosquito/Arthropod Parks, to phrase it in the popular government/military style, complete with slashes. But perhaps I should
rephrase that idea, eliminate the scientific terminology designed to hide the
ugly truth, and get back to basics. I propose we establish the Tick Park.

My idea has so many advantages I don't know where to begin enumerat-
ing them, but it's logical to start with the biggest problem: waste. Some of my
best friends are fervent environmentalists. They backpack into the wilderness and carry out all their waste products for disposal in a landfill handy to
their vacation spot. Of course, that's not where they live and pay taxes, but
we can't have everything. These people don't just haul out their peach pits
and candy wrappers, if they are undisciplined enough to eat candy. No. They
also deposit their fecal matter in plastic bags and proudly carry it around until they emerge in a place civilized enough for a garbage dump. I hear that
some groups pass summer evenings passing the feces-laden bags around in a
circle of like-minded folks who cooperate to mix it to a consistency easy to
transport. Anyone who can do that is tough. They don't carry firearms, even
for emergencies like waking to find a grizzly gnawing on your head. Some

folks who have grizzly teeth marks on their foreheads say they'd be proud to be a bear's lunch.

I am filled with admiration for these folks. I'd hike with them. I'd even carry out my—er—waste, if they'd have me. But while they are discussing their menu of dried kelp, dehydrated milk products, peanut butter, and macaroni, they pointedly look away. They'd be surprised how friendly we meat-eaters can be if they'd only ask. We're often lonely, especially with vegetarians re-producing so rapidly. But I'm hurt when they don't ask, and I stumble away in tears, thoughtfully filing my teeth and cleaning my fingernails with my bowie knife. We need to bridge these gaps in understanding.

But back to the subject. If you mention to the most avid wilderness fa-natic that he or she has a tick crawling across his or her forehead, love of na-ture vanishes. The environmentalist may shed clothing faster than an ecdysi-ast on a hot tin roof. Try it—choose for your experiment a person who gently carries spiders outdoors rather than swat them or spray poison. The minute the word "tick" passes your lips, he or she will whip a spray canister of tick repellent out of a backpack faster than Wyatt Earp at the OK Corral, and proceed to aim it everywhere but his or her forehead, with no regard for in-nocent bystanders. By now (I don't keep up on these things), someone has probably developed a machine-gun tick spray. The stuff makes me break out in a nasty red rash, but I've been showered with it several times without my consent, even while I screamed, "NO! No means NO! Just say NO!"

Somehow, our native love of wildlife doesn't extend to ticks or to many other members of the species I'm sure must be essential for some reason, like ants, spiders, or fleas. Or scorpions.

Some experimental mosquito repellents even kill the poor innocent predators. Eight volunteers once spent a day wearing a combination of repel-lent and toxicant while walking in a Florida park, and were proud to report they'd have killed ninety-four percent of the biting mosquito population. What if we kill them all? What if mosquitoes become endangered? How would we ever enforce a fine for slaughtering them, especially in Wyoming where the citizenry regularly declares open season on animals the feds de-clare endangered?

And who is to say mosquitoes are not vital? Without them, the woods would be even more crowded. Consider this: Lyme disease benefits mankind by doing more to make parks empty of tourists, and thus bearable, than any of Edward Abbey's strategies. Unfortunately, new studies indicate Lyme disease isn't nearly as deadly as we've thought; one researcher said, "The bigger epidemic is Lyme anxiety." If you like the woods quiet, don't spread the news.

On the other hand, perhaps we should consider the bottom line. If mosquitoes and ticks become endangered, we would soon have shops packed with T-shirts proclaiming "Save the Mosquito." Rock and roll stars would conduct "Tick Aid" concerts and proudly drop their pants to display their own collections of small crawling livestock. Volunteers might donate their naked arms, keeping their own personally saved mosquito on a leash so it could be taught to bow in gratitude for its meal. Wouldn't that be cute? The Japanese, who are adopting prairie dogs as pets, would offer an entirely new market. Think how low the shipping costs would be! Maybe I should reconsider.

Another advantage of U.S. Mosquito/Arthropod Designated Wilderness Areas (hmmm, that spells USMADWA, which doesn't fall trippingly off the tongue as a good acronym should) is that they could be very small. A company with a heart, like Exxon or Union Carbide, could establish a park with plenty of wildlife even in an office building hallway. Precedent exists for parks inside buildings since some marketing genius has apparently decided that nature makes folks feel rich. Shopping malls already contain collections of plastic flora intended to give shoppers the illusion they're outdoors. With a little more research, retailers might discover that introducing real greenery and a few ticks would cause sales of polyester and other gimcracks to rise.

Perhaps I'm hopelessly immune to advertising ploys. I've never understood why a car built so low to the ground that a man has to crawl out of it enhanced his sex appeal, and I don't see any appeal in drinking a beer advertised by a bull terrier or a cigarette smoked by a camel.

But I digress. Again. Companies with interior parks devoted to the display and feeding of spiders, ticks, ants, and fleas could hail their working atmosphere as more beneficial to workers. At the same time, they'd have a handy testing ground for the latest chemical, all without sacrificing an inch of space usually devoted to creating money and hazardous waste.

In states overendowed with cities and people (usually called "growth climates"), real creativity could be exercised in putting the parks where people gather. An open wall of plantings covered with ticks in, say, the welfare building could serve the double purpose of entertaining the clients who wait with their screaming children for hours until some overfed bureaucrat has time to insult them, *and* providing varied snacks for the insect life. Ticks carrying Rocky Mountain spotted fever might even trim the welfare rolls a bit and save our tax dollars. What politician could be against that in his secret heart? I'll leave the details to speechwriters who have experience translating something that creates poverty into a beneficial-sounding program.

Even impoverished states, and cities with little wilderness land, could devote enough space, a quarter of a block perhaps, to a park filled with indigenous species of insect life. In populous areas where dogs must be leashed, officials could provide a sturdy fence and invite the folks to turn Fido loose inside. Fido gets exercise even when Mr. and Mrs. Suburbia are too busy to walk him, the wildlife gets a varied diet, and the whole family gets to study nature up close and personal when they try to pry the critters out of Fido's hide.

I simply haven't time to enumerate all the advantages of my plan, and they'll be obvious to most people anyway, so I'll move on to the few problems I still need to solve.

How about calling it Terrain Infested with Crawly Kritters?

Naturally, people who want to live in the country will build expensive homes near the park so no one else can build beside them, and they'll have a wonderful view from the deck. Then they'll complain when the wildlife for whom the park was established inconvenience them. Irate poodle owners will point out that Phideaux never had fleas when they lived in the city. Barechested folks in shorts who gather around the smokeless, odorless, flame-free barbecue grill to toast tofu hot dogs will want the government to keep the mosquitoes away from them. They may demand fences to keep the vermin out of the entire subdivision.

Ranchers will exercise their independence and ingenuity to develop uzzzzzzi, the Terminator Machine Gun Bug Bomb, to defend themselves and whatever brand of ruminant they graze on leased public land, in the name of American freedom. Children will ignore posted warnings, plunge into the swamp, and emerge as pale ghosts of themselves, sucked dry by the resident insects. The wildlife will be harder to confine than wolves, and even harder to brand or ear tag for identification.

On the other hand, none of these problems are new. They are nearly identical to the worries facing workers in other national parks—with one crucial difference.

Almost anyone can kill a tick. It's a little harder to kill a grizzly or a wolf and difficult to "shoot, shovel, and shut up" to hide the evidence. Tick parks will give 50 percent of Americans an improved chance to restore their manhood. No longer will stockbrokers have to endanger themselves and muss up their hair stumbling around in the brush trying to kill a moose or a bear that might bag them instead. They won't have to pay some guide to haul the kill out of the woods, or pay a taxidermist to mount it. One stickpin and a quarter inch of space over the fireplace will display their trophy for everyone to admire.

So let's warm up those computers, phone lines, and whatever it is that carries e-mail, and contact your congressperson, folks. Ask for a huge federal grant to hire a consultant—me, of course—to travel the country advising states and cities how to establish a truly new park: Totally Integrated Crawly Kingdom, or TICK Park. The "truly democratic park" where folks in wheelchairs and campers can experience the wildlife just as completely as healthy hikers. We won't need to spend a dime for new highways, concession buildings, parking lots, or park ranger salaries, or build new toilets. Why, individuals could even adopt a tick—much smaller and easier to feed than a horse—and establish a tick park in their very own homes.

COILED IN THE
PRESSURE COOKER

...

Nearly everyone who ever stepped outside the house on the plains has a snake story. I remember a fresh fall day my husband George and I moved a few head of cattle. We wanted to take one bunch to the summer pasture across the railroad tracks, while holding back a few we wanted to keep closer to home. We thought the job would be so easy we didn't take the horses. The cows were fat and slow, and anyway, the broken ties and rails discarded in the right-of-way by railroad workers made it dangerous to use horses there.

Then a wild Charolais heifer jumped through the rickety fence. I scrambled up the steep embankment and staggered along the ties behind her. Then she wriggled through another hole in the fence. Amazingly, she'd gone into the pasture where we wanted her. That's not usually the way cows behave.

Still, we weren't finished sorting the cattle, and I knew if we didn't fix the fence right away, others would jump through it and cause more trouble. That's one reason ranchers work such long days—every job seems to lead to another.

A few years before, along this same stretch of fence, my father had stopped pounding steeples into rotting posts long enough to mutter, "Damn—excuse me—darn railroad never fixes fences. They got the land free, the least they could do is keep the fences up."

Pressed, he told me how pioneering railroad companies talked the government into giving them a strip of free land clear across the country. Officials insisted the railroad was a public service, a way to encourage farmers to move west, homesteading the "Great American Desert." After the farmers got established, the same tracks could carry their produce east to feed the populous seaboard.

Of course, even though the companies got millions of acres of free land, neither the farmers nor the goods rode free, so the railroads made enormous profits. Some companies didn't lay any track at all, just got rich selling land several times to different settlers. While I listened to my father fume, I picked up the soda cans the train crews tossed into our pastures when they sprayed chemicals to kill weeds. Later in the summer, when the dead weeds had dried enough, the railroad's dilapidated engines would throw sparks and set prairie fires.

Remembering my father's comments, I climbed back over the tracks in waist-deep weeds lugging a bucket of fencing supplies and a shovel. I repeated my father's story to George, who was just beginning to learn our ranching business, adding details like the company truck that followed every train for a few days after the company set a big prairie fire. The truck carried no fire-fighting equipment, only a radio. If the train started a blaze, the driver radioed our volunteer fire department, consisting of my neighbors and myself, and we fought the fire. After a particularly fiery summer, a pack of ranchers would sometimes sue the railroad. If they felt especially pugnacious, they'd tell each other over coffee how easily a train might be tipped over if a few of those discarded ties were placed strategically on the rails. My vehemence left me breathless and a bit off-balance. Besides, George had already crossed the tracks to the fence on the other side.

Reaching for a clump of grass to pull myself up the steep slope, I heard my subconscious say, "Great place for a snake." I stopped in midstride, telling myself the heifer had scared away any snake when she ran through this grass. I took a deep breath, heard the unmistakable chatter of rattles, and knew I'd been hearing it since I started up the slope.

Coiled under the clump of grass I'd almost grabbed, within two feet of my face, the rattlesnake was warning me with every ounce of energy it could spare. If it had felt inclined, the snake could already have struck my face as I leaned forward, or my leg as I raced after the fleeing heifer.

I set down the bucket, slid the shovel under the deadly package, lifted it to show George, and tossed it out into the pasture, away from our work. Anger at the railroad seethed in my blood. I tightened wires so hard I pulled a couple of steel posts out of the ground, creating more work for myself.

For years, beginning in childhood, I periodically endured two nightmares. In the first, I stood in a pit below a circular opening too high to reach. Screaming or trying to climb brought snakes slithering from the rock walls to coil around my ankles. Some rattled or hissed. Others simply struck until the light above me darkened, or I awoke.

In the second nightmare, I wandered along the streets where my grandmother once led me to kindergarten. New leaves fluttered on young trees between the sidewalk and the street. At the end of the block, a black panther crouched, fully visible, in the spindly branches of a sapling. I kept taking steps until the panther was directly overhead, snarling. Terror usually woke me as the cat leaped.

Lying in the dark after either dream, I'd try to recall any actual event that might have inspired it. Experts say females who dream of snakes or any animal with a long, snaky—and thus automatically phallic—tail may be afraid of sex. I certainly was. My mother's only sexual advice was given the day I married for the first time, almost twenty years after the dreams began. "Men have to have it," she said, and a woman's role was to "lie there and put up with it." Much later, I learned that in cultures where snakes are respected for their earthly connections and used in healing ceremonies, women do not have such dreams.

As soon as I moved to the ranch, encountering snakes as a normal part of life, the dreams gradually stopped. When I was ten, a blue racer slid down inside my collar as I walked under a juniper. I stood still while it inched across my stomach, cool muscles flexing against mine. Its tongue skimmed my unformed breasts. When I pulled my shirttail out, the snake zipped away in the grass. I chased it, thinking of taking it to school. When it saw me, the snake raised its head. I watched it go, and had no nightmares.

In recent years, I've read a great deal about women's concerns; at the same time, I have been evaluating my own connections with my physical and spiritual home, the prairie. Our ancestors respected and worshiped serpents' closeness with the earth, the royal mother of all life. Later cultures damned them for precisely the same reason.

Certainly some past cultures appear to have been ruled by people who seemed to fear the female as much as the snake, and to link them as representatives of evil. In many parts of the world where the snake became a character of dubious repute, it was associated with women. Both European and Near Eastern cultures often picture their warrior gods killing a snake or dragon. The ancient and profound image of the spiral goddess may have been transformed by later, male-dominated societies into a whirlwind hiding a snake. Christianity adopted many of the same beliefs. Saint Anthony wrote, "When you see a woman, consider that you face not a human being, but the devil himself. The woman's voice is the hiss of the snake." Methinks the comment reveals more about the saint than about women and snakes. When I began reading modern female scholars of archeology and religion, I was pleased to learn they shared my distaste for many of the doctrines, symbols, and practices common to Christian churches. The effect of such practices has been to separate humanity, literally and figuratively, from its ancient bonds with the earth.

Fear of vipers is planted in us so early that few of us can be objective about reptiles. Pious adults who tell toddlers how the snake seduced Eve the Woman and ruined Paradise may not appreciate the child's ability to draw broader implications from the lesson. Snakes and women, the child may believe, not only kill but also condemn a person to everlasting hell. Further, when a child's mother squawks, "Get up off the floor" or "Get out of that mud puddle. Wash your hands—you're filthy!" the child may come to believe that being in close contact with earth is nasty. Most Christians swallowed these tales with their morning oatmeal, singing hymns to God's benevolence, without conscious realization of the subtler lessons.

Once past the delicious sensual years of childhood, most adults infer that they should remain upright in stance as well as thought. We hold ourselves, literally and figuratively, above mud. We school ourselves to forget those down-to-earth delights, shudder at the thought of lying naked in cool ooze. Admonishing our children that to be clean is to be godly, we neatly teach them to identify evil with darkened fingernails and slime between the toes.

We have tried to deny and forget our grimy history, insulating ourselves from earth. Instead of toughening our hides, we devised clothing and shoes to protect us from thorns, snakes, and other natural elements we perceived as dangerous. We built floors, lifting our beds so far above insects it's easy to forget how they outnumber us. Our notions of discomfort have dwindled to the trivial, as our entertainment became expensive.

Remember the bliss of being barefoot in warm mud? Can you recall how gently it oozes up between your toes, how softly it caresses the soles of your feet as they slide through it? Watch a baby rub its hands in mud. Almost inevitably, the child then looks at them with an expression of pure joy. Our feet have become tender. "Ow! Ouch!" we holler, tiptoeing on naked feet. How long has it been since you deliberately took off your shoes and walked through a puddle? Those of us who garden may deliberately forget our gloves, but would rather not admit we do it partly for the pleasure of getting our hands dirty in a socially acceptable way.

Think of this: Snakes slide their whole bodies, that whole long ripple of undulating muscle, through silky mud. They slither between rough chunks of gravel that would tear human skin. They descend through cracks in bedrock into cavities, divine earth's secrets in grottoes a human can never know. Gliding among grass stems, snakes inhale leaf mold and taste the planet's skin. No matter how deeply we immerse ourselves in nature, no human can do the same, and few are willing to try.

I believe our protective devices have served to detach us, literally as well as figuratively, from the landscape. We have transferred our ambiguous feelings about the actual earth to those who work most closely with it, to anyone whose work requires getting dirty. Farmers may be the subject of odes about their closeness to the soil, but few of us want our child to grow up to be one. "Go to college," we say, teaching the underlying lesson that professions that require handwork are inferior to those requiring a degree, that suits are superior to coveralls.

I was raised to understand that rattlesnakes are the most dangerous native animal left in our plains ranching neighborhood. As I child, I wasn't allowed to go outside barefoot. Grumbling, I had to lace my stout boots above my ankles. Getting out of the truck at a water hole, I once tripped over a coiled rattlesnake, unable to hear its anxious warning over the engine's noise. I was glad of my high boots, but the snake did not strike.

When I grew into a hurried adult, I sometimes violated the rule about running barefoot. Bootless, I'd run to my car in the driveway or to the gar-

den. Several times I nearly stepped on rattlers. Each time, the shock catapulted me several feet away. Once, so early in the morning I hadn't yet had
coffee, I put on my boots, got a shovel, and diced the reptile as a penalty for
scaring me. I never went outside barefoot again, but the next time I stumbled
over a snake in the driveway, I used the shovel to carry it to the other side of
the garden. I've never killed another rattler, either.

On a window ledge in my father's garage was a dusty jar full of rattles. Until I got old enough to argue with him, pointing out how snakes helped us by
eating gophers and moles, he probably killed every rattler he met. He once
found a rattler stretched alongside an old fence post he'd picked up to reuse
in a fence. He couldn't find the crowbar, so as the snake tried to escape, he
took off his shoe and beat it to death, telling me, "Didn't realize until later
he had the reach on me." Soon after George moved to the ranch, he noticed
my father's jar of rattles, and helpfully explained how to tan snake hides
with antifreeze. A few evenings later, when my father returned from his
regular evening walk with my mother, he walked to our house and called,
"I've got a snake skin for you. Heard him in the alfalfa." From his outstretched cane dangled a tattered strip of hide. Laughing, George shook his
head. "Nothing but a few scales wrapped around holes, John. Nothing left to
tan." My father said, "Guess I got a little carried away. I hate being startled."

After George and I built our home on a hillside, we began planting and watering shelter belts of bushes and trees. Drip hoses parceling out meager
drops attracted birds, butterflies, moths, moles, and mice. Predators, including snakes, followed the small game. Several times, kneeling to check the position of an outlet, I touched a snake coiled under a tree. My ability to cata-
pult backward amazed and reassured me. Checking the shelter belt, I often
walked too fast for Frodo, our West Highland white terrier, who wandered
into the bushes on business of his own, then climbed to the porch to keep
track of me. Several times I heard him bark in a tone I recognized as "Snake!
Snake! Snake!" When I found him in the grass, he and the snake were posed
in a showdown. First the snake lunged forward, then the dog. Carefully not
touching each other, they might alternate charges for an hour. Frodo quivered, his small body hot, while I carried him away, leaving the bull snake in
peace.

One day when I was gathering and rolling hoses scattered in the tall grass, I heard a whisper of sound and felt a robust roll of muscle under my moccasin. Leaping high, I may have hovered a few seconds, long enough to see long grasses rippling downhill as the snake escaped. I followed the trail and found a radiant twist, a translucent husk shed by a bull snake. I held the cast-off length as high as I could reach and gaped at the span still on the ground: the snake was wider than my big hand and at least seven feet long. I hung the skin on the wall of my study, a reminder of the ancient sentry guarding the prairie.

The next spring, as I drove back up the hill after checking first-calf heifers, I saw a huge bull snake stretched out across the trail. I got out to look. Dead. Perhaps I ran over him on the way down the hill, though if I saw a snake in the road, I drove around him. More likely, a neighbor who'd visited the day before deliberately crushed him. He was as big as bull snakes get, longer than the pickup, his girth the size of my upper biceps. Two moles bulged his belly. That year, the rabbits and gophers girdled several bushes and trees in my windbreak. Snakes increase the odds that some bushes will survive to attract insects to make fruit for the birds—and for me. Frodo bustled through the windbreak and around the woodpile daily, and gobbled more moles than usual, without reptile competition. I mourned all spring, sure the guardian spirit of my trees was gone.

In spite of my Christian background and ranch training, I've always loved to crawl or lie in the grass. I've learned to appreciate the importance of snakes to the community around the shelter belts on my hillside, knowing that besides patrolling the windbreaks, a bull snake often gulps his weight in digging pests who destroy crops that feed our cows. Likewise, I've read the words of writers who say any evil force, including mental, emotional, physical, or spiritual pain, can be transformed into creative power by someone with the right attitude. Snakes were once accepted as symbols of beneficial change because their venom, so dangerous to others, is harmless to the snake producing it. The nomadic tribes whose descendants still live near my ranch saw snakes as tokens of earth's fecundity. Considering both my knowledge and my experiences on the plains, I worked out a compromise: I stay alert to natural warnings and attentive to risk, but I refuse to be consumed by fear.

So I lie in the grass and imitate a serpent, breathing to the earth's slow pulse. Sometimes I doze, dreaming of ancient times when some folks worshiped snakes. In ancient Europe, spirals, vines, and serpents symbolized the life force. All three grew from the depths of water and earth. Celtic symbols for snakes, the tree of life, and the spinal cord were all interchangeable. Snakes represented the way dreams weave through our lives, and a snake shedding old skin to hibernate denoted both death and rebirth. Aztecs pictured their god Quetzalcoatl as a snake with feathers, a canny union of earth and sky that contains four important elements of life: water and earth, fire and fertility. Instead of separating worship from reality as modern folks tend to do, the Aztec belief system fused mundane and celestial, the everyday life with the promise of paradise. Each of these venerable ideas endowed the snake with power and respect. In modern times, the precise observations of biologists have taught most of us that reptiles are a vital part of a nature that is neither hostile nor loving. These days, some folks venerate golden girls and coins, expensive cars and politicians with stiff hair. All are more liable to double-cross us than an honest rattlesnake.

I once led friends through a deep gash in red sandstone cliffs in the Black Hills to see prehistoric pictographs. I warned everyone that the crumbled rock littering the floor of the crevasse provided perfect shade for reptiles. At the end of the passage, I jumped several feet to the canyon floor, barely clearing a baby rattlesnake coiled against the stones. Its pencil-thin spiral was no larger than my cupped hand, its vibrating tail tip the size of my little finger. I leaned close and heard no sound. The infant had only one button, nothing to rattle. Head raised, it hissed meagerly and struck anyway. I directed each hiker to vault over it. Briefly, we debated the snake's fate. The country people present that day live close to rattlesnakes but don't read nature writers. They argued that the snake was just as deadly as its parents, and wanted it to die. The city folks held the opposite view. I cast the deciding vote and allowed the baby to slither safely away.

A few years ago, I visited a chic woman whose husband ranched and raised exotic wildlife, and who, she said, just loved nature. She told of seeing a bull snake coiled in a tree above a meadowlark nest and angrily turning the hose on it. When I tried to suggest that, to nature, a bull snake in the bushes was worth several meadowlarks, she exhaled fire. I explained why bull snakes, sometimes called pine-gopher snakes, are a rancher's ally, gobbling gophers and ground squirrels. Like most of humanity's favorite emotions, love of nature requires choices. Meadowlarks serve us well, eating mosquitoes and grasshoppers, but they are one of the most abundant and resilient of species. The bull snake's nature causes it to do humans many services, but it is more likely than the meadowlark to die at our hands. When we stop a serpent from swallowing a bug-eyed, naked bird, or scatter birdseed but shoot snakes, we're allowing prejudice, or ignorance, to corrupt our judgment.

Victims of centuries of bad press, snakes are among the few critters to escape today's vogue of romancing the wilderness. After my diary of a year of ranch life was published, a man who planned to visit the ranch wrote to ask how he should protect himself against rattlesnakes. Reading his letter, I thought he must picture the prairie grass writhing with deadly vipers. I chuckled, but the wide screens of movie theaters are regularly filled with ordinary animals corrupted by cinema into threats. No wonder some folks are terrified by wilderness.

The truth is, a person who walks the plains with awareness—without chatter, listening to noises in the grass—may never see a rattlesnake. Sometimes I leap aside from what turns out to be dried seed pods. My jittery legs react before my sluggish brain can analyze the sound. When I really hear a rattlesnake, my mind and body don't debate. Instinct—perhaps so old my conscious mind is hardly aware it's there—snatches me from danger. But each fall local newspapers carry a standard set of warnings alongside the latest item about an unwary visitor rushed to the hospital after being bitten.

The first warning usually seems self-evident: not to put your hand in a spot you can't see. But most of the unwary are bitten on the hand.

Rattlesnakes are more visible on the prairie than in the Black Hills, but no place can be certified snake-free. One fine warm day, several of us hiked an old flume route. On a narrow trail between pines, we walked in single file. The city folks wore tennis shoes or sandals, while we country people clopped along in our high-laced boots, dragging our habits. Millie, a nurse about my age, walked ahead of me, wearing shorts and tennies. I teased her about forgetting her respect for rattlers. She'd been born on a reservation but lived in the city too long. What if she was bitten? None of us were nurses.

"Don't worry," she said, laughing. "I'll tell you what to do."

We all heard the rattle at once. Three hikers in front leaped aside while I blinked at Millie, who hung in space, back straight and legs tidily folded. An inch below her ankles, the snake hovered at the top of a strike, three feet above its rattling tail.

Millie landed well away from the snake. We circled, laughing nervously, until someone found a long branch to lift the reptile off the trail. Our fast pace hadn't given it time to hide. Like bull snakes, rattlers usually vanish before hikers see them. Even cornered, they warn. Wouldn't it be nice if all armed humans broadcast their deadly intentions a dozen times before they fired?

Rattlesnakes know they can kill. They'll shake their tails quite a while before striking if the enemy keeps its distance. Venom is their final defense, one they try not to waste. Being bitten by a rattlesnake is a little like saying you were attacked without warning by a brass band playing the "1812 Overture." If you walk the prairie wrapped in contemplation of your own neuroses, snakes are the least of your dangers.

If rattlesnakes would actually keep humans from crowding the plains, I might start a rattlesnake ranch. Reptile herds, less conspicuous than cattle, would leave no piles of manure or deeply scored trails. Ranchers afraid of environmental warriors who think it's courageous to cut fences and shoot cows might try preserving rattlesnakes, or even raising the critters. A cow is a big, slow-moving target with a benign reputation, but shooting snakes might be considerably more hazardous. Naturally, reptiles would be harder to fence in—but we could give up branding. And the advantages to parks and wilderness areas where cattle now graze, causing public outcry, are obvious: reduce the crowds without resorting to higher fees. In fact, a rattlesnake ranch might combat the crisis underlying most environmental questions, the single problem no one wants to discuss: population control.

During the autumn after George died, a friend came to help repair the wiring in the barn, bringing a portable radio. Listening to an oldies station, he and I discovered we liked to sing the same songs with tuneless vigor. We spent the afternoon in dissonant harmony, song fragments bouncing among the rafters of the barn loft as I handed him pliers and wire.

With the sun hammering on the sheets of tin covering the weathered shingles on the roof, the heat nearly choked us. At each step, dust rose to whirl in shafts of light eddying through cracks and broken windows. Around us lay the detritus of several generations of ranchers. A buggy with traces of yellow paint on its gray boards stood in the center of the floor, filled with boxes of antifreeze and motor oil my father had forgotten buying on sale. Along one wall, dust lay an inch thick on a quilt over his mother's treadle sewing machine. The workhorse team's jumbled harness hung from wood pegs over boxes of books my first husband forgot while he was busy claiming the antique furniture we'd refinished together. A wire live trap stood beside the stairs. My father got it to catch skunks raiding the chicken house, but didn't use it because he wasn't sure how he'd haul a live skunk away without getting sprayed. Meanwhile, we used the trap to capture stray cats. I'd haul them at least ten miles away before opening the door.

Gradually, as the electrician and I sang and chattered, I became aware of a steady drone beneath our voices, a sound like wire brushes on a drumhead. At first, I was afraid the hum was electrical power and ran to be sure I'd flipped the current off. Coming back upstairs, I noticed Frodo whining and growling, pawing at a pile of rubble.

Rattlesnake! I thought, dragging the dog away. As soon as I let go, he lunged forward, barking. I used the tip of a hand scythe to push a piece of canvas off the open cardboard box. Inside was an old twenty-gallon pressure canner, its lid at an angle. The whir echoed louder.

My friend climbed down the ladder to stand behind me. "Let's just leave it alone. Do you ranchers have to kill everything?"

If the barn was harboring a poisonous snake, I had to know. Otherwise, each time one of us rummaged in a corner for a sack of salt, or knelt in the hay beside a sick calf, we might be bitten. With the scythe, I flipped the lid the rest of the way off the kettle. Coiled inside was a huge snake, hissing energetically. Snake stew, already bubbling.

Each time the reptile inhaled, the speckled body swelled to twice its normal size. Even relaxed, its upper body was larger than my biceps. For a minute, my skin felt cold before my breathing steadied. Frodo pounced and retreated, barking as the snake struck. Coils adjusting as smoothly as flowing oil, the snake undulated until the pointed end of his tail slid by, revealing bands of color running all the way to the tip: no rattles.

During that first maniacal moment of confrontation, many bull snakes die. The hides of both bull snakes and rattlers are mottled with tan and brown spots divided by patches of beige. Both coil and quiver their tails, lunging at intruders. A bull snake's head is blunter than a rattlesnake's, not so flat and triangular. The tongue does not flick in and out but quivers with each breath. Frightened people rarely notice such detail, so the bull snake may die for its impersonation.

"Aren't you going to kill it?" the electrician asked, holding Frodo's collar. Shaking my head, I used the scythe to lay the canvas gently back over the kettle, leaving the lid off, thinking what an ideal den the round, smooth-sided kettle made. I left the agitated reptile concealed in his paradise of mice. While the electrician helped bring light to the old barn, the snake explored dark recesses, a living glory in a ranching mausoleum.

THE DUCK
IN THE HIGHWAY
DEPARTMENT

...

Once upon a time I married a man who dreamed of being a writer and singer. Conscious of what I was giving up, I forsook the ranch where I ripened, and used my fallback skills to teach journalism and English while I acquired more insurance—in the form of an M.A. degree—and settled into wedded bliss in a small southern city.

Steaming in the heat of Memorial Day weekend in Missouri, I sat on a blanket at the edge of a lake, doing homework while getting a tan; I grew up trying to do two things at once, and still follow that pattern. Each time I began to grasp intransitive verbs, I was distracted by a clamor of quacking ducks. Squinting, I saw a drake circling over a bare peninsula where a family had cooked hot dogs on a concrete fireplace an hour before. Their laughter, as they ate at a picnic table on a little spit of land next to a clump of cattails, had irritated me. I wondered if the drake's hen and her nest were in the weeds, and the family's excitement had upset him.

I watched him circle a while, thinking of procreation. Even the animals— everyone but me, it seemed—were multiplying. But my husband had three children from a previous marriage and wanted no more. He'd switched his major from philosophy to English, and obscure magazines had begun to publish his poems. He was letting his hair grow, and smoking a pipe. Vocalizing in saloons at night, he groomed his mustache and sported the splendid plumage my paycheck provided: Edwardian coats and ruffled shirts.

Perhaps an hour passed while I concentrated on my reading before I smelled smoke. My ranch training in being alert for prairie fires will never allow me to ignore that odor, no matter where I am. Gusts of wind ruffled the lake as I looked for fire and spotted flames reaching from the fireplace into the tall weeds at the end of the peninsula.

Cursing stupid people who didn't know enough to douse a campfire, I threw the book down, grabbed my plastic water jug, and ran. I doused the fire's beginning at the firepit, then refilled my jug among scorched weeds at the lake's edge. The fire hurled itself against the sheet of water and fizzled out while I stamped sparks around the picnic table. I filled the jug several times, even wetting the unburned branches, perversely making life harder for anyone else who wanted to roast hot dogs that weekend. Afterward, I moseyed through the weeds, saturating smoldering sticks and stomping on clumps of sparks.

Grumbling to myself, I couldn't hear the ducks over the blare of motorboats until they were close above my head. Around and around the pair flew, tilting their heads to look at me. At my feet, a circle of charred sticks held four blackened eggs.

I took my water jug back to my blanket, but instead of opening the book, I watched the hen land on the point. She waddled through charred grass, her feathers flashing in sunlight. Now and then she raised a webbed foot and shook it. The sight should have been funny.

At the nest, she bent her glossy neck, turning her head back and forth to peer down. Then she rolled an egg over with her bill. Deftly, she tumbled it to the edge of the water. She adjusted the egg's position, then pecked hard until the shell broke. One by one, she pushed shell fragments into the lake. Finally she pushed away the half-cooked center, scattering bits of flesh with her bill, tilting her head to watch the chunks bob away on slow waves. Then she plodded back to the nest.

She destroyed each egg at the water's edge, pecking the half-formed ducklings apart until the fragments drifted away. Honking, the drake circled above her.

Finished, she fluttered her wings and lifted into faltering flight. The pair wheeled a broad circle over the nest. Wings beating in unison, they flew straight toward the trees at the south end of the lake.

The singer/writer/philosopher and I later moved back to South Dakota, where we failed to repair our shaky marriage. After the divorce, I returned to live on the ranch. Each fall, I awoke one morning to see the grass coated with frost, brittle and gleaming in sunrise. Each time the ice fell, I knew the next three nights would be hushed, sound suspended while the air chilled, while frost blackened blooms and green tomatoes. During the busy sunlit hours, I found time to sit for a few minutes against the south wall of the house or in a sheltered corner of the barn, inhaling warmth, storing it for December. Eventually, I married George, a man who wanted to harvest the garden with me in the fall, and curl up with me under wool blankets in winter. He was sterile from radiation given to counteract Hodgkin's disease, so we could have no children.

After the quick freeze finished off the garden, we usually enjoyed balmy nights and toasty days for another month as the pace of prairie life quickened. Two or three skunks visited the compost every night, a cavalcade in formal suits. Two dozen finches hung upside down on the sunflowers at one time, pecking seeds faster than a secretary can type. A coyote hunted the field below our house at noon, pouncing on mice as though his life depended on each leap. Crows and meadowlarks all exclaimed at once in adjoining trees. If I stepped outside, the flocks shot into the air like tiny rockets to revolve around the house in spinning clouds. After the birds finally shut their beaks to fly, the air seemed still as a lake, almost serene. Winter tenants were more laconic, reserving their strength for survival.

Standing still in the sun, caught in the spell of warmth and half-forgetting what I came outside to do, I'd hear geese and cranes shouting their litany of stations overhead: "Canada, North Dakota, South Dakota, Nebraska." Their cadence sent me to work. Three days before, those big wings flapped through snow. They'd outflown it for the moment, but winter soared behind them.

One warm autumn morning after the first wintry warning, my father and I drove down the rutted trail to a stock pond. "Time to get the salt out of the pasture before the snow's so deep we can't get back up the hill," he said.

We each picked up a fifty-pound block and hefted it over the tailgate. "Get those little chips, can't waste those," he said turning toward the dam. I wasn't supposed to notice his pallor, the pulse fluttering under the fine wrinkles on his throat. I kicked a few chunks of salt under the pickup, knowing the antelope would enjoy them all winter.

"Huh," my father said. I looked where he pointed. The dam was frozen over, after four nights of zero temperatures. Five feet from the shore, a duck paddled in a pool of open water the size of a washtub. Father hooked his thumbs in the back pockets of his jeans and shrugged thin shoulders. "You suppose she paddles all night to keep that from freezing?"

"Maybe she's hurt, can't fly."

"She's too close to the bank. A coyote will get her." He turned away. We had stacks to haul, fences to fix in the winter pasture. We needed to repair the floor of the loading chute to hold the big fall calves we planned to sell next week.

The next morning, we headed east to the summer pasture for our annual closing tour to pick up the salt and shut the gates before snow drifted the trail closed. When we drove out of that pasture, we were saying good-bye until June. On the way home, near sunset, my father turned south, off the trail. I opened the gate without a question and he drove to the stock pond.

"Couldn't sleep last night," he mumbled. "Kept thinking about that poor damn duck swimming in circles to keep from freezing down. Hell of a life."

Rummaging in a sack, he brought out several ears of corn and tossed them down the slope toward the duck. She was standing on the bank, head under her wing, but her little pond remained clear of ice.

Three days later, while we took a breather from nailing planks in the calf chute, my father pushed his cap forward and scratched the back of his neck. "I slipped down to the dam before breakfast this morning," he said. His hat shaded his face, but I could see his white teeth. "The duck's gone, the pond's frozen over." I waited.

"She ate most of the corn. Maybe a coyote got her, but I didn't find any feathers." He shrugged, and picked up the hammer.

Only people who live in the country, I later wrote, could form a relationship with nature so intimate that they feel concern for one lonely duck. People who live in cities, I said, only glimpse nature from high windows or speeding vehicles. Even wilderness lovers who probe deeply are only passing through. We who live on the land truly live within the land, each of our lives only one among the other inhabitants of the place; as Wendell Berry says, we are "one kind among many kinds."

A reader countered in a letter, telling how he cultivated wildflowers and vegetables on vacant city lots, reminding me that determined people grow gardens even on windowsills and roofs. Such minute particles of nature, he said, may be as important and eloquent as the thousands of acres around my house. After all, city people longing for green space conceived the idea of parks; the first outdoor miniature golf courses appeared on rooftops in New York City in 1926.

For most of my life, I have visited cities only when forced to by the necessity of making money. His remarks made me raise my eyes and pay attention to rooftop trees whose green steeples caught my eye against the city's gray vertical wall. Still, after each trip, I hurried home to the plains, saying, "I could *never* live in a city."

Then my husband died. Two years later, I moved to Cheyenne, Wyoming, at 50,000 people, a city by my standards, to join my friend Jerry. He had never married, and I had never borne the children I longed for that Missouri spring.

Here in the capital city of Wyoming, I cherish every hint of green, every particle of earth. I brought bags of wildflower seeds from my South Dakota hillside to tuck into cracks in the concrete shroud. When I saw the first redwing blackbird in spring, I cried as if he was a faithless lover cavorting in the trees with a new sweetheart.

Sometime during that first urban spring, Jerry, who works for the Wyoming Department of Transportation, told me about the duck in the highway department. An interstate highway storms past one side of the office complex, while on another lie open fields around a military base. Nearby is a golf course containing a small lake. Other ponds sprinkle the green belts surrounding office structures. The highway division's building contains a courtyard in the center of a vast asphalt parking lot, a green eye in a concrete hurricane.

One year, workers in an office with a window half-underground noticed a duck's nest in the window well. The duck stayed on the nest when they moved about the room at normal work, but fluttered off the eggs if they approached the glass. They covered the glass with dark fabric and cut a tiny observation flap. The whole staff peeked, entertained and educated while the duck hatched and fed her downy brood.

In warm weather, the lively adolescents overflowed the nest, scrambling up and down the window well, tumbling back when the hen came with food. During one lunch hour, a group of employees formed a human corridor from the window across the parking lot to the nearest pond. Someone encouraged the duck and her brood to scramble out of the window well. Composed, the hen led her dozen fluffy offspring across the tarmac between two lines of people.

Newspapers publish pictures of ducks crossing highways a dozen times a year. The scene is always popular, but the next day the photographer looks for a new subject. The duck in the highway department, though, didn't go away. She returned for the next couple of years, but not to the window well. Instead she tucked her nest under a bush in the enclosed courtyard. Workers eating lunch on the sunny benches watched her, occasionally feeding her bits of bread. Each year, when her ducklings were ready to swim, rumor informed everyone who worked in the building to assemble in corridors around the courtyard. Someone opened the door. People whose primary job is concocting concrete and steel alleys and bridges, people who are accused by environmentalists of hampering wildlife migration, lined the halls to escort the duck and her retinue across parking lots to the nearest pond.

One spring, the courtyard bustled with several different repair projects, and no one saw the duck. Workers speculated she was disturbed by the commotion and had nested elsewhere. She figured in dozens of conversations, as people realized how much they would miss the spring ritual of escorting her to safety with her family.

But one day the duck appeared with several ducklings at a door from the courtyard to an interior corridor. Word spread and work on the state's highways and bridges stopped. This time, however, they did not herd the duck out into the parking lot. They rounded her up with her brood, and transported her to the lake at the golf course.

Next day, curious about how she had eluded notice for so long, someone searched the courtyard and found the hidden nest. One egg was left. For a week, people who worked in the complex—engineers, secretaries, maintenance personnel—watched the nest in shifts so if the final chick hatched, it could be reunited with the family. The duck never returned to the highway department complex, but every spring someone mentions her, and wishes her well.

PART · II

HUNTER AND
HUNTED

RUNNING WITH THE ANTELOPE

...

Yesterday, I drove my favorite plains road between my ranch in South Dakota and my home in Cheyenne, Wyoming. The narrow two-lane winds ninety miles through broad desert and beside narrow creek bottoms, among rolling hills and tree-covered mountains. Every time I make the trip, I know antelope will materialize on a certain stretch, testing my eyes and reflexes by sprinting in front of me. Yesterday, I didn't see a single one, and I was puzzled until I remembered that it's hunting season. They move away from roads, where every other pickup has a rifle sticking out the window. I relaxed, pushed the accelerator up to seventy-five.

Two miles down the road, when my car popped over a knoll, a big pronghorn buck lay in the borrow ditch on my right, head up. I touched the brakes while deciding he wouldn't bother to get up. Thinking about antelope behavior, I braked again. The antelope leapt toward the right fence, then in one motion whirled and charged across the highway. Neither of us died. I needed new tires anyway.

Today, after Jerry got home from work, two of his friends deposited antelope bucks at the back door. One likes to hunt but doesn't like the meat. "Have you ever tasted it?" I asked.

"Well, once." Turns out he sampled a buck that had been shot from a pickup after running a couple miles on a hot fall day. When the animal's tissues are gorged with blood and fear, the meat will always taste of terror. The other man loves the meat; he stalks his prey so well the antelope seldom realizes he's around until the bullet strikes. But his wife doesn't like to cook antelope. In our suburban backyard, both men sawed off the horns to keep, leaving the rest for us. We'll deliver neatly packaged steaks to the quiet hunter, who will save them to cook on his solitary hunting trips.

All afternoon Jerry sawed bones and cut meat in the basement while my terrier, Frodo, lay under the table catching scraps. Upstairs, I counted steaks and chops, slapping them on the slick side of white paper. I folded, turned, wrapped, and taped, scrawling messages about winter meals of stew and chops across the packages before stacking them in the freezer. I tossed bones and odd scraps of maroon flesh into an enormous pot, and added onions, garlic, thyme, a chile pepper, and a pinch of sage, along with the peelings from all the vegetables we'd eaten this week.

The long leg bones are heavy as stone, much thicker than the bones of a deer. The pronghorn's predators and prairie habitat designed these legs over millennia for speed straight ahead, and for strength when the animal pivots on the padded front hooves. During the twenty-five million years the pronghorn has spent on prairie ground, its trachea, lungs, and heart enlarged and evolved to take in and use oxygen at triple the rate of other animals the same size. I've read that pronghorn can cruise comfortably at more than forty miles an hour for miles. When racehorses run thirty-eight miles an hour, their lungs sometimes bleed.

All day and all night, bones shaped by plains water and sagebrush dance to the rhythm of heat. Golden fat made of prairie grasses rises in the kettle like cream. The scent permeates the house, forecasting winter's thick soups, a benediction for plains flesh made grass made meat.

At 2 A.M., I pushed the dog off my pillow and tiptoed downstairs. By the dim stove light, I watched shining bones bounce in the kettle of antelope stock and remembered something I'd rather forget.

The whole thing started in the community hall at the fairgrounds. I put down my plate of cold turkey slices and looked around. My husband, David, sat alone, eating a piece of chocolate cake. I'd started toward him through the murmuring crowd when someone took my arm firmly.

"Are you too high class to speak to old friends?" said a thick voice directly in my ear. I jerked away and looked into dark eyes. "Whattsa matter, Linda. Don't recognize me with the brush?" His hot breath on my face was thick with whiskey. His mouth was grease-smeared, his black beard matted. "Mark?"

He took my arm again. "How about that? You remember. Thought I'd liven up the party a little and come drunk. Every county fair needs at least one drunk. I didn't think old Phin Johnson could uphold the honor alone; all he can uphold is old Phin."

I tried to jerk free, but he gripped harder. "Oh, you're not going to escape, little girl—not yet. That's part of the role you have to play: visiting daughter from the East, safely married to the college professor, is captured by the resident drunk, who turns out to be her old flame, Mad Mark. The peasantry will love it." He steered me toward a pair of isolated chairs.

Leaning closer, he whispered hoarsely, "See the heads begin to turn, the eyebrows twitch. I'm becoming a legend in these parts." He threw me toward a chair and half-fell into the other.

His plate was heaped high with turkey, roast beef, sweet potatoes with marshmallows, three kinds of gooey Jello salad, and two whole wheat rolls. "This is the best meal I've had for quite a while. I kind of lean toward cans of beans and whatever ran in front of my truck and got hung in the shed last week. Sometimes it gets a bit green." He wiped his mouth on his sleeve and grinned. "Have to give the folks a show when you're a legend. How's your life? I haven't seen you since you married the professor."

"Really? That long?"

"I remember because I really hung one on. Here I'd been sitting around thinking how I'd sweep you off your feet when you came back, and you didn't come back. I went out and drank a fifth of whiskey, and then we got to betting who could eat the most raw eggs. I won; sixteen. Damn near made me quit drinking whiskey. When I threw those eggs up they were fried."

He wiped the plate clean with a roll and stuffed it in his mouth. "What you need is to get out of here. Let's go shoot something."

"I can't. This is practically a family reunion. Besides, you're drunk, though you don't seem nearly as drunk as you did a minute ago."

He grabbed my wrist and pulled me out of the chair. "Wish we could get your dad to come along; he looks like he's slipping. You know, if you'd married me, I'd be taking care of things. I used to go over to help him fence and stuff, but your mother run me off."

I leaned close to his ear and whispered a line that always worked with pushy college boys, "Let go of me, you son-of-a-bitch or I'll rip your balls off."

He laughed. "Then quit trying to escape fate. And shut up." He shoved me forward. "You know, the last time I went over there, I was going to help your dad butcher. But your mother didn't want the mess in the house. So he asked me to help him load the heifer, and drive her to the packing plant. By the time we got that bitch loaded she'd tore down half the corrals, knocked your dad down, and about broke his back. When we got her tied in the truck, he said, 'You know, someday I'm going to quit listening to that woman.'"

"Stop shoving and I'll go outside with you to talk."

"Ah, now we open Scene Two: the gallant professor gallops to the aid of our heroine." Mark leaned against me drunkenly and pointed toward David, advancing with a worried expression.

As Mark's grip loosened, I jerked away. "Do you do this all the time?"

"Haven't kidnapped a woman in weeks." He looked sober. "This is actually kind of a special occasion; I was a little nervous. Now can't we get out of here? We can even take him. You never did answer my question."

"What question?"

"How's your life? Is he good to you? Are you happy? How come you don't have any kids?"

"That's four questions."

"Stop stalling. It's four ways of asking the same thing."

"We're very happy. I just love teaching and I have a good position . . ."

"I don't give a damn what you do for cash," Mark said. "Are you happy?"

"I'm not finished with my degree yet, and David thinks it would be better if we waited a while to have kids, until we get established financially." I felt tears gather.

Mark leaned to take one tear on the tip of a grimy finger. "Yeah, Linda. OK. That's kind of what I thought." He licked his finger.

"Linda?" David's voice was higher than usual. "How—how are you doing?"

I was smiling when I turned. "Just fine. David, I want you to meet my old friend, Mark Degnan. I've told you about him."

Mark smiled and stuck out a hand. "Glad to meet you. Must be pretty difficult to be a stranger in the middle of a county fair where everybody's known everyone else since birth."

David, swollen with marital indignation and prepared to drag his wife away from a drunk for the benefit of my parents' neighbors, looked puzzled. Usually, I was on my own with drunks. "Why, why yes, it is—rather awkward. I'd met some of them before, of course. What—what do you do, Mark?"

"Oh, a little bit of everything. Worked construction and hauled garbage—that was in Alaska, Linda; got to tell you about that sometime. I went up there about the time you two kids got married. Right now I'm working double shift in a uranium mine and saving money to go back to college next year. Enroll in a few art classes."

"Where did you graduate, Mark?" I'd never expected him to manage college.

"Didn't. Remember? I had quite a struggle just getting through high school, what with the old man drunk. I took a year or two at State and they tried to draft me and found out my back was no good. So I got behind and I quit. But I've been doing a little woodcarving. Welded up a cowboy and the boys at the mill figured it looked like a cowboy, so there might be something to this art business after all. Say, David, we were just getting out of here; we haven't seen each other for years, and there's a lot of catching up to do. Care to ride along?"

"Oh—well, Linda, do you really think you should leave?"

"Why not? I've had about all of the old home week I can stand. Come on."

"My truck's right outside," Mark said. "Let's drive back to your place and look at that east pasture of yours. Shoot some of those prairie dogs. Maybe we'll scare up a deer."

"I know Dad hasn't been near that pasture for a while, so we'll be doing him a favor."

We began to work our way through the crowd, hearing snatches of conversation. "She just comes to things like this looking as though it wasn't nothing and brings that little baby along just like it had a daddy and she was proud of it, don't she?" was my favorite.

I detoured to tell my father where we were going. He nodded and half-smiled at me. "Hello, Mark. Say, when you get some time, stop by and help me fix that chute. How are you standing it, David?"

When we reached Mark's battered green pickup, a black dog sat up wagging her tail. "How are you, you slimy mutt?" He tucked the corner of a tarp down under a box and the dog licked his hand. "Go on, cut it out," he snarled, scratching her ear. "She's worthless. Shoot over her head once and she stays right by your heels the rest of the day. Started out to be a good hunting dog, but I guess I beat her too much."

I slid into the middle of the seat; David brushed dirt and torn papers to the floor before following. At our place, Mark got the house key from its hiding place in the cellar while I was still untangling my legs from the gearshift. "You seem to know your way around," David said.

Mark looked at him without expression. "John ain't had a son or a son-in-law, so I've helped him; fenced, hayed, branded, a little bit of everything. I know where the keys are." He walked toward the house, throwing them in the air. I started to speak to David, but he turned away. By the time I got inside, Mark was rummaging in the cupboard where Dad kept the rifle. I went downstairs and changed clothes without speaking. When I got back, he was standing by the truck with my old .22 and a .30-30 that looked familiar.

"You can use the .30-30, Charley. In case you want to take a poke at them."

"My name's David," he said.

Mark laughed and handed the rifle to me as I slid into the middle again, saying, "Put the barrel down between your feet; it's not loaded."

"Dad says those are the ones you shoot your foot off with."

"Right, my girl, so don't put it on your foot." He reached across me and took a pint bottle from the glove compartment. "Have a snort, Charley?" He uncapped it with one hand, driving with the other.

"No. Thank you. David. My name is David."

Mark gulped from the bottle. "David, you're on the outside; open the gate."

David slammed the pickup door, and Mark chuckled.

"Have you got a girlfriend, Mark?" I asked.

"My God, Linda, we're thirty years old. 'Girlfriend.'" He took another swig, capped the bottle, and stuck it inside his jacket. His eyes glittered. "I guess you could say that. I got over waiting for my true love and now I just pick up whatever's lying around loose enough on Saturday nights."

"There must be lots of girls who would be—good for you."

"You mean who aren't overeducated for my way of life? Yeah, I guess so. Say, Charley, you know how to open a gate, at least."

"I've been out here before, when Linda and I were first married. I'm not completely ignorant. Why aren't you settled down on a place of your own, Mark?"

"Not everybody's old man's as rich or as good a manager as Linda's. Mine spent most of my tender youth drunk, slamming my mother and the kiddies around, and kind of lost his grip on the financial end of things." He pulled out the bottle and sipped.

"Remember, Linda? The neighbors always used to call when he was coming home drunk. Mother would grab me and hide out in the canyon. If we had time, we'd grab a sandwich. We'd drink out of the creek; she'd tell stories. He'd break every dish, the chairs, anything he could get his hands on. We could hear him yelling for us to come to the house. Sometimes he'd only go into town for a part for the Farmall and be gone two weeks, then come home like that. One time Mom got tired of it and threw two or three dresses in a bag, and started walking. Told me she'd get a job and send for me. Hundred and ten degrees. I cried all day. The old man came home and grumped about how much better off we'd be without her, and how we'd cook for ourselves and hunt more. Along about dark she came in and started fixing supper. When I heard her and ran in the kitchen, she said, 'Damn, it sure is a long way to the highway.'" He thought for a minute. "Guess my sister Della was born the next fall."

He sipped from the bottle again and shook himself. "Anyway, after Dad lost the place, he went to work in the gold mine and just works like hell all the time." He looked at me. "Mom says he never touches a drop now, except once in a while for a ball game on TV, never slaps her around. I think she kind of misses it." He braked the truck sharply and threw us all against the dashboard. "Hey, prairie dogs!"

He was out of the truck before it stopped rolling. "Lean up, Linda—my .22-250 and my pistol are behind the seat. I haven't got around to getting a permit yet. Charley, you take the .30-30. Where the hell did I put those shells?" Mark stuffed cartridges into the pistol, scanning the dog town and pushing his hair out of his eyes.

"Linda, use your little .22. Your dad let me use it, said he guessed you wouldn't need it much. Must have another box of shells under the seat. Get your ass out of there, Charley."

David fumbled with the .30-30 until Mark jerked it away, pulled back the bolt, jammed six shells into the magazine, and handed it back in one motion.

"Here you go." He smiled. "Bet you hit one the first time." He shifted a chew and spat on the ground near my foot. "As for you, baby, I'll bet you ain't nearly as good as you used to be."

David rested his rifle on the truck hood, aimed carefully, and fired. Dust spurted. A prairie dog dropped to all fours with a squeak, ran around in a circle, and sat up again. "Harder to hit than deer," he said.

At Mark's gesture, I lifted the little .22. The round bead slid down easily into the notch. Easing the hammer back with my thumb, I squeezed the trigger and heard the familiar tiny pop.

"Right in the eye," Mark purred. "We used to call her One-Shot." Mark fired as he was pulling down, and a prairie dog fell over.

"You know, Mark," I said, "if you'd *pretend* to aim, or even maybe miss once in a while and then swear, other people wouldn't hate you so much."

We fired until the dogs refused to come out of their holes. Mark shot ten, I got six, David two. Mark's black dog quivered with each shot, but stayed in the truck.

"Well, children, we'd better hit the road." Mark put the truck in gear, taking another drink from the bottle. He offered it to David, who hesitated, then waved it away. The grass surged like silk over the rounded hills, fragile as strands of hair, gold, green, brown. Red mallow sparkled among the blades like scattered rubies. When we reached the top of the hill, we saw far ahead the breaks of the Badlands, sunstruck and gold.

"God, this is beautiful country," I said, relaxing against the hot vinyl seat. Mark smiled.

"It looks pretty bleak to me," David said. "I was raised in Iowa. I love all that corn. Green rows, stretching for miles."

We crossed another pasture in silence. When David got out to open the gate, Mark said, "This is getting too quiet. Got to relax old Charley a little."

"Aren't you ever serious, Mark?"

"All the time, but this isn't a situation that will bear much seriousness. Say David, I'll get the next gate, OK? Give you a break."

When Mark got out, David went around to the driver's seat. As he put the truck in gear, he said, "'One Shot.' I can just see Dr. Burke's face if he ever heard that."

I laughed and put my hand on his knee. "It doesn't exactly fit my prim image in the department, does it?"

"What about 'I'll bet you're not as good as you used to be, baby.' What the hell were you so good at?"

"Shooting, you idiot. I was fourteen. I didn't do anything but work."

"So where does he get off calling my wife 'baby?'" His jaw was clenched.

"I have no idea; he never called me that before. Christ, I haven't seen him since we were in high school!"

"You act as if you're enjoying this insane venture."

"This is the most fun I've had in years."

"Now kiddies, don't squabble," Mark said, opening the truck door. "Let's see a shining example of that marital bliss; I need encouragement."

When we began to see our cattle, David drove slowly among them. "They look good," I said, surprised because it had been such a dry year.

"I think that's a winter calf," Mark said in a friendly tone. "He had a few this winter. I kept asking him if they were late from last year or early for this year. You know your dad, Linda; he'd just grin and say, 'Think how big they'll be by fall.'"

He was silent for a minute, then laughed. "I asked him once about that old John Deere, the one with the stacker on it? The thing runs so slow when it idles, you think it died. I asked him how it fired and he looked kinda thoughtful and said, 'I guess it just fires when it needs to.'" He laughed, shaking his head.

We dawdled along, talking of cattle. Mark took the bottle from his jacket and sipped, then handed it to me. I took a swig and held it in front of David.

He started to wave it away, then sipped delicately, choked, and looked at the label. "My God, Mark; do you drink Wild Turkey all the time?"

"Not all the time. Special occasion." He winked at me.

A muscle in David's jaw jumped for a second and then he said, "A friend of mine got some once as a gift. He always drank Jack Daniels, so he thought it was some cheap stuff, like Old Rocking Chair or Wild Tennis Shoe. So he stuck it away and forgot about it until another guy and I were there one day. He was out of booze and brought out the Wild Turkey; said something like

'Well, we'll have to drink this, it's all I've got' and the other guy almost went out of his mind. Said he'd been trying to get some, and told us how good it was. And it is," he said, and took another swig.

"My husband has learned that college professors are required to prefer expensive liquor," I said. "When we worked for the newspaper in Sioux City, he was reading about wine and found out that some priest ordered a particular kind by the case from Italy. He whined until the liquor store sold him a bottle, and spent a week talking about the bouquet, the nose. After that he talked them out of two bottles a month; he had to pay extra." David's jaw was tight again.

"Then one day I got a story off the international wire about a raid on some wineries in Italy. The officials shut them down to protect the image of fine Italian wines. It seems that several of the most popular export wines contained no grapes at all. They were made from ox blood. Guess which wine was prominently named?"

Mark snorted. "That sounds like something that would happen to me; a peasant getting above his station."

I jabbed David in the ribs. "Come on, honey; you might as well start thinking it's funny, because I'm going to keep telling it."

He bent his lips up at the corners. "One of my revolutionary buddies says that I'll get to be head of the department, and I'll be celebrating on my porch with a good cigar and a bottle of wine when his little ragtag army comes up the street. Somebody will holler 'Aristocrat!' and I'll be the first one shot."

Mark nodded, and they both chuckled a little.

We circled the water tank, noted that it was running over, and turned back toward the ranch. I looked at my watch; already past two. The truck rolled along in the precious flat heat of early autumn, with cool crisp air flowing over our faces. The smell of drying grasses rose around us. The men began to talk idly of experiences they'd had hunting or fishing, little anecdotes about male interests. Content to be left out, I smiled.

David drove through a gate into a neighbor's pasture. We were rolling along having another round of Wild Turkey when a pronghorn—we call them antelope—trotted easily out of a swale ahead of us. An antelope's silhouette is so slender it gives an impression of barely contained flight, a sketch of wild speed momentarily arrested. This one crossed the track and stopped to look over his shoulder. Without alarm or haste, he trotted over the next rise. He was old, heavy with muscle, his horns sharp and wide. He had seen our truck many times.

"Gun it," Mark said softly as the antelope disappeared, and the truck raced. We popped over the rise just behind him. He'd stopped to graze, and he raised his head and looked at us, standing broadside. Instead of running like hell, he stared, for he was old and wise. No one had ever shot at him from this truck.

Before the tires stopped rolling, the two men were out on each side of the truck, firing the rifles.

One of the antelope's hind legs snapped at the top joint. He leaped and stumbled, back legs working. Wobbling, he slipped down the slope out of sight. Almost immediately he ran up the sidehill, craving height, needing to face the danger. Across the gully, he stopped again to look back before limping out of sight.

"Jesus, David. I think I missed him. Where were you aiming?"

"At his shoulder, but I think I hit him in the leg."

"I was aiming at the left eyeball, but I think I shot high. Christ, now we've got a wounded antelope. Hell of a rack though."

"You drive, Linda." Mark slid into the middle of the seat, the .22-250 between his feet, David beside him with the .30-30. "Let's go get the son of a bitch."

I shifted and raced the truck ahead to the next rise, watching them reload out of the corner of my eye. They were both smiling.

We topped out to see the antelope lying just below the top of the next rise. Both men leaped out and aimed. In one motion the antelope shifted from lying in the grass to standing, a big target, and then was gone. His white rump flashed with muscle as he crested the hill and ducked under a fence without slowing down.

"They can go a hell of a long ways with just one busted leg," Mark said, cradling the rifle in his arm. He sighed. "Well, I'll drop off to the east there and try to haze him back up onto Hasselstrom land. That pasture he's in now belongs to the Triple 7 and they don't take to hunters much. You guys watch from up here with the binoculars, so you'll know where he goes. I'll keep watching you, and if you see him you wave me the direction he goes, OK? You have to stand on top of the truck so you're against the sky or I'll never see what you're waving. Just like old times, eh, Linda?"

David took the binoculars and began to scan the rolling land. I slid out and watched Mark walk from sunlight into the black shadow of a gully. I studied the darkness ahead of him, following the shadows until the gulch flattened out.

October. The sun rises far south, so daylight is harsh, contrasting flat white with black shadows. In six years' teaching in Missouri, I'd missed the ranch, and yet I'd forgotten how beautiful it really was. The land below us looked like a hand, spread open, palm up, almost clenched. The deep creases were little dry washes. The deeper ravines were the long spaces between the fingers. I felt the sensation of walking in one of those gullies, feeling the earth close over me, shutting out the wide horizon.

"I don't see a sign of that antelope, Linda," David said, handing the binoculars to me. The sun's warmth made me feel like honey sliding off a slice of toast. Lazily I backed against the truck to steady myself. The land leaped at me through the binoculars as I scanned each wash, each ridge. No antelope. Mark was standing where two gullies came together, spreading his arms. I stood on the truck's hood and made a huge circle with my arms. He began trudging up the nearest gully west of him, toward our pasture.

Sitting on the hood, I said, "Let's go around through the gate and pick Mark up at the fence. He may spook him up that way. Or maybe he slipped up that way and we didn't see him." As I started the pickup, I glanced at David; he was smiling. "Feeling better?"

He looked at me, eyebrows raised. "I'll be happier when we get rid of this goon. 'My girl' indeed."

"For God's sake, I wasn't his girl, and anyway that was years ago. Unlike present company."

"What's that supposed to mean?"

"It means you say I'm your last wife one minute, and the next minute you're telling some girl I believe in open marriage."

"What do you mean?"

"I mean that's what you said to Crystal when you were trying to get her into bed."

"You know Crystal? What did she say?"

"Not a brilliant response, my dear. She came to the writing group. Somebody told her my last name. She went white when she found out I was your wife. She said you told her I didn't mind a bit if you slept with other women. For once you picked the wrong one."

"That was way last spring; it was a mistake."

"It would serve you right if I did sleep with Mark. But I'd have to sleep with every man in town to catch up with your record."

"I really don't think you ought to," he said. "He sounds pretty careless. The way he waves guns around." He shook his head solemnly. "Probably wouldn't use a condom."

"I can't believe we're having this conversation. I don't want to sleep with anybody but you, and I don't want you sleeping with anybody but me. That's what marriage is. Can't you get that straight?"

"OK, OK. I told you I won't. God, it's three o'clock. Just what we need, spend hours looking for a wounded antelope."

"You were right in there blazing away, Mr. Sportsman. You're the one who shot him in the damned leg."

"Well, your lovely Mark was shooting."

"He didn't hit him, did he?"

"No, he sure didn't." David looked smug, then alarmed. "What do you mean?"

"I've never seen him miss anything at that range before."

"Oh, great. Now it's all my fault."

"Open the gate."

He got out, cursing under his breath, and slammed the door. When he returned, I said, "Why does something always have to be someone's fault? We're in this together, aren't we?"

"Damned if I know. I was just trying to take care of my wife."

"Why don't you think of things like that when you spot a new little chickie?"

He grunted. "I just hope we find the antelope soon, and I get out of this alive."

"What are you talking about?"

"Don't you think it's a little strange to leave a county fair to go hunting? Get a novice out with a gun and have a little shooting accident. Only he might be surprised; I used to hunt with my dad."

"You've been reading too much Hemingway."

"You're crawling all over him. I'll bet he'd shoot anything, or lay anything, either." His face was red.

"You're making something ugly out of nothing. I was really starting to enjoy being out here."

"We'll see." The rifle stood upright between his knees; he clutched it with both hands.

We drove in silence until we saw Mark standing along the fence line. While David stayed in his seat, I got out and held the rifle as Mark climbed through the fence. "Now what?" David asked.

Mark stood by the driver's side, leaned on the rearview mirror, and scratched his beard. "Well, we can follow this gully on up a ways. He probably got up it while we were looking somewhere else. It gets kind of rough on the other side. I'll ride in back and keep a lookout."

David stared straight ahead when I got into the driver's seat. As I drove, I watched the breaks on my left, and the broader valley where they converged.

Something thumped on the roof. I stuck my head out the window. Mark leaned down and said quietly, "He's over to the north. On that sidehill, just below the ridge. Drive slow, and kinda angle that way. When you're below the dam, out of sight, run it hard up the gully and you'll come out right by him."

I explained to David. When I hit the gas going up the gully, he clutched the window frame. "For God's sake, Linda, are you trying to kill us?"

"Getting close," I shouted. "Get ready now."

The truck burst out of the gully twenty yards from the antelope and slammed into a rock. Mark was already firing. David dropped to his knees as he left the passenger seat, glancing over his shoulder at Mark, then blasted. The antelope leaped, seemed to falter, and then was gone over the rise, out of sight.

Reloading, Mark bellowed, "Let's go!" I backed the truck off one rock and hit another. Swinging the wheel hard left, I shifted into low. The truck lurched and tipped. Then something underneath clanged and we moved ahead.

"You're going to wreck this truck." David muttered. "What do you care about one damn antelope anyway? Can't we just let him go?"

"Oh, come on!" I shouted. "Code of the West. We don't leave wounded animals running around; even Hemingway knew that. Chasing antelope is supposed to be half the fun." He gave up trying to reload and hung on as we jounced.

We spotted the antelope crossing the gully. He stopped again to look at us. His wounded leg hung useless, and he was breathing hard.

I swung the truck into a relatively clear patch, came up fast on the antelope, and heard Mark firing. David reloaded and fired one shot out the window. When the antelope trotted, one front leg was gimpy. He gathered speed, raced down across the head of a shallow valley, and started up another slope.

"Hey, David," Mark yelled, "Ever shot from a truck box before?" He jumped down and jerked the passenger door open. "Out."

Mark pushed past David and got inside while David was making up his mind. "Hang on, son; she drives like hell, just like I taught her." He laughed.

I watched David climb into the truck. He glanced at Mark's dog, huddled in one corner, and took a firm grip on the framework behind the window. When I roared off, Mark began to reload. The box slipped from his fingers, and shells flew around the inside of the truck.

"You're going to blow us all up!" I shouted, and looked back to see David's legs dancing around, avoiding tools bouncing from the bottom of the truck. The dog was still crouched in a corner. The truck swept up the hill, and lifted into the air as it hit a rock.

We dropped into a little swale on the far side, and the sky filled with antelope.

Mark, pumping shells in, began to laugh wildly, and let go of the rifle. It slid across the seat and bumped into my thigh as I held the wheel, unable to react. Antelope flowed and leaped and flew over the truck's hood, twenty or thirty of them. The wounded buck almost collided with another, turned, and wobbled toward the fence. Then the herd was gone like blown leaves. The single antelope ahead dropped to his knees to go under the bottom wire.

"Stop, Linda; got to get him before he gets under that fence or he'll be gone in the breaks," gasped Mark. Then the .30-30 blasted from the back of the truck. The buck's right front leg buckled. He went down.

"Damn it to hell!" David yelled, ejecting the shell. He lunged out of the truck, raised the rifle, and fired again. The dog leaped out of the truck, racing after the antelope as it ducked under the fence, running again. Mark followed with the pistol, laughing. He and the dog dived under the fence almost together, racing down the gully. Once, Mark stopped and fired downward. The dog ran ahead, and he followed and disappeared.

I looked at David, red-faced and struggling with the rifle. "Take Mark's," I hollered, and ran for the fence. I could hear Mark shouting as I dropped and rolled, hoping I'd miss any cactus or rattlesnakes. At the edge of the gully, I looked down.

The dog had her teeth in the antelope's throat. Mark was close, shouting, trying for a shot. The buck shook its head. The dog fell and rolled, and the antelope ducked his head, horns pointing at Mark's chest. They slammed together. The gun went off. I saw hair part on the buck's neck as the bullet struck. The antelope backed off and tottered toward the other side of the gully. Mark lay on the ground, his chest covered with blood.

Then I heard a gasping breath, and a rifle fired behind me. David. Paranoid enough to think Mark might shoot him. Would he shoot Mark instead?

He fired again. The bullet struck the antelope's shoulder, spinning him around toward Mark, who was half-sitting, trying to reload the pistol. David fired again, and dust puffed between the man and the antelope. Mark flattened and turned to look toward us.

"No!" I yelled, turning toward David. He fired. When I looked back, Mark lay facedown in the grass and the antelope was on its knees.

Antelope and man stared at one another, hunter and hunted, no knowledge between them of difference.

Then Mark lifted his head, and shouted, "Die, damn you," and extended the pistol. The antelope surged to his feet, lunging forward, trying to reach Mark. David shouted hoarsely, "Down!" Both men fired at once. One bullet exploded the antelope's brain. The other struck his windpipe. He crumpled beside a boulder. Blood burst from his nostrils.

I ran, hearing footsteps behind me. The antelope's lips were tightly closed over his black tongue. His eyes were open. Without getting up, Mark extended his knife and cut the antelope's throat. Then he stood, panting, and grabbed a hind leg.

"By God, we got him!" yelled David. He dropped the rifle, and grabbed the other leg. Mark smiled slightly, and looked up at me.

One of the antelope's front legs was broken clean off. The white shard of bone was caked with dirt. The other front leg was torn open, the blood clotted. A wound in the shoulder dripped blood. One hind leg was smashed. The hide tore as David lifted. Through an open hole in the skull, I saw the brain quiver. Air puffed out in a little gasp through the jagged hole in the windpipe.

Mark slashed between the antelope's hind legs, starting the gutting stroke. The knife blade snapped, and he cursed and opened another. As soon as the knife pierced the belly, David reached in and dragged out the bleeding entrails, then wiped his bloody hands on his new gray suit trousers. With the belt knife Mark offered, he began to cut around the anus.

"Some things you don't forget," he said. "I used to hunt with my dad." He tossed the liver to the dog, who lay panting where the antelope had tossed her. She nosed it, put her head down, and closed her eyes. The antelope's torn lungs pumped gently once, pouring blood into the grass roots. As the men worked, the eyes lost their gloss, turning dull as the distances faded.

I picked up the rifle and sat on the boulder watching. The breeze cooled me, drying sweat from my back and tears from my cheeks. The rifle across my knees was scarred. Mark had carried it behind the seat of his truck for years. The low sun of late afternoon slanted across the grass, spotlighting the men. Beyond them, beyond the antelope, the gully was black. Surely, I thought, none of us would escape the darkness.

David steadied the carcass as Mark deftly cut off each leg at the knee joint, and flung them down into the shadows. He shook his head as he looked at the shattered bone. "Tough devil. Want the rack? It'll probably go fifteen inches."

"I guess not. You take it." David glanced at me.

"You could hang it in your office; let the kiddies know there's another side to the professor. If you don't want it, I'll leave it here." Mark was sawing at the neck hide. "He belongs out here." He grunted as he tried to work the knife between the vertebrae. "Anyway, it's safer to make a smaller package, since antelope season doesn't start for another month."

I laughed, a little hysterically, at David's face. One minute he was the Compleat Sportsman, eagerly digging the guts out of the animal he helped pursue and kill. The next he was an English professor tricked into a bloodbath and covered with the evidence. He stepped away from the carcass. "What?"

Mark looked at him, and then at me. His smile was cold. "Relax, Charley; we're five miles from the highway and fifteen from the nearest game warden, who is still eating his head off at the county fair. And nobody bothers much about stuff you shoot on your own place anyway."

"This isn't your place," David said.

"No, but it's her dad's place and you're her husband or something, so you have squatter's rights. Me, I'm just cutting him up."

David stared at Mark, then turned to glare at me.

They dragged the amputated carcass slowly up the hill, and rolled it under the fence. I followed with the rifle and pistol; the dog limped behind me. At the fence, I looked back. The antelope's head lay half in shadow, eyes gleaming in reflected light, white neck collar red.

After Mark had covered the carcass with his tarp, "always kept handy for such occasions," he got out the Wild Turkey and handed David a jug of water. With a bloody hand, he raised the liquor to his lips. David poured water into one hand, set the jug down, and rubbed his hands together, scraping at the blood with a fingernail.

Mark's eyes were bright. He throbbed with energy. When I touched his arm, he turned toward me, and put the bottle in my hand. I raised it, and sipped. He strolled to the back of the pickup, took the jug, and poured water over David's hands. Then David held it while Mark washed. When Mark turned again to look at me, his eyes were opaque. Like the antelope's.

David took the Wild Turkey from me, laughed, and drank deeply. Mark stuffed the guns behind the seat and drove toward the ranch through the twilight. When Mark began to speak, his voice was so soft he might have been speaking only to himself.

"You know, something like that, you put your life on the line—just like the antelope. But your life doesn't mean anything. You don't respect the antelope, except that he fought with thirty-five bullet holes in him. You don't respect the dog, but she kept fighting like hell. You, too, David. You don't know anything worth knowing out here, but you got the fever up and fought, too. I respect you more right now than I ever will again, or ever thought I would. Not because you killed something, but because you fought."

After a while, I took the Wild Turkey out of David's limp hand and gave it to Mark. When he passed it back to me, I rolled it slowly on my tongue, tasting its autumn fire, watching sunset blaze and fade.

A flicker of blue flame keeps the stock bubbling, the antelope bones drumming gently against the bottom and sides of the pot. My muscles are stiff from sitting so long at the kitchen table. Do I think that making use of scraps of meat and vegetables will atone for that death? I haven't seen David since our divorce twenty-five years ago, though I saw Mark more recently at a party. I wonder if they remember, if either of them ever wakes, as I do, to find the antelope staring, eyes gleaming in reflected light, white neck collar red with blood.

BLACK POWDER SMOKE
AND BUFFALO

...

Narrow rumps to the north wind, the two buffalo bulls graze slowly among drifted clumps of curly grass, working at what they do best: surviving a harsh plains winter. The kinky hair on their necks and shoulders is clotted with snow.

"Tell me again why we had to do this in January," Jack says.

"Cold. Hides are prime," says Jim.

"Real prime," my husband, George, says. "Forty below for two months."

"Let's get this over with so I can get back to the ranch," I say. "I don't want to have to call my father in Texas and say I'm snowed in someplace in Nebraska in a blizzard instead of feeding his cows."

"I want a Coke," says Mavis. "With lots of ice."

We all turn to stare at her. The last time we looked at a thermometer the mercury hung at twenty below zero. A north wind blows chips of ice from old snowdrifts into our faces. This piece of prairie offers little cover from the wind. No trees or rocks to serve as rests for the rifles, to make aiming more reliable. We stumble through the drifts, circling the sod house until we're as close as possible to the buffalo. The men crouch, rifles across their arms.

The buffalo stop grazing, raise their broad heads and look toward us, black eyes nearly invisible among the spirals of frosty hair. Jim speculates that the two-year-old he is going to shoot will weigh nearly a thousand pounds skinned and gutted; the yearling George and Jack will shoot probably weighs half as much.

Jim raises his rifle, a dramatic picture in his long black horsehide coat. He and George, as well as Mavis and me, are dressed in our authentic buck-skinner garb—the kind of clothing the mountain men would have worn on a similar hunt in the 1840s—wool and leather, including our moccasins. Jack wears modern clothing—jeans, rubber boots, and a down coat. We are all hoping he'll get cold, proof enough for us that the old clothes are better than the modern.

The men have agreed Jim will shoot first because he won't miss, and his heavy .54 caliber might knock the bull down with one shot. George and his friend Jack squat behind him, right hands tucked in their armpits to keep their fingers flexible. If Jim's buffalo is wounded, and doesn't drop, George will be ready to fire his .50 caliber cap-and-ball rifle. The animal may charge, and George's rifle carries more power than Jack's .45. If George fires, Jack's rifle will still be loaded so he could shoot the wounded bull again, or take his first shot at the yearling. Meanwhile, both Jim and George will have time to reload in case either buffalo gets up and heads our way.

Jim paid for the privilege of shooting an older bison. George and Jack split the cost of the yearling, and Jack drew the lucky straw for first shot. He'll take the skull and George will get the hide.

George tugs his ski mask down under his chin and glares as one buffalo turns toward the sound of Jack's down coat rasping. "We'll never get any closer with you making all that racket," he says.

"I'll bet I'm warmer than you are," Jack responds, adding a traditional mountain-man saying: "And if they'd a' had down, they'd a' used it."

"No, they wouldn't," George snaps. "Too noisy. An Indian would have killed them the first day. Besides, nothing's warmer than wool and leather."

Cheek against his rifle stock, Jim murmurs, "When you two ladies are through gossiping I can shoot."

Mavis and I, armed only with cameras, realize we are too far from the mud walls of the homesteader's soddy to reach its flimsy protection if the bison go berserk. We lie down, trying to imitate snowdrifts. My feet have been numb for a half hour. A reflection catches my eye, and I glance over my shoulder at the ranch house, so distant I can't imagine walking there. Let alone running there ahead of a wounded buffalo. I remember the last words of Crowfoot, a Blackfoot warrior, as he died in 1890, "What is life? It is . . . the breath of a buffalo in the wintertime."

Last night the herd's owner, Lanny, entertained us with tales of other hunts on his western Nebraska ranch. One bull, maddened by a neck wound when a hunter shot at his head and missed, ran for the protection of the herd. Lanny, driving his pickup, chased the bull, trying to turn it away from the other buffalo. Enraged by the smell of blood, the herd surrounded the truck, ramming it repeatedly with their massive heads. Lanny dodged and accelerated, but the bulls demolished the truck. When they drifted off to stand around the wounded animal, the hunter was still crouched on the floorboards, whimpering. Lanny wrenched a modern rifle out of the rack behind the seat and killed the bull himself. A week later, he drove another hunter out for a hunt in his brand new pickup. The man tried for the vital shot behind the shoulder and hit the bull's kneecap instead. Yep, the herd wrecked that pickup, too.

"I can't even tell you what all happened," Lanny said, shaking his head and shutting his eyes. "Just don't kneecap him. And don't shoot him in the head. The skull and hide are so thick at that point it's almost impossible to penetrate."

Such disasters compelled him to make new rules for hunters, to preserve his equipment and his sanity. Once the hunters have chosen the bulls they will shoot, Lanny herds them into a pasture away from rest of the herd. He accepts each hunter's money, makes sure no one has a modern weapon, and drives the hunter to the site early in the morning. He wishes him luck, and goes home.

"Kill 'em with a stick, your bare hands, anything but a modern rifle. I don't care. When they're dead, walk back to the house and I'll come help you load them, but that's it. If you don't show up by the time I deposit the check, I'll pick up your carcasses and notify your next of kin, but I won't rescue your ass."

During our long drive here, all three of the men discussed bison anatomy, agreeing to shoot only at the bulls' hearts. Each of them will reload as soon as he fires; so theoretically two rifles will be on reserve at all times. They didn't need to discuss what this means: that any one of them might have to shoot to save another. I hope they would shoot to save one of us women too, but no one mentioned us.

The wind is blowing so hard even the buffalo don't want to stand still. They move slowly upwind, scouring snow away from the grass with their heads, nipping off dry grass. Jim lowers his rifle, sniffs the wind while blowing on his fingers, raises the rifle and fires.

Blue smoke blossoms at the barrel's end. Dust billows from the lead buffalo's shoulder. He pauses, glances at us, and shrugs as though a fly is pestering him. He nips another morsel of grass, moving ahead like a glacier.

All three men drop as if they've been shot. Jim grabs his powder horn, muttering, "I do believe I'll double-ball."

"Will the barrel stand up to it?" George asks. "Have you ever done that before?"

"Only on the firing range. But I never shot a buffalo before either."

Rifle barrels vertical, Jim and George pull their powder stoppers with their teeth. Jack jerks out a brass powder measure and yelps as it sticks to his naked fingers.

"You're gonna measure?" Jim drawls.

"My barrel's lighter than yours. I don't want to pour too much and have the barrel explode."

"I don't know if there is such a thing as too much," Jim announces, ripping off a strip of patch cloth with his teeth.

George seats one ball on his patch, taps it down, tops it with another and rams the load home on the new powder charge while Jack sifts powder into his measure. "What do you think, two hundred grains?"

"I used about two-fifty, or maybe three hundred," Jim remarks, slapping the ramrod back into its slot under the barrel.

Jack's hands shiver, scattering powder on the ground. "Close enough!" He dumps most of it in the rifle barrel.

George says, "If they were Indians, you'd be dead by now."

Mavis's camera clicks and the shutter stays open. "Oh, great! Here I'm about to become a widow and I won't even have pictures of the death scene." She blows on the lens and takes another shot. The shutter is slow, but it operates.

Rifles loaded, the men turn toward the buffalo. "Hell!" someone grumbles. "Too far away."

"Gosh, you'll have to come out here in the open like us women," I say, jumping up and down to encourage blood circulation in my feet. Maybe if one of the bulls chases me, I'll be able to run and get warm. Or maybe he'll kill me and I won't feel the cold.

Jim strides past the sod outhouse into the open. George slinks off to his left, out of the line of fire, while Jack edges close to the soddy's woodpile.

Mavis and I flounder behind them. "Here's a little swale. Maybe if they charge, they'll miss us," I say, snuggling into the snow.

"And we can get close-ups while they kill Jack," Mavis says, flopping beside me.

The buffalo Jim chose has stopped grazing and ambles faster, tossing his head to look at his pursuers. Jim stops, raises the rifle. In the cold silence I hear him gasp, winded from the walk and feeling the cold burn deep in his lungs. Then he inhales once and holds the breath. The rifle booms.

The buffalo drops, then raises his head, scrambles for footing, and begins to pull himself up. Jim drops to one knee, dumps powder down the barrel, and rams a ball home without bothering to patch it. Then he sits down, legs outstretched in front of him, arms extended to steady the rifle, and fires again. The impact knocks him flat on his back. The bull lunges forward, bellowing.

"Maybe you ought to measure that powder next time!" Jack calls, raising his rifle to aim at the yearling as the older bull's head drops. Jim runs forward, reaching for his knife, yelling, "Shoot! Now!"

The second bull is trotting toward the fallen one, uttering a guttural moan. Jack fires. Dust puffs from the bull's shoulder, but his stride remains even.

"Did I miss?" Jack howls, waving smoke away with his hand. "I couldn't have missed!" He holds his rifle at port arms, staring.

"George!" Jim calls softly, stopping ten feet from the fallen bull. "Any time now would be fine." The second bull has reached his downed companion. He snuffles at the blood on its shoulder, shakes his head vigorously, and spins to face Jim. Mavis whispers, "Oh, God."

George has dropped to one knee in front of me. I hear him murmur, "Lord, please don't let me kneecap him." Then he mumbles, "I can't feel my finger on the trigger." His rifle thunders. In the middle of a bellow, the yearling bull chokes and falls.

George is already dumping powder down his rifle barrel. "Did I hit him?" he says without looking up.

"Oh, yeah," I say in my most encouraging voice. "He's down."

Running to his bull, Jim bends over it and slashes its throat. The legs flail briefly. Blood gushes. The bull's tongue slowly slides out of his mouth.

Mavis and I snap pictures wildly, blowing on the cameras between shots. But neither of us gets in front of George.

Jack dashes to the second bull. "Is he dead?" He prods it with his foot, jumps back as the body spasms.

George spits a ball out of his cheek, rams it down before it can freeze, slaps the ramrod home and moves toward the others. He holds his rifle in both hands, ready to lift and fire.

"Let's make sure," Jim says, poking the knife into the second bull's throat.

A muffled cough spins us all around. Lanny stands by his pickup. "Nice shooting," he says, handing Jim a bottle of Jack Daniels. "On the house."

"Where the hell were you?" says Jack. "I thought you went to the bank with our money."

"I say that. Keeps people alert. But I keep an eye out." He gestures toward the binoculars on the dashboard. "Don't want wounded bulls rampaging around the countryside all day. Irritates the neighbors." He grins. "Besides, your miserable carcasses woulda been snowed under by dark. Hard to find."

We all look up. Overhead the sky hangs blue and cloudless. George tips the bottle back, wipes his mouth on his sleeve, then points with his chin to dark clouds lying on the northern horizon. Jack takes a tiny sip of whiskey. Blinking, he extends the bottle toward Lanny. Behind him, Mavis snatches it, gasping, "We're at least as cold as you guys," as she passes it to me. I make it glug twice.

"Hold it," Lanny says, snatching the bottle. "Got a ceremony to perform." He strips off his glove and dabs his bare hand in the pool of blood under the buffalo's open throat. "I'm part Sioux, you know. My wife's full-blood." He shows perfect white teeth. "Turn around, Jim."

Jim hands Mavis his furry bearhide coat as Lanny raises the long fringe across the back of his white buckskin shirt. Mavis screeches, "Not on his new buckskins!" while Lanny makes a bloody handprint on the white leather shirt.

"Will that wash out?" Mavis asks.

"You wash these and I'll have to shoot another buffalo," Jim growls. "With my second wife."

A neighbor has arrived driving Lanny's tractor. He lowers the grapple fork while Lanny whips a chain around the neck of Jim's buffalo. The neighbor drops it in the pickup bed while Lanny dabbles his hand in the second bull's blood and asks, "Who fired the killing shot?"

Jack points to George and explains, "Besides, I didn't wear my skins and I wouldn't want blood on them anyway. And Ellie'd wash it out as soon as I got home."

George hands me his air force great coat. Lanny marks the back of his fringed buckskin shirt, then smears blood on his cheeks and Jim's, saying, "Old warrior's custom. Shows you've killed."

"Don't we get some award for crawling around in the snow without anything to defend ourselves with?" Mavis asks.

"Sure," says Lanny, lunging toward her, bloody hand outstretched. She ducks away.

"This is sure fun, guys," Jack says, "but I'm cold. Let's go back to the house now."

George snorts. "Serves you right for wearing that down jacket instead of your 'skins." By the time the second bull is loaded, Jack is sitting in the passenger seat of the pickup, staring intently at his fingers as he tries to bend them. Jim, Mavis, George, and I climb into the rear and embrace the dead bulls, absorbing the heat rising from their bodies.

At the ranch buildings Lanny uses his loader to lift the first bull out and maneuvers the carcass onto its back.

"The Indians propped them on their bellies and split them down the back," I mention.

George says, "Then to hell with authenticity. I want the hide split down the belly. Besides, it's easier to gut 'em."

"Isn't this where we men go in the house and have a drink while the women do the butchering?" Jack asks.

I wave my skinning knife under his nose. "George said it. 'To hell with authenticity.' Start carving." All we have to do is skin and gut the animals. Lanny will deliver them to a local butcher to be cut, wrapped, and frozen for us.

Jim and George, stripped of their leather shirts and gloves, work fast. In minutes, both buffalo are open, guts steaming.

Lanny reappears, followed by his five-year-old son and carrying a large basin. "We're not quite through with the formalities here," he says, cutting a liver free. He holds the quivering mass of maroon flesh aloft, then slices off a chunk and holds it to George's lips. "Gotta eat that while it's warm. Good medicine for the next hunt."

"I can't afford another hunt," George says, trying to keep his lips together.

Lanny pushes the chunk between his teeth and George begins chewing. He chews and chews and chews, while Lanny whacks off another piece. Jim takes it from his hand, eyes George, then tips his head back and tosses the piece down his throat. He gulps and beams at George.

"I knew there was a trick to it," George grumbles, swallowing hard.

"Look, Daddy!" Lanny's son has smeared blood on a strip of buffalo hide to stick it under his nose. "A mustache! Does this mean I'm old enough to have some liver?"

"Sure." Lanny cuts a small chunk and bends to slip it into the boy's mouth. "Hold your breath and swallow."

Lanny rummages in buffalo guts and begins pulling at ropes of intestine. "Anybody want the stomachs?"

I do, for a gift to an Indian holy man I've interviewed about sacred and historic topics. I'm hoping he'll invite me to next summer's Sun Dance. Lanny hands me a slippery bag that looks like pink honeycomb and smells like the inside of a buffalo. "Rinse it off under that faucet."

At George's suggestion, I hang the washed stomachs on the rear vertical supports of the framework he built to carry our tipi poles on the van. Neither of us realize that they will freeze to the metal. Next day we'll drive home with the odd shapes hung on the van, drawing puzzled or horrified looks. For three days, until the stomachs thaw a little so we can pry them loose, we have to explain what they are. No one really wants to know what we're going to do with them.

Finally, we toss them in my parents' freezer to await better weather when we can drive to the reservation. They're still there when my mother opens the freezer in March. Her shriek nearly shatters the windows. While she collects her nerves, we wrap the stomachs in plastic bags and hide them under the steak until July. Our delivery trip isn't monotonous, either. We arrive at the holy man's house in the middle of an American Indian Movement rally, complete with fiery speeches against the lowdown, sneaky whites who stole

Indian lands. The gift is accepted and we escape unscathed, but it's quite a while before I'm invited to a Sun Dance.

We work in couples to skin the buffalo while Jack offers advice and fondles a bottle of peppermint schnapps. "Get as much of the meat off the hide as you can," Jim advises. By the time the hides lie flat on the ground, the fragments of flesh adhering to them are frozen solid.

"This is easier to do now than in warm weather," George observes, slicing his finger for the third time. "Look at this!" He's found the ball from his rifle, lying inside the rib cage. "So even with a couple hundred grains behind it, the ball only penetrated the hide and ribs once. Didn't have enough zip to go on through."

The men carefully inspect the carcass, inside and out, and conclude that Jack's .45 caliber ball, driven by more than two hundred grains of powder, simply bounced off the buffalo's thick hide. Jack's eyes widen, as he absently raises the schnapps bottle, gulping enough to make him cough for several minutes.

Meanwhile, Lanny painstakingly squeezes partly digested grass out of the intestines. When each is empty, he washes them under the faucet, handling them gently, lifting wobbly chunks of white fat so water flows everywhere. Then he turns each long rope of gut inside out and washes it again. His hands turn red, then white. "I'm not sure I should ask, but what are you doing?" Jack says, when he can breathe again.

Lanny grins. "Old mountain man custom: *boudins*. This is part of your package. My wife'll cook 'em up for you tonight. We'll bring them to the soddy when we bring supper."

"No, thank you," Jack says, upending the schnapps again.

"Oh, this is an offer you can't refuse," Lanny says, winking at me.

While George and Jim spread salt on the hides, Jack decides he can be most useful by returning to the soddy to build up the fire. "I'll get it good and warm. I'll get our sleeping bags out of the vehicles, and everything set up."

"Don't forget to bring in wood so you won't have to get up in the middle of the night for it," Jim says. "You aren't taking the bottle, are you?"

"Yeah. I'll need to restore my energy after hauling all that wood and blankets."

"Well, give it here first." The bottle makes the rounds, and when Jack finally tucks it into his coat pocket, he doesn't notice only a swallow remains. He drives off toward the soddy in Jim's pickup.

"Shovel the snowdrift away from the outhouse!" Mavis calls after him.

George and Jim roll the stiffening hides with the hair inside, and strap them on top of our van. We'll deliver them to a man who will tan them the old way, with the bulls' brains, in time for rendezvous. With a flourish, George hands both Mavis and me a buffalo scrotum.

"What are you going to do with yours?" Mavis asks me.

"I'm sure I'll think of something." After all, I take feminism so seriously my powder horn came from a female buffalo. Maybe I'll make a medicine pouch, just to wear to rendezvous.

Meticulously, the men peel hide away from the buffalo skulls, scraping hide and bone clean, then salt and roll the scalps and pack the brains in an ice cream bucket. They move slowly, hands raw and chapped from the cold. Blood and fat streak Jim's white buckskins and George's wool pants. Mavis and I pick up the buffalo steaks cut earlier and wrap them in a canvas bag. Then we perch on the sleeping bags Jack didn't take, inside the van, picking bits of frozen meat and blood out of each other's hair. George washes knives at the faucet, while Jim straps the skulls to the front of the van. The bulls' empty eye sockets stare down the ranch trail as a rising wind begins to toy with the snow, idly sifting little drifts across our tracks, then sweeping them away. Clouds mute the setting sun.

The buffalo stomachs thump against the van's back doors as we drive around drifts to the soddy. Smoke rises from its listing chimney. When Jim shoves the door open, Jack is lying on a cot beside an old cookstove, snoring. "Bet that's the only cot in the place."

It is. We pile our sleeping bags and blankets on a platform near the ceiling. When we climb the ladder, we can see the ranch house through cracks in the old sod bricks.

"I figured since heat rises, you'd rather sleep up there where it's warmer," Jack says, yawning.

"Hasn't been much rise yet," I say. "Throw some more wood on that fire."

"I don't want to run out in the middle of the night," he says in response. But he piles more wood inside the firebox, while George digs in a bag and hauls out a bottle of Old Bushmills.

"Now, isn't that a coincidence?" Jim says, holding up another.

With her bloody gloves, Mavis brushes bits of hay and dirt off the surface of the stove, while I rummage through a lopsided cupboard, looking vainly for a frying pan. George wipes the stove with the tail of his coat.

By the time eight or ten small steaks are sizzling nicely on the stove top, we've all swigged enough from one of the bottles to think we're warm. My feet and hands throb and itch from frostbite, as they will for days. George hangs our candle lanterns from convenient nails in the rafters and roof beams. In the warm yellow glow, we shed our heavy coats, dig out clean socks, and hold our aching feet and hands close to the stove.

Lanny told us the soddy was nearly a hundred years old, built by a home-steader. Watching snow blow between the blocks of sod to drift in the air overhead, Jack remarks, "This is way too authentic. Why don't we just drive back to the motel in Alliance?" No one bothers to answer.

Lanny and his wife arrive with their little boy, who promptly crawls into Jack's blankets and falls asleep. The woman places a pot of chili on the stove, stacks bowls on the rickety table, and slices homemade bread.

Lanny drags intestines out of a plastic bag, flourishing his knife as he chops them into six-inch chunks. He drops a chunk on the stove. "Now you're in for a treat!" he crows as the fat sputters and pops. He pokes the pieces with his knife point, moving, turning, caressing them until he judges one to be done, then spears it and turns. "Hunters first."

Jim shrugs and opens his mouth. Adroitly, Lanny flips the *boudins* inside, then spears a piece for himself. Grease runs from the corners of Jim's mouth as he chews; his eyes grow round, his back straightens.

"Like this." Lanny demonstrates, holding one end of the *boudins* with his left hand and deftly slicing off the bite he's chewing with the knife in his right hand. "Watch your nose."

George hesitates, takes the next piece from the knife and nibbles. When Jack shakes his head and grimaces, I finally get one.

Crisp on the outside, tender and flaky inside, like pie crust. Perhaps a lit-tle like the fried pork rinds we used to gobble as kids. Meaty, but rich. Fatty, but light. Moaning with delight, we gobble them as fast as Lanny lifts them from the stove on the tip of his knife. Our chins shine with fat.

After his fifteenth chunk, George rubs his hands over his chin, then wipes them back over his hair with a broad smile and offers a buckskinner's praise:

"Waugh!" Jim wipes his hands on Mavis's long black hair, ignoring her squeals of protest. Lanny's wife smiles, her dark eyes bright, gesturing to her own shiny black braids and nodding.

Lanny opens the plastic bag again and brings out bulging lengths of gut tied on both ends, arranging them across the back of the stove beside a pot of water. "These are even better," he says. "Stuffed. They're for dessert."

His wife ladles chili into bowls. Jim and I sit on the edge of the sleeping platform, legs dangling. Mavis is snuggled into a blanket between us. George leans against the wall, possibly because he might not be able to stand without support.

Jack grabs the bottle every time it comes around. "I usually like to eat chili with a spoon," he says, as Lanny's wife hands him a fork.

"Tough." It is the only thing she has said so far. Jack eats.

By the time we've polished off the chili and two mincemeat pies, Lanny has swept the stuffed *boudins,* nicely browned, from the stove top into the boiling water. He lifts them out, dripping juices, as his wife hands him our bowls.

"What are these stuffed with?" Jack says. "Never mind."

"Did you eat any of the fried ones?" I know he didn't. I'm just making trouble. Lanny stiffens, glares at Jack.

"You mean—who is this guy? Didn't he come with you? Didn't I say not to bring anybody that wasn't a mountain man?" Lanny's hand is on his knife hilt and he looks truly fierce. His son's head pops out of Jack's sleeping bag, eyes wide.

"He built my rifle," George says defensively. "That oughta count for something."

Lanny scowls, then spears a generous piece of stuffed gut and holds it to Jack's mouth. "Eat. Or sleep outside."

Wincing, Jack nibbles at the meat as if he's trying to keep it from touching his lips. "Hey! That's good." He scoops the chunk into his bowl and picks it up in his fingers.

I'll admit my memories of the rest of the night are hazy around the edges. We sing parts of all the mountain man songs we know. Each time we toss an empty bottle of Bushmills under the stove, we seem to find a new bottle. Every time Jack lies down, we send him outside for more firewood.

At various times, each man rises ponderously, goes outside without a coat, and reappears buttoning his pants. Finally, I know my time has come. I grab my blanket coat, called a capote, pull the door shut behind me, and stumble around the corner of the cabin toward the outhouse. Still half-blind from the lights inside, I don't realize until I have floundered halfway through a huge drift that there are no footprints in the snow. The outhouse door is open and a bank of snow extends from the seat through the opening. No one has used it in a long time. Jack did not shovel a path.

My eyes have adjusted. Somewhere above the clouds and falling snow is a full moon. I plod to a corner post, raise my capote, and begin working my way through my wool pants and red long johns toward relief. Leaning back against the ice-crusted fence post, I spend a long time staring upward into the weak moonlight, watching the snow fall.

When I open the cabin door, warm light illuminates the snow around my feet. A dozen yellow holes melted six inches deep make a perfect circle around the doorstep.

"Mavis!" I bawl. "Come and look at this. Jack didn't shovel out the outhouse, and these guys are too lazy to walk five feet. They've been pissing on the doorstep."

On the sleeping platform, Mavis raises her head. "I'll take your word for it. We'll kill 'em tomorrow when we run out of meat."

Telling time in a soddy during a blizzard isn't easy, but it's late when Lanny and his wife bundle up their son and leave. Then Jim says, "It's gone."

"What?" George glances out the window at our vehicles, then reaches up to check the rifles under our blankets.

"The bill of my cap. Did I cut it off?" Jim asks irritably. "That's my favorite wool cap."

"Get a little wild with your knife, did you?" On the ladder, George leans back to look at Jim's head and laughs so hard he slides down the rungs and hits the floor. Mavis raises her head. "What's the matter?"

"I can't find the bill of my cap," Jim gripes. Laughing, we wake Jack. "What's the matter?" he mumbles.

"The bill of my cap's gone. Have you seen it?" Honestly puzzled, Jim tries to turn his cap and fails. George rights it and Jim feels the brim and grins. "Put some more wood on the fire, Jack," he says, toppling backward. Mavis groans and drags him into his sleeping bag. George piles blankets over us all.

The roof beams pop with cold every few minutes. Every hour, one of us wakes up cold and yells at Jack to build up the fire, waking the other three. Jack snores on. Once Jim bounces a winter moccasin off Jack's head. The next time George throws a boot. By the time we run out of footwear and are discussing the merits of throwing our knives, the horizon glows softly with sunrise.

Lying close beside me, George whispers, "I shot a buffalo."

"Look at the ceiling, George. It's full of holes. No wonder we're so cold."

"I can see stars. Stars."

The Hugh Glass Rendezvous is named after a fur trapper who enlisted as a hunter with Major Andrew Henry's party in 1823 and became a legend on the northern plains. The group ascended the Grand River, exploring and looking for creeks and rivers full of beaver for pelts that would eventually become top hats for English gentlemen. In what is now northern South Dakota, Hugh was attacked and terribly mutilated by a grizzly that broke his leg and gnawed on various body parts. Ashley took one look at the mess and ordered two men to stay with Glass until he died, to bury him, and then catch up with the party.

The men waited a couple of days—reports vary—but Glass refused to die, and the men grew nervous, alone in Indian country. So they took his weapons—the worst crime a man could commit against another in those perilous days—and left him. Glass's fury when he came to and realized he'd been betrayed may have helped him survive. He crawled nearly two hundred miles, to Fort Kiowa, near Chamberlain, South Dakota, where he outfitted himself and began a long search for the two men, and revenge. His story has been told by writers John Neihardt and Frederick Manfred.

The rendezvous named after Glass was first held in 1982 on a ranch along the Bad River in South Dakota, a region Glass probably came to know well as he scrambled through the cactus on his hands and knees, mumbling about what he'd do to his faithless partners when he caught them. Modern mountain men respect the old boy's stamina, but we went to the event in pickups and vans. The first year George and I attended, he explained that this was a special event, open by personal invitation only to buckskinning aristocracy: people who preferred "primitive" camps. The unspoken rule allowed nothing modern—manufactured after 1840—to be visible in camp.

We followed rumors thin as smoke along a dirt trail marked sparingly with silhouettes of tipis instead of signs. In a grove of cottonwoods along the trickling river, we unloaded and piled our belongings where we'd erect our tipi, then parked our van behind a dusty hill a half-mile away.

Shadows lengthened toward dusk as we sat on blanket-covered wooden boxes to catch up on news. A buckskinner in his sixties, properly dressed in breechclout and leggings, squatted in the grass near us, talking about his winter trapping.

Abruptly, with energy belying his gray hair and lean shanks, he exploded into the air howling and prancing.

"Bee in his breechclout?" George muttered.

Then two men and a woman sprang into the air, yelling. We looked at each other: this strange affliction was apparently contagious.

Then one man grabbed a shovel and whacked a coiled rattlesnake while the first man explained how he'd reached down to brush an ant out of his breechclout and patted the snake on the head. He was embarrassed about his outburst, considering such cowardice unbecoming to a mountain man.

The tumult scattered us to put up our tipis and dig firepits before dark. Soon whoops and shouts shattered the drowsy afternoon. Rattlesnakes everywhere. One was coiled under a stack of blankets a woman had dropped only minutes before. A child reached for a stick of firewood that crawled away. George grabbed his hatchet to pound in a tipi stake, and saw a rattler gliding under the tipi cover toward our bed. Soon a whisper of sound was enough to send crowds of folks soaring skyward.

Parents collected their children in a bare spot near the center of camp and lectured them on rattlesnake etiquette, while someone gathered car keys and rummaged through everyone's glove compartment for snakebite kits.

Around the night's council fire, debate raged over methods of treating snakebite. The folks who adhered to the traditional method of cut and suck tended to be conservative in other ways, too; some of them used flint and steel to light their pipes. Younger folks favored the more modern technique of skipping the cut, and applying suction while racing toward the nearest hospital. After a grizzled man whetting a knife interjected quietly that the nearest town, thirty miles away, had no hospital, several people admitted to being nurses, doctors, or to having had CPR training.

A young man told the joke about the hunter bitten by a rattler as he sat on a log to answer an urgent call of nature.

"What should I do?" the victim wailed to his companion, looking over his shoulder at his fang-marked buttocks. "Aren't you supposed to suck the wound?"

His friend studied the bite a moment, then said firmly, "You're gonna die."

At dawn, a 'skinner who'd strolled across the prairie behind camp reported that it looked like a colander, a rattlesnake New York City. A few mothers warned their children to stay away. A horde of bloodthirsty tots ran whooping into the field, waving tomahawks and knives. By noon, several pots of rattlesnake stew bubbled, and several camps were preparing snake shish kebab, conducting friendly disputes over recipes and flavor.

Several 'skinners fastened rattles to a hat or necklace. One woman made rattle earrings. When buckskinners pirouetted or sprang into the air abruptly, everyone enjoyed the sight—even more if they'd been frightened by their own ornaments. One minute a burly mountain man might be strolling solemnly through camp, resplendent in deerskin shirt and leggings, dignified under a tall bearskin hat. A minute later, the hat hit the ground as the man leaped six feet in the air with his legs crossed, yelping.

"First time I ever saw buckskinners levitate," George remarked.

Around the nightly council fire, we proposed prizes for the highest and broadest bounds and the most creative dance steps. Not one person mentioned the rattlesnake's double penis. Given the nature of camp humor, they must not have known. In those days, I was liberated enough to think of it, but too shy to bring it up.

By dark of the first day, the score was buckskinners seventy-five, rattlesnakes zero. George told me his snake stick was magic. "When I'm walking through camp, it's seven feet long. The second I see a snake, it shrinks to two feet." As he skinned six rattlers, he insisted, "I only killed the ones that attacked me." Acting on the advice of more experienced snake hunters, he found a spare bottle of antifreeze in the van—George was always prepared for emergencies—and tucked the hides into a bucket of it to tan. I wear the supple and shining hides as hat bands.

The next year's gathering was scheduled during South Dakota's deer and turkey hunting seasons. Even hidden buckskinning camps attract a few morons who use gasoline to start fires, throw cigarette butts on the ground, or come only to gawk at our outfits. So many people had asked to attend the gathering that veterans began calling it the "Rattlesnake Rendezvous," and lied about the location and dates. Once in camp, we appointed a few tough dog soldiers—camp police—to eject anyone who wouldn't behave.

A true snake-lover, I am also prudent; so the next year when we went to the Rattlesnake Rendezvous, I was wearing brand-new knee-high moccasins made of thick buffalo hide, *almost* guaranteed to stop rattler fangs. I vowed never to get out of the lodge without them; I became skilled at wrapping the ties around my legs very quickly. The first morning, stepping confidently out of the lodge at the command of Mother Nature, I wore my new moccasins and a tan dress over red long johns. I hiked the dress above my knees, and tucked the hem into my belt. A layer of white frost softened the leaves so my steps made no sound.

Buckskinners with deer licenses had been out hunting since sunrise. Their tracks in the frost pointed toward the foothills on the other side of the snake metropolis. Skilled at hunting with muzzle-loaders, they'd creep within a hundred yards of their prey, sighting so carefully down their old-fashioned open sights that a single shot would probably kill. Most would be back in camp with a deer or turkey draped over their shoulders, mouths watering as they anticipated fresh meat for breakfast, before most of us finished our first cup of coffee.

Ambling along the river's edge, I stopped to scan a clearing. Ten feet away a mule deer buck ringed by does stared calmly back at me. I almost laughed out loud, thinking of all the hunters a half-mile away.

Movement drew my eye to the other side of the river, where a man in full camouflage and an orange cap stepped around a tree. He carried a high-powered rifle with a scope as big as my arm. He hadn't seen the deer. But if he'd parked by the gate, he'd passed our vehicles, so he knew people were near. Yet he raised the scope to his eye—with the rifle barrel pointing straight toward the sleeping camp—and began scanning the woods through the scope. The rifle bore looked like a railway tunnel. If he fired at the deer and missed, the bullet would hurtle straight toward camp.

Therefore, my next action was inspired by concern for the safety of friends. I vaulted into the open, screeching in raucous imitation of a levitating buckskinner. Then I dodged into the woods and dropped behind a tree.

Unlike humans, deer don't form a committee and discuss their options before coming to a decision. At the second whoop, they sprang up and clattered away, hopping deadfalls and bouncing over fences. Within seconds, they were running up a hill on the other side of camp. I swear it was only an accident that they were heading toward the black powder hunters.

Across the river, the modern hunter began screaming obscenities and possibly threats. Since he looked the type to shoot at noises, I realized it behooved me to depart without sounding like a deer. Since my clothes blended with the landscape, the trick was to be so completely invisible he'd think I'd run away when the deer did. A little test of my woods skills.

I sank into the leaves, trying to think like a buckskinner of the early 1800s. In those days a man trapping this wooded river had to assume he'd be hunted by all the predators within five hundred miles, including grizzly bears, wolves, and Lakota warriors. All I had to fear was a hasty shot from one careless human with a high-powered rifle and a scope sight.

Swearing, the hunter scrambled down the riverbank and started splashing across the thin stream, headed straight toward me. Meanwhile, I inhaled deeply and studied fat trees and thick brush. With my skirt tucked up, my bright red legs would be acutely visible. I hoped the hunter only looked at deer height. The early frost was gone. The leaves were supple, but I had to watch for twigs.

When I heard him grunting and cussing as he pulled himself up the riverbank three feet beyond my tree, I stood and walked deliberately away, moving to the hunter's right. When his curses grew louder, I knew he'd gained the top of the bank. I stepped behind a broad-beamed cottonwood and risked a glance. He sat with his back against the tree I'd left, still swearing. His shouting provided cover. I dashed straight upstream, keeping close to a line of trees.

When a branch snapped underfoot, I dived into a thicket of plum bushes. The hunter bellowed, "Who's there?" He yelled twice more, but when I peered out through the branches, he was looking at the spot where the stick broke. My hideout was out of his line of sight. He raised the rifle and scanned ahead, then swore again and started confidently off—directly toward our camp.

Some of the men in camp, alerted by his clamor, were doubtless already moving to intercept him. They'd explain in words of one syllable why he shouldn't point a rifle toward their children.

But I'd enjoyed the game. Pretending he was still a threat, I crept to the edge of the thicket to plan another route, mentally colonizing the woods with danger. I spent a couple of hours creeping through the underbrush, watching turkeys drink at the stream, smelling flowers, leaning against tree trunks to watch birds. Later, when I told George how much I'd enjoyed the morning, he cringed and said, "Uh-oh; you might be turning into a real buckskinner." The hunter, he said, had been politely informed he was hunting on private land, posted against hunting with modern rifles. A couple of brawny lads had walked with him back to his truck, and then followed him in another truck until he was well out of the county.

An hour after scaring the deer, and two miles along the winding channel, I crept close to the riverbank, hoping that if I was silent I'd see something unusual. Below me, a golden eagle sat in a cottonwood, intent on ripping at something held in his talons. His back looked wider than my body. Each dark feather was outlined in burnished bronze.

I watched him for a moment before he straightened and turned his head, glaring at me with one great golden eye. Swiveling his shoulders, he spun his head to focus the other eye. Then he belched.

Plummeting from the branch, he dropped toward the water thirty feet below. The great wings snapped open, roared as they caught air. One beat, two, three. He rose, wheeling back over me, climbing above the trees and gliding straight away down the path of open sky above the river. A rattlesnake writhed in his talons.

SLEEPING WITH
THE GRIZZLY

...

Dusk filters through the ragged branches of lodgepole pines as thirty horses stumble along a narrow, rocky trail. The riders ahead slump, hitching one knee over the swell below the saddle's horn to rest weary legs and blistered thighs.

As our trail crosses a stream at the edge of a broad meadow, the horses silently separate. Dropping their heads, they slurp loudly, taking deep, gusty breaths. We haven't crossed water since the noon break. Saddles and leather pants creak softly as riders dismount to loosen cinches.

B. Joe, our guide and outfitter, grins over his shoulder at us, white teeth bright under his hat in the falling darkness. "We'll camp in the trees," he says. Pulling hard on the lead rope, he rides across the narrow end of the meadow to a group of pines. Five mules tied nose to tail behind him carry supplies we couldn't fit on our horses. B. Joe piles the panniers in a heap near a rock fireplace before brushing the pack mules.

One rider, still on his tired horse, peers into the water as the animal drinks. All day, this man has shattered every silence with his loud jokes and singing. When he utters a hoarse cry, I grimace, expecting another chorus of "Roll Me Over."

The loud man is pointing at the creek bottom and flapping his lips, but no sound emerges. He clears his throat and tries again. "Grizzly track. Big one. Fresh." Meager words compared to the racket he made earlier.

The watchful man beside me grunts; his blue eyes flick left and right. He loosens his belt and reaches inside his jacket to touch the pistol beneath his arm. Deliberately, he turns in the saddle. Crow's-feet at the corners of his eyes tighten as he studies the trees behind us. Another man unbuckles a rifle scabbard. Several check the loads on heavy black powder pistols. The new bride squawks and clutches her husband's mighty arm.

We stare at shadows under whispering trees. When our horses finish drinking, we lead them toward the loud rider, now standing in water nearly to the tops of his black thigh-high boots. Bending, he places his hand on the creek bottom beside the grizzly print in the mud. The track is twice as large.

We knew at the time we signed up for that summer ride in 1987 that we'd be in grizzly country. All day, we've seen tracks in the dust. Scratches on trees beside the trail—higher than any of us could reach—made us more vigilant. The sight of this track close to our camp at dusk silences us.

I glance across the meadow toward B. Joe, the wrangler. Last night at the campfire he entertained us with tales of rampaging bears shot to defend unwary campers. His voice was soft, his manner modest. He's thrown a rope over a short tree limb ten feet over his head and is hoisting a food pack. Grizzly country, indeed.

The horses toss their heads, work the bits, scratch their heads against our legs. I slide my hands under Ginger's bridle to rub her cheeks, and talk softly to her.

The loud man bellows, "That son-of-a-bitch comes into camp, I'll shoot his ass." He pats the big-bore twin pistols hanging from his hips. "Old Marvin and Betsy here will blow his skull apart."

The new bride giggles shrilly. "We'll camp close to you, then, but I'm not worried. Big Slim will take care of me." She gazes up as her massive husband pats her shoulder. I allow myself a tiny vision of a grizzly, attracted by the perfume and makeup she wears even to bed, licking her face.

The quiet man, who has spoken only ten words in two days, glances toward my husband, George, who has been silently scanning the trees. Grinning at each other, they raise their bridle reins and mount. The horses snuffle and fling water as they trot toward camp.

Reaching camp, George and I swing down off our horses. B. Joe turns from hanging a pack and says in a carrying voice, "Hang all your food, and anything that smells. Use these big trees with the chopped-off branches in the middle of camp. Don't unsaddle. Loosen the cinches, breathe 'em a little, but we're riding over to a hunting camp in a few minutes. They'll have supper waiting for us."

While the two men help inexperienced riders hang their packs, I loosen the cinches on the gelding, Ringo, and his sister, Ginger. We rented both horses from B. Joe, who advised us not to bring our flatland horses to this altitude. I shift the saddles a bit, and rub their necks, watching the other riders grab their gear. By the time I collect our packs, most of the others have chosen sleeping sites, and I can pick a spot far from the new bride and her collection of reeking cosmetics. The quiet man has slung his bedroll at one end of a massive fallen log, thirty feet from the central fireplace. He unrolls the bag and drops a water jug, and he's ready for nightfall. Scratching his reddish beard, he stretches and adjusts the pistol holster under his arm. A leather-clad hunter with a well-used rifle leans it against the log's other end. I place our bedding on the opposite side of the log, between them.

We'll be riding home in the dark, so I arrange what we'll need as we slip into our bedrolls. George's .357 and two pairs of dry socks go inside his bag. I tuck the flashlight under the head of mine. When he takes off his belt, George will put his possibles sack containing matches next to the rolled-up coat he uses as a pillow. Our heads will be nearly under the curve of the log, so an animal leaping over it is likely to land on our legs, not in our faces.

When I finish arranging necessities, I join George as he and B. Joe finish hobbling the pack mules to graze in the meadow. I'm just in time to hear how a grizzly once charged through a camp of hunters here.

"He was trying to get at the packs, so I just laid quiet. He'd have moved on when that didn't work. But then one of the dummies sat up and hollered, and they all started thrashing around trying to find their rifles. Made the bear nervous. He went over to the noisy one to look him over, and practically tripped over an empty sardine can." He shakes his head.

"They kept yelling. I think he went after them to shut them up. Anyway, I figured I'd better shoot before one of 'em really irritated him." He glances around, leans toward George, and lowers his voice. "We're on a trail they use for water, but no sense mentioning that to anyone else. Load that .357, if it isn't already." George nods.

He turns to me, smiling. "Break any ribs when that Ginger mare came apart today?"

Every time I breathe, strained muscles throb, but I say, "Nothing to mention," and watch his eyes.

"You stuck with her." That's as close as B. Joe comes to praise, and I'm pleased to hear it. "Wish somebody'd had a movie camera. I'd like to run it in slow motion and see how you got from her rear end back into that saddle."

"I looked over my shoulder at those rocks and sprouted wings," I say, trying not to take a deep breath.

He pushes his hat back, shaking his head. "You were *gone*. I was already trying to figure out how to tie a stretcher between two mules." He turns away, and yells, "Let's ride. Roast turkey and dressing."

Groans echo among the trees. Someone shouts the question we heard fifty times today, "How far is it?"

B. Joe repeats, for the fifty-first time, "Not far now."

We tighten cinches, drag ourselves back on the horses, and line out for dinner at a hunting camp a couple of miles up the valley. I've never been this tired after a day on a horse. Between spells of bucking, Ginger kept me tense by shying at rocks and snorting at trees, looking for some reason to buck again.

All day, the group rode close together, experienced riders looking out for others. Now the ride to supper becomes a stampede. Ginger likes to stay close to her brother, Ringo, so George and I cross the meadow far behind the other riders' clatter. Just before we plunge into darkness under the pines, George's son, Mike, rides into sight from the back trail. All afternoon, he has dawdled behind us, perhaps dreaming of being a mountain man or lost in some teenage sexual fantasy. But B. Joe's hired wrangler was with him, leading several more mules, so we figured he was safer than if he were alone.

"Where we going?" Mike asks.

We tell him, and he drops back with the wrangler again. He doesn't know about the grizzly track. After a whispered debate, we decide George will tell him on the ride back.

When the trail widens, George eases Ringo up beside Ginger and says, "Do you remember what I told you about being attacked by a grizzly?"

"Yes, dear. Dive toward him while he's raking my back with his claws. Find his balls, and cut 'em off."

He beams. "Probably won't save your life, but you'll die happy, knowing he'll bleed to death."

"Ecstatic. My luck, it'll be a female, and she'll think I'm making advances."

The glow of lanterns in the hunting camp reaches down the trail to meet us. Groups of people sit on stumps around a half-dozen square white tents. Bonfires throw gold sparks high. Dark figures in white aprons carry platters from the cook shelter into the dining tent. We fill our plates. Only the new bride sits down on a bench. Her husband looks at her, then follows the rest of us outside where we slump on tree stumps, shoveling food down our throats. Unlike our collection of blanket-covered bedrolls a mile away in the dark, this is a permanent camp, where certain guides bring hunters every year. This party has been here a week, and the neighborhood grizzly is mentioned like an acquaintance in fragments of conversation.

"He tips over rocks the size of Volkswagens along that trail every night, but he mostly stays up on the mountain during daylight," one man says.

A guide who comes here every fall adds, "We've had enough trouble over the years, we put in a better food cache."

In this region, rangers dump "garbage bears"—grizzlies from Yellowstone who have learned humans leave tasty tidbits in their trash. The outfitters built a small log shanty in a tree outside their circle of tents. Each evening, someone hauls camp food supplies up a ladder to the platform fifteen feet off the ground.

"Then we take down the ladder," says one of the guides, adding earnestly, "Griz hardly ever gets into it."

George finishes eating and calls to Mike to ride with him. He'll add bear warnings to his regular evening lecture on responsible behavior. Mike hasn't been brushing his horse, and last night he dumped the saddle he borrowed from me under a tree where his horse stepped on it. "And if you want a ground cloth under your sleeping bag," I hear George say, "you'd better get to camp in daylight so you can see what you're doing."

"I'll just use your flashlight," Mike says. George rumbles a reply as they jog out of earshot.

I start toward camp with a group of riders, but Ginger, angry that Ringo has left her, begins to buck, smacking trees close to the path with her heels. When she stops, gasping, the other riders are gone, and the mare is so tired her ears droop sideways. I'd like to relax, but she tries to stumble into a trot, wanting to catch up with Ringo. Keeping the reins taut, I wonder if she'll warn me if one of the wavering shapes along the trail is a grizzly instead of a rock.

I dilate my nostrils, breathe deep of air fragrant with pine and dust kicked up by the horses ahead. I hear riders yelling faintly. Perhaps they are deliberately making a clamor to discourage the bear. I whistle, then try to hum. My voice flutters and evaporates among the sighing trees. I listen for cracking brush and hear only hooves clicking on rock.

Butch, one of our friends in the buckskinning club, used to guide bear hunters for a living. We pulled into camp at Sunlight Basin one night when he was the only one there. For five hours he sat beside our fire, passing the whiskey jug and telling of his conflicts with bears. Unfortunately, I remember most of them on the ride back to this camp.

An outfitter had left Butch alone in a permanent camp while the rest of the crew made a three-day trek for fresh hunters and supplies. The first night, three grizzlies sauntered through camp. Scurrying around the tents, trying to stay out of sight, he rooted through sleeping bags and other gear, and discovered his fellow workers had taken most of the guns. His arsenal was one shotgun and a single-shot .22, neither capable of killing a grizzly.

He crouched in silence while the grizzlies sniffed through camp. "I'd watch 'em go by, and then tiptoe along behind 'em with the shotgun, hiding behind a tent if one of them turned its head." He snorts. "Like if they didn't see me, they wouldn't know I was there."

Frozen elk and deer carcasses hung inside the provisions tent, fortified with log walls. The bears climbed the logs and slashed open the canvas roof. Then each bear seized a half carcass and ambled into the clearing by the fire-pit. Snarling and skirmishing, they ate until they belched, then ambled off into the woods.

Butch went to bed. "I figured they wouldn't bother me, with all that meat, but I didn't get much sleep. Woke up every time I quit hearing bones crack."

The next night, Butch barricaded himself in the cook tent. Searching his friends' camps, he'd found a few bullets for the guns, and confiscated a hidden bottle of whiskey. "I expected a medical emergency."

He'd heard grizzlies were afraid of fire and loud noises, so he lit the stove and collected wood for torches. Then he piled up most of the big pots and pans. He arranged long dining tables against the sides of the tent, and hung lighted kerosene lanterns everywhere. Inside the fortified square, he stacked the guides' most valuable camping gear.

"I even brought in all the knives I could find. Spent the last daylight sharpening them. But I was too scared to drink any whiskey."

That night, according to Butch, eight grizzlies ambled into the lantern glow. Two of them finished off the leftover carcasses, while the other six rampaged through the provisions tent. They batted fifty-pound sacks of flour as if they were hacky sacks, and lobbed canned goods out of the tent like stray bullets. Every time one of them sniffed at the cook tent, Butch banged pots and pans together and screamed.

"Didn't get any sleep the third night, either," he muttered. "Drank a little whiskey, though. Sometimes there was a bear on each side of the cook tent, sniffing at me. I made a lot of racket running back and forth, tripping over the pans I dropped. I counted fourteen grizzlies that night, but the rangers said I was crazy—there weren't that many in the whole drainage."

He shook his head and tipped the bottle back. "I mighta been seein' a little double, but when the guys came back the next noon, they came creepin' in with their rifles out. Said there was so many grizzly tracks they didn't expect to find anything of me but my fillings."

By the time I unsaddle and brush the mare, and turn her into the meadow, most of the riders are rolled in their blankets. A few candle lanterns flicker. The man who hasn't ridden in fifteen years sits in his sleeping bag making strange motions: rubbing over his raw thighs the hand lotion I gave him. He's so grateful he tells me to look him up if I ever come to Chicago.

The quiet man leans against the log writing in a notebook, eyes shielded against the light. He nods. On the other side of the clearing, the bride rattles tin cups as she shuffles through a pile of gear. "Where's my toothbrush?" she whines. "And I can't find my facial cleanser." Her husband, a shapeless bundle on the ground, mumbles and growls. The loud man has fallen asleep leaning against a tree again, a bottle loose in one hand, and a pistol in the other.

Mike is snoring, but George leans against the log. Mutely, he hands me the flashlight. He knows I have one more chore. "Holler if you need me," he whispers, then chuckles. "I'll send B. Joe."

Flashlight off and being careful not to step on sleepers, I creep between the trees to a bushy area I've scouted earlier.

Unbuttoning my riding skirt, I remember another story Butch told. Tracking a grizzly one of his hunters had wounded, he followed it down across an open valley and up a hill past a stand of trees.

"When I went past those trees, the hair stood up on the back of my neck, but I looked pretty careful and couldn't see nothing. Over the hill there was another open valley. I could see the tracks circled around to the right. I cut across, and the tracks kept circling back. Pretty soon I was in that stand of trees, looking at my own trail." He shivered. "That bastard stood up so he blended into the tree trunks. Tracked me while I was trackin' him. Big pool of blood. I finally found him under a cliff a half-mile away. If he hadn't a lost so much blood, he'd have got me."

I shouldn't be here. Menstrual blood can attract grizzlies. Some female hikers have died because they went into wilderness during the five days out of thirty when their presence attracted grizzlies the way a torch draws moths. When I realized my monthly cycle fell during the trip, I considered staying home to protect myself and others. But, I reasoned, my cycles have become irregular. Some months I hardly bleed and this might be one of them. I've always wanted to ride through these mountains as the fur trappers did, with primitive gear and appreciative companions. This might be my only chance.

"No bear is going to get near us," George had said. "Don't worry about it." I carried tampons rolled in an extra shirt, hoping I wouldn't need them. Still, I felt guilty as riders including three other women gathered the first night. Of course, my flow arrived on schedule. When I slipped away from camp to find privacy, I discovered another woman crouched in the willows, covering the same kind of wastes. We nodded without speaking.

The first morning of the ride, while B. Joe supervised packing the mules, I noticed some riders had brought other items guaranteed to annoy bears:

dogs, sardines, even perfumed makeup. In a businesslike way, B. Joe listed the risks, and a few people stowed some dangerously attractive items in their trucks. The dogs came along, as did the bride's makeup. Besides their muzzle-loaders, several riders carried modern rifles or large-caliber pistols specifically for protection against grizzlies. Most of the men have hunted in bear country. I paid particular attention to the experienced hunters. Where our trail wound through thick timber, I casually rode close to them.

Now, in the dark, I focus on my task, hoping any grizzlies in the neighborhood are more attracted to perfume or turkey and dressing than blood. And I remember a comment Ed Abbey made somewhere that bears are omnivorous, and "will eat anything, even authors."

Handmaiden to the cycles of my body, I crouch to perform the ceremony, listening intensely for sounds of ambush. Every muscle screams with strain, but my nerves sparkle with the joy of being alive in this place and time. Moonlight flows down the blade of my belt knife, planted upright beside the hole I dug with it.

From the meadow, the lead mule's bell jingles. I'm glad she's there. At noon, I remarked to B. Joe how loud she could bray. He said the yodel I heard was a whisper compared to the sound she makes when she smells a grizzly.

My ears catch each sound, interpret and judge its importance while I work. Women have done the same for centuries: stood or squatted outside the shelter of humanity, tending personal needs after the regular workday.

The faint sound of my own footsteps as I walk back to camp obliterates other noises. At the edge of the clearing, I stand to listen to my companions' soft breaths, rustling as they shift position.

George waits, his back against the log, to hug me. Just before he sleeps, he whispers, "I hope if there's a grizzly around, he eats me before I have to get back on that horse."

I lie awake. The dark is saturated with sounds intimate as a leaf's rustle and a bird's single note. From the meadow rings the treble tune of mule bells, and from far away a howl. Within a mile, perhaps, a grizzly tips over rocks, licks ants from great thick paws. He sniffs the wind, turning his great head from side to side. Every sound vibrates. Each crackle of brush raises my vigilance until I am rigid. But hearing him if he is tracking me will change nothing. I loosen muscles one by one until I sleep.

A snap wakes me to the moon caught in branches overhead. A doe stands at my feet, lowering her head to sniff my toes. A buck and another doe tiptoe behind her, taking dainty steps around sleeping bags. The does stop at the smoldering fire to lick at B. Joe's frying pan. The buck paces gravely to one of the trees with suspended packs, and sniffs the ropes. Standing in front of the man who snores as loudly as he talks, the buck raises and lowers his head several times. I hope he charges.

George snorts in his sleep, reminding me of a night when we drove into the rendezvous camp at Sunlight Basin just at dusk. As the van groaned through the last curve in the winding trail to camp, a brown shape galloped across the road, headed uphill.

"Uuggh-er-ugh," I said.

"Shit! That was a bear!" George replied.

"That's what I said. Was it a grizzly?"

"What?" said Mike from the back where he'd been reading all afternoon except when I yelled at him for missing the Tetons. "What did you see?"

"Not sure. Too dark," George mumbled, shifting into low. When we got to the clearing, the blue van was alone. No one else had arrived yet.

"I'm too tired to set up camp tonight," George said, yawning ostentatiously. "Let's sleep in the van."

"And besides, grizzlies can't get into a van. Right?"

"Ah." He scratched his beard. "Not as easy as they can get through canvas. We've got frozen meat in the cooler, don't we? Let's leave it outside."

Mike slept rolled in his sleeping bag between the front seats. George slung some gear out on the ground. I leveled the rest of the stuff as well as I could, and spread our bags on top. When we lay down, George's face was only six inches from the roof.

I woke at sunrise and looked out. Growing light revealed a herd of Hereford cows grazing on all sides of us. Just then, one of the cows belched up her cud.

George bellowed, "Bear!" and tried to sit up, .357 in hand. His forehead whacked the van roof and he fell back, groaning.

Tangled in his bag, Mike screamed, "Is it a bear? Where? A bear?"

Gathering himself to defend his only son, George sat up again, flinching, and shoved the pistol barrel out the open window. "Cows? I thought we were far enough from the ranch to get away from damn cows."

I guffawed for a while before I was able to explain the sound. Neither of them spoke to me until after breakfast.

Smiling, I sleep. I wake just before sunrise to find George has rolled away from me, and cold air divides us. Chilled stiff, I crawl out and put on the blanket coat I use for a pillow. As I step away from the log, the quiet man raises his head. He stands up with his coat in one hand, his pistol in the other.

Before I step into the meadow, I survey the view, sniffing danger. Thirty feet away, a moose raises his royal head from the creek bottom, yanking up a mouthful of grass with a sound like a toilet flushing. He stares, then chews. I stand in knee-high grass drenched with dew. Somewhere on the peak before me, a grizzly naps. I can still taste his heat, almost see his fur shimmer in sunrise light.

Riding up the trail after breakfast, we see a stone upended during the night, and claw marks in the wreckage of the ant apartments underneath. Massive tracks alternate with horse hoofprints in the muddy trail. Standing in the stirrups, I reach as high as I can. The gashes where he sharpened his claws on trees are higher still.

Later that afternoon, we reach a campground littered with human waste, including the kind I've been burying for the past few days. As we unpack our gear, we're quieter than usual, perhaps gloomy at the evidence we're back in civilization.

Ten years later, I met the quiet man again, in a noisy bar in Elko, Nevada. He was driving a bulldozer for an open-pit gold mining operation. We caught up on each other's news—he was divorced, my husband was dead—and recalled the ride. Neither of us had ever gone back, but we smiled at each other, quiet in the company of someone else who had been where we had been. Each of us had felt the fear differently; we didn't speak of that. Each of us could see the mountains shining in the other's eyes, the knowledge that grizzlies are still out there. We didn't speak of that, either.

THE SECOND HALF
OF LIFE

. . .

In my forties, I was cheerful about middle age. My second husband, George, accepted both my need to write and my compulsion to stay on the ranch where I grew up. There we'd built a house adjustable to the likely demands of our aging. George worked patiently with my irascible father, and my writing was beginning to appear in print. Not long after I gave up my independent press and stopped publishing books by other writers, my first two books of nonfiction were published by separate companies, and I signed a contract for another book. I could *never,* I said to several people who interviewed me, live in a city.

At last, I thought smugly, I'd grown up. I saw myself gliding on the smooth stream of a responsible and well-ordered life. My husband and I, separately and together, had already seen plenty of white water. We knew how to maneuver the marital canoe around big rocks and whole fleets of rapids. I pictured a placid lake somewhere ahead where we would drift together as the sun—eventually—set on our lives.

For the sake of brevity, I'll list here the biggest hidden boulders the canoe struck in that calm creek:

—George died;

—my father, his mind damaged by strokes he wouldn't acknowledge, ordered me to stop writing or leave the ranch;

—knocked off my bearings, I moved in with a friend in a city five hours'
drive away from the ranch I love;

—with no income, I rented my ranch home to strangers;

—my father died, leaving exclusively to my mother everything on the
ranch where I'd worked for forty years;

—connections between my mother's body and brain parted; she entered
a nursing home;

—my best friend, a ranch woman with whom I talked every day, died
of AIDS;

—the job of settling my father's estate fell to me;

—I sold my father's cattle to pay his expenses;

—I sold my own cattle and borrowed money to acquire the ranch;

—with no cows and no home on the ranch, I leased the land to a
neighbor.

When I glanced up and saw my fiftieth birthday on the horizon, I was living with an old friend in a new condition of romance, staggering from the
effects of change. A week before, I'd packed up or discarded the forty-year ac-
cumulation of my packrat parents in three days so my land renter's hired
man and his wife could move into my childhood home. I was ready for a
break from the routines of loss, but unsure which ritual would be appropriate. I considered adopting the old Viking custom of loading the deceased's
possessions on his ship and burning it.

I recall cavorting on a Galveston, Texas, beach at three or four years old, discovering the ocean's thunder in a conch shell and the dangers of starfish. I
think it was there, in a vendor's stand, that I first saw a kaleidoscope, a cheap
cardboard tube with bits of colored glass locked inside. When I held it to my
eye, the gray ocean disappeared, and I entered fantasy. My single mother
couldn't or wouldn't buy it. A few years later, she married my father, who
didn't waste hard-earned cash on frivolities. Each time I spent a quarter,
they'd remind me I was wasting money reserved for my college education.

For forty-five years, each time I saw a kaleidoscope, I snatched it to stare.
In airports, I sometimes saw little plastic tubes with faceted glass eyepieces,
artless diversions from my primary job of holding the wings on the airplane.
Even the simplest scene, observed through a repeating pattern of, say, hexa-

gons like the multifaceted eyes of a fly, adopts a fresh and possibly symbolic importance. I told myself I was doing research for my poems.

Heir to my parents' philosophies and economies, I caressed kaleidoscopes, but never bought. I saved my money for emergencies rather than wasting it on trinkets. A kaleidoscope was a bauble, a knickknack. Not a tool for my varied trades of writing, teaching, or ranching, not something I could *use*, not something for work.

Since my birthday falls in July, the middle of a plains rancher's season for haying and other preparations for winter, I grew up expecting little in the way of birthday celebrations. My family might take an evening drive into the hills after we had birthday cake and opened my presents, but that was about as exciting as the celebration got.

So when I married for the second time at age thirty-five, and realized that my birthday would fall in the middle of rendezvous season, I was already trained not to expect a birthday cake or a bouquet of flowers in the middle of a camp full of people wishing it was really 1840. Still, the birthdays I spent in camp created a new standard for celebration of my natal day.

On my thirty-ninth birthday, for example, we obtained a permit to cut tipi poles in the Uinta Mountains of northern Utah. A tipi eighteen feet in diameter requires eighteen to twenty poles to hold it up, and since George had promised to cut a set for a friend, we needed to cut at least forty trees. While George and his friend Jim searched for perfectly straight lodgepole pine trees to cut, Jim's wife Mavis and I took charge of transport. Dutifully, we followed the men, tramping miles through the deep woods. As soon as they'd cut two slender pines, our job was to haul them back to the van.

The trees weren't heavy, at first. But we soon discovered an unusual botanical fact: straight trees grow only on top of the highest mountains. Once Jim and George had felled two trees, they strolled off in search of more. A lodgepole pine that achieves thirty-five feet of height always stands in a crowd. Mavis and I would each grab a tree butt and lunge in the direction of the van. Approximately thirty feet into woods, I'd veer around a cluster of trees so closely packed I couldn't slide between them. Turning while dragging a long, straight object isn't easy; ask any long-haul trucker. Each detour hooked my tree's branches on some protrusion, yanking me to a stop. I'd pull my log hard, and stumble on. At first, Mavis and I kept track of one another by hollered curses. As our stamina waned, we were too short of breath to swear. Resting, we counted closely packed rings—a sign of the arid climate—to determine the tree's age. At two hundred, we gave up, knowing these slender saplings were mature when the real mountain men camped in these peaks.

Several times I reached the truck, dragging a tree, and found the men chatting, seated on a comfy rock. "Just drop it," George said. "Not enough straight trees here. We're going to look somewhere else."

"Don't you want to load this one?" I'd pant.

"Naw. We'll wait till we have enough for a whole set." We changed locations twice, abandoning five trees we women had hauled a couple of miles through the underbrush, before I managed to get back to the van before the men. I shoved my tree crosswise through the two front windows, and sat behind a bush to catch my breath. As soon as Mavis saw what I'd done, she dropped her tree and joined me.

"Hmmm," said George when he and Jim emerged from the shady woods. "I think the women are getting testy."

"I expected it," Jim declared. "We better make do with the trees here."

As the van lumbered back to camp that night with forty treetops sweeping its tracks from the road behind, I mentioned how tired I was, how much work I'd done, and all this on my birthday, too. Most women my age, George replied without missing a breath, were not in my superb physical shape because their husbands didn't love them enough to provide such exercise. The day's workout, he added, put roses in my cheeks and would help keep me young. His deft combination of compliment with rationalization left me speechless until a neighbor singing birthday greetings came to our campfire carrying a single cupcake lighted by one fat candle.

The summer I turned forty, George arranged for us to go fishing in Canada with friends, as a change from rendezvous and a surprise. Many times, I've written and rewritten the story of my birthday celebration from that summer, but it's still unpublished. Even in this permissive age, some episodes—involving fly-fishing, mosquitoes, and mayonnaise—are apparently just too shocking for most markets.

The next summer we were back at rendezvous, setting up our lodge at nine thousand feet on a Colorado mountain with several thousand other buckskinners. Each morning, George dropped a handful of fresh grounds into the coffeepot, softly waking me to the scent of brawny campfire coffee. Each afternoon, gentle rain tapping on the canvas lulled me into a nap, cooling the air. Each evening, we wandered among glowing tipis until we found music to suit our moods, whether it was bagpipes, fiddles, or mouth harps.

On my birthday, we went out to lunch—to a lean-to where two sweating women sold Indian tacos. Unfortunately, right after lunch, George reported that the latrine closest to our camp was overflowing, an unnecessary announcement since he was holding at arm's length a four-year-old boy who'd fallen into it head first. The child's mother shrieked, snatched the child, and headed for the creek.

"If he was mine," said George, "I'd have pushed him on down. Easier to have another kid than clean that one up."

Both George and I were dog soldiers—camp police—so providing a new latrine was part of our job. "I can't ask you to help me," George said, "since it's your birthday. But digging is healthy outdoor exercise."

First we removed the canvas privacy shield, along with the toilet seat and the open-ended fifty-gallon drum supporting it. We shoveled dirt over the remaining human wastes, and found a site for the new facility in a grove of aspen, where three trees served as a framework for the canvas wall.

Then we dug a deep hole in the Rocky Mountain soil. The name of those mountains is no metaphor. We dug a while, borrowed a pick to shatter bedrock, and shoveled some more. Operating a spade while wearing moccasins is painfully authentic to the mountain man era. As we dug, we reflected on the thousands of people excreting in the vicinity. We discussed dog soldiers in other areas of the camp who were neglecting latrine duty, forcing people in their vicinity to go elsewhere. Then we swore an oath to tell no one the location of the new toilet. "Let 'em scout for it," said one tired dog soldier, "like real mountain men." Since mountain men really do live in the same world as liberation and feminism, he may have realized that he should take some notice of my contribution, so he turned to me, adding, "You did a damn good job of diggin' fer a girl in a dress!" I thanked him modestly, resisting the urge to curtsy. His was a compliment compared to other remarks I endured as one of the first female dog soldiers. Still, women who wear belt knives every day and beat their husbands at tomahawk throwing get considerable respect.

After digging the latrine, we closed the tipi door, knowing our gear would be safe in camp, and headed for Linda's Birthday Revenge. I'd persuaded George to attend a reunion of my mother's family, a group of sober, law-abiding folks who drive recreational vehicles, shave, never drink liquor, and probably iron their camping clothes. My theory was that George, wearing a beard and shoulder-length locks that almost hid his earrings, might be nearly as uncomfortable for a day as I was for a week on his Canadian fishing trip. For maximum effect, and because we couldn't find our civilian clothes, we wore our rendezvous garb—my long leather dress and his fringed leather pants and shirt. I didn't think to remove the businesslike Green River skinning knife I wore in camp.

As soon as we entered civilization and stopped for gas and cold drinks, I encountered a modicum of trouble. Relishing the chance to use a flush toilet and wash my face with hot running water for the first time in nine days, I stood in the ladies' restroom, scrubbing at hands blackened by cooking over an open fire. I may have taken a wee bit longer than the usual visit. When the door handle rattled, I called politely, "Just one minute."

I dried my hands and was grasping the doorknob when the door began to shake as a woman pounded on it, yelling abusive curses of a distinctly vulgar nature.

Startled, I pulled the door open, jerking a short, red-faced woman into the small bathroom. Crashing into me, she lurched sideways, swearing. Then, perhaps startled by my attire, she jumped back and tripped over the toilet. She grabbed at me, probably an instinct to keep from falling. I may have been a little too absorbed in the 1840 fantasy, because I was convinced she was assaulting me. I shoved her with one hand, and reached for my knife with the other. She fell behind the toilet, jammed against the wall with her arms over her head. I moved my hand away from my knife and commented on her indiscreet language. Her eyes bulged, and she breathed deep and tried to stand. I stepped out the door. She slammed and locked it.

Catching my breath, I heard a murmur in the darkness near my knees. A small boy trembled there, his eyes on the knife at my belt. I reached to pat his head, but he shrank away, howling something about being scalped. More oaths erupted from behind the door, but it stayed closed. The kid was on his own.

I slipped up one aisle as the manager rushed down another. George was peering over shelves, unruffled. Another man trotted a few steps toward the bathroom, and glanced nervously at us, but retreated from the wailing child. We departed in armed peace and headed for the reunion camp.

Various unidentified relatives of mine gathered around the van as we arrived, asking us merrily what we thought about "what the Democrats did this morning." I explained that radios aren't allowed in rendezvous camp, so we had no idea what the country was doing. I've found that the benefits of missing two weeks of national news far outweigh the disadvantages. In this case, however, we'd missed the nomination of the first woman candidate for vice president. One of my cousins, laughing hysterically, yelled, "The Democrats nominated a *woman* for vice president!" The crowd whooped with laughter.

"Right on!" I cheered, waving my knife in case anyone disagreed.

Following a moment of horrified silence, they all laughed at my hilarious joke. The in-laws most inclined toward the far right end of the political spectrum gathered to look at our knives. The men pressed close, testing the balance of each blade and asking George how he polished the bone hilts. Then they stood around shaving heaps of hair from their bulky forearms, and decided that as George knew how to get an edge, maybe he was an acceptable relative.

Meanwhile, I drifted off with the women and showed them the parts of my weapons collection I happened to be wearing, including the Green River I used for camp cooking, and the push dagger that looks like a belt buckle. I might have mentioned that liberation requires a woman to be prepared for emergencies. They might have retorted that they didn't have to be liberated to be prepared.

By then, we'd all congregated at the campfire, where we entertained ourselves for several hours, eating and talking and whipping out concealed and semiconcealed weapons, muttering about food caches and the best places to be when the Big One drops. We also discovered that the only family members attending were members of a single religious faction notorious for its sobriety. Not only was the camp free of beer, they hadn't even brought coffee.

After a while we opened the van door to show them the weapons and buffalo hide we'd put in the van in case buckskinners weren't as honest as we thought they were. Long into the night, we all compared firepower and sharpening stones, and debated ballistics. We were sober and clearheaded the next morning for breakfast, and the pancakes were delicious. But on the way back to camp, we stopped seven times for coffee, and proclaimed it one of my most unusual birthdays.

No matter how happy our childhood birthdays are, we usually stop having parties soon after we decide we're adults. In our thirties, we may live out wistful memories through the parties we hold for our children, enduring lame jokes from friends whose smiles betray their own fear of age, rather than display pleasure that we've all lived another year. Childless, I missed all that. So during my fiftieth spring, I primed myself for a party. Unfortunately, the relatives and friends in my private life-support system—mostly writers, artists, and musicians—couldn't make the five-hour drive to Cheyenne. Instead, I decided to invite colleagues and friends of my new partner, Jerry. An engineer in the Wyoming Department of Transportation, he'd just turned forty. Our guests would be geologists, engineers, and technicians, all in their thirties. Most knew me only by rumors about my environmental writing or my age.

I snarled as I opened cards depicting the inevitability of decline and death, picturing women with sagging flesh and gray hair in despair at their loss of sex appeal. From a few friends came gifts more in harmony with my mood. An artist who liked the cover photo on my latest book of poems—me peering through a cow pelvis—sent a signed piece of his work: a deer pelvis affixed to its own skull. We hung it over a living room door, and enjoyed watching people glance up, and then gawk, asking, "What the hell kind of animal is *that?*" Another artist sent an icon called Horse Charmer, in memory of my horses, who had all died during the previous year.

For the party, I wore a purple dress with matching tights, hinting at my hopes for the years to come. As we all filled our plates in the dining room and sat cross-legged on the back lawn, I listened, not always passively, as mothers in their twenties whined about gray hairs and fat, listing the minutiae of their decaying bodies. The party guests didn't all know why I grew furious at demeaning jokes about age. They may not believe as I do that a steady diet of banter on the theme of how useless and disgusting old people are can prematurely bend your body and calcify your mind. I laughed a lot that day, ignoring pain from past wounds—physical and otherwise. I wanted the day to symbolize how I mean to face the future. I'll wear my scars, but I refuse to trace them every day.

Between jokes, guests visited a sixteen-gallon keg of my favorite beer—H. C. Berger's Red Banshee—chosen not only for its flavor but for its name. In legend, the banshee wails to forewarn of a loved one's death. If she'd been hanging around me, her throat was sore and she'd probably appreciate a little liquid refreshment before she delivered any more omens.

Two longtime friends, Sue and Carolyn, seemed to symbolize the divergent directions my life had taken. Sue and I had met as children when our fathers bought cattle from one another forty years before. She and her sisters regularly rode a horned Hereford bull they named Winston. When my father bought him, I rode him to impress my friends. With Sue's younger sisters, we'd once scrambled through the brush along the river, and examined rattlesnake dens in the bluffs. On their rare visits to our ranch, we romped over my hillsides. But after high school, we rarely met; our mothers provided Christmas updates until we reconnected a couple of years ago in a store where I was autographing books.

Frankly, below the party noises, we discussed our different lives. She'd read occasional articles about me, and pictured me as living a free and rebellious life, in contrast to hers on a remote ranch raising kids and teaching school. I've always believed I'm too conservative as a writer. In my thirties, I'd chosen her life as my preferred daily reality, but lost it to divorce (first husband) and death (second). I'd envied her curly raven hair and recalled her low, bubbling laugh; she'd coveted my long, straight blonde hair. Though her hair is short, mine long, both hairdos are dusted with white and our opinions on many topics—education, the environment, women's place in the West—are as similar today as they were when we rode old Winston, and we could still disagree with laughter. The long gap between our walks in her pasture and our talk in my city yard vanished, leaving only memories of her cantankerous father and mine, and laugh wrinkles around our eyes.

Carolyn, a friend from Minneapolis, had come to the party with two teenage sons. We'd met at a writing workshop fifteen years before, and exchanged commentary on each other's writing. She visited our ranch in spring to help pull calves and take pictures, and I've spoken to her high school writing classes. She wanted to meet Jerry, and cross-examined me, suspecting I might have misplaced my mind by moving to town with a young man. Her own fiftieth birthday was two months in the future, and she was anxious to make it a celebration instead of a requiem.

When the party was at its peak, I slipped upstairs to don the gray wig I'd found in my mother's dresser drawer, styled in the short poodle curls women in my home community wear after they turn thirty. Busy, and proud of their efficiency, these ranch women get a haircut once a year from a neighbor who subjects them to a home perm so tight the curls last until the next "do" six months later. Identical curly heads bobbing, the women congratulate themselves on not having time to bother with elaborate styles. I have no idea when or why my mother bought the wig. She regularly dyed her hair blue-black until my father died when she was eighty-three. Then she appeared with pure white hair, announcing that she no longer had a reason to look pretty.

Adjusting the wig, I looked in my mirror and faced my grandmother, who never wore cosmetics either. She didn't "waste money on such foolishness," but her clear skin was always lit by a smile as it crinkled year by year into a topographical map of her life.

Returning to the party, I strolled among the crowd unnoticed—proving to myself for the hundredth time writer Sue Hubbell's notion that middle-aged women are invisible—until I found our brashest young friend. Mark is a brilliant engineer who loves rock climbing, and snatches any chance to travel to some unexplored spot on his world map. Recently he'd shown us slides from Mexico, and talked of his adventures in Australia. Eavesdropping at parties as he tossed back a nasty drink called a cement-mixer, I had often heard him say, "Gotta do it while I'm *young*."

I put my arm across Mark's shoulders, and watched patiently while dismay and puzzlement appeared on his face as he wondered, "Who's this old gal? Somebody's mother?" As recognition reached his eyes, I said, "This is how it works, Mark. One minute you're thirty, then *pow!* It's *over!* You're *old!*" He reddened as a camera flashed and the crowd laughed, parts of it uneasily.

Occasionally, I encountered remnants of past lives drifting through the party. Daniel, my first husband's son, was working on cleanup of Rocky Flats' nuclear mess. He remembered how much I love cheesecake and brought two. A woman who was my student in freshman composition twenty years ago, and later dated Jerry, divulged a vicious streak, presenting me with a tiny bottle of tequila, a shot glass, and a lime in memory of my thirtieth birthday, which struck a week after my divorce. She was a witness to that disaster. Years later, I occasionally met people who said, "I was at your thirtieth birthday party, but I'll bet you don't remember me!"

A stickler for accuracy, Jerry had insisted on putting fifty candles on a huge chocolate cake. Someone put the cake in the front hall of our old Victorian house, and lit the candles. With the help of a couple of guests who admitted to being *over* fifty, I blew them all out. I had to. The heat was intense and I couldn't find the fire extinguisher.

But the best part of the day was observing the line snaking through the living room as children and adults squabbled over Jerry's gift to me: a kaleidoscope he'd designed and made in his garage woodworking shop during two months of evening labor.

The scope is a tapered tube, a cylinder of woods: purple heart, from a tropical American tree, and padauk, an orange wood from a tree native to Southeast Asia. The mechanism of my kaleidoscope is simple: three mirrors run the tube's length. At the wide end is an object chamber, a space a half-inch deep, with a removable lid so I can replace the objects reflected and tripled in the mirrors.

To contain the scope, Jerry built a golden oak box nineteen by eleven inches and nearly a foot deep, fastened with a brass lock and key. In the lid's center, framed by thin slices of purple heart, is a lightning bolt of a deep brown wood called moradillo, a symbol, he explained, of my effect on his life.

Inside the box, beside the velvet-lined cradle for the scope, stand three tiers of oak trays with twelve divisions each. Jerry filled most of the compartments with assorted colors and shapes of beads, and with fragments of colored glass left from his other hobby: making stained-glass windows. He left some niches empty, awaiting new discoveries. We spent that evening changing the objects in the chamber, and swapping the tube to savor shifting designs. Everyone who gathered in our home and yard that day—no matter their age—delighted in luminous pictures reflected in the angled mirrors.

The next day, we began a game of putting different trinkets in the kaleidoscope's chamber. A necklace chain, string, or rubber band are all opaque, drawing snaky black lines through a glitter of beads. A black plastic ant becomes a swarm. Each day, one of us challenged the other to identify something new. A paper clip became an interlocking puzzle. Cog wheels form a whirl through a glitter of beads. When I found a baby's christening ring and an earring in a heat vent, I looked at them through the scope. Dry beans. Glitter. Macaroni. Fake diamonds from my mother's old jewelry. No two views are the same. Each slight movement, each second, changes the tableau.

The intuition and skill of an engineer enabled me to begin the fifth decade of my life looking into a bright cache of ingenuity. The kaleidoscope was invented in 1813 by a Scotsman trained for the ministry. Sir David Brewster, a religious leader in the early nineteenth century, believed in minimizing the gap between science and religion. He studied the qualities of light while developing a philosophy in which art and science blended, choosing to call his creation "kaleidoscope" from a combination of Greek terms meaning "to view beautiful forms."

My kaleidoscope is not only a sculpture, but a treasury of creative relaxation, a toy filled with spiritual possibilities. I waited for it fifty years.

The second half of my life? A kaleidoscope.

PART · III

WHO CARES FOR
THE LAND?

CATTLE RANCHING
IN SOUTH DAKOTA
...

I own a South Dakota ranch that has been in our family since my grandfather, a Swedish cobbler, homesteaded here in 1899. Since 1980, I've been active in various environmental affairs, including several statewide battles to
contain uranium mining and prevent the establishment of a nuclear waste
facility and radioactive waste dump in the state. I now live full-time in Wyoming, visiting the ranch only in summer, so I lease my land to a neighbor
who grazes his cattle on my land under conditions calculated to enhance the
land's condition. The lease limits the number of cows he can run, and includes provisions requiring him to maintain improvements that benefit
wildlife as well as cattle, such as windbreak trees that shelter deer and grouse
in winter. Clearly, I'm a rancher as well as an active environmentalist.

Because of my interests, I've been disturbed by a steady escalation of the
"war" between ranchers and environmentalists. In 1985, David Foreman, a
founder of Earth First! published a technical manual on "monkey-wrench-
ing," a modern environmentalist's version of sabotage. The book, reprinted
several times, devotes fourteen pages to instructions on vandalizing ranches:
stealing salt blocks, plugging water pipes, smashing water tanks, disabling
windmills, cutting fences. "Some experts estimate that 100 people cutting
fences on a regular basis around the West could put the public-land ranchers
out of business," wrote Foreman encouragingly. The April 1998 issue of the

journal *Earth First!* noted "rampant fence cutting" in Wyoming, and advised, "Dust off those wire cutters, folks!"

In June of 1998, during the Wyoming Stock Growers Association annual meeting in Casper, someone still unidentified drove a hundred miles on dirt roads in the rough Gas Hills uranium mining area of the Rattlesnake Range, cutting barbed wire fence in hundreds of places. "Just in time for the welfare cowboys' convention," read signs nailed to fence posts. No group admitted the action, and no arrests were made.

Wyoming agricultural groups acknowledge that fence-cutting has increased in recent years, explaining the incidents weren't publicized because members hoped to keep the conflict quiet. One Wyoming rancher whose fence was cut in sixty places said in June: "For their own safety, they better lay off. If the right group finds them, they might get shot." Another notes, "Any number of my neighbors are now carrying rifles."

While ranchers in some states use millions of acres of public land, in my home state of South Dakota the percentage is low. Still, in this state where nearly everyone knows everyone else or their cousin, we experience most of the misunderstandings that arise nationally between ranchers and environmentalists. For years, in my writing and in talks before varied groups, I've urged ranchers and environmentalists to get acquainted, to listen to each others' positions instead of squaring off. Though I am highly visible as a writing rancher, with connections to dozens of environmental groups, neither ranchers nor environmentalists have ever asked me to sit in on a discussion of the conflicts between the two "sides."

If asked, I'd explain my views on land use as follows. No one driving past our pastures could ever have seen the difference between the land we leased from the government and the land we owned. My father treated both kinds of pasture the same: with care. (As soon as I bought the ranch, I gave up the public land lease we had held for more than fifty years.)

My father lived on the ranch almost all of his life, and knew exactly how many cows a particular pasture would comfortably support, in wet years or dry. Damaged grass will not recover in time to support our cattle next year, so in a dry year we start selling cows in early summer to avoid overgrazing. If anything, he habitually undergrazed, keeping grass in reserve in case a prairie fire or a hard winter reduced the amount of pasture we expected to have. Most of our neighbors do the same, as does the man who now leases my land. The ranchers we know might not call themselves conservationists, and certainly not environmentalists, but they know it's good business to take care of the land. And most, like us, are equally respectful of the other life forms that share this land with our cattle. On several occasions, neighbors have told me of seeing unusual wildlife—a pair of wolves, a mountain lion—and cautioned, "Don't tell anybody! Somebody'd come in and shoot it," implying the killer would be an outsider, not a fellow rancher.

When I first began driving the tractor to mow and rake hay in the summers, my father warned me that one field was a favorite spot for does to hide their fawns. The noise of the tractor scared the little fellows so much they wouldn't run, so the mower would hit them. Speed is everything in getting hay into the stack in good condition; our primary purpose was to get the alfalfa cut down, dried, and stacked. Still, he advised me to mow slowly in that field, maintaining just enough speed to keep the cutter bar moving, and to watch for fawns just ahead of it. That's just one example of his concern for our co-residents on this land.

My father was also known as one of the few ranchers in the area who allowed no one, not even game wardens, to shoot coyotes. Other ranchers insist that coyotes kill calves, but he noted that in eighty years he'd seen no evidence to prove it. I follow his example; coyotes are welcome in my pastures. Once a calf of ours caught his head in a tree and was apparently helpless to escape for at least a week. The coyotes didn't bother him. After we freed him and nailed a board across the hole in the tree, he died. Then the coyotes cleaned up the remains, the job they do best.

The day I wrote the first draft of this essay, back in the 1980s, my husband and I had been trucking cattle to our summer pasture, a ten-mile trip across land owned by a couple of neighbors. As usual, we saw herds of deer and antelope, including a pronghorn buck still limping on the leg some hunter had wounded the fall before. We went out of our way to avoid disturbing him and, like the others, he merely made a token run when he saw our pickup coming. We always talked about bringing a rifle to fire out the windows, to teach the animals fear of vehicles, but we always forgot. When the pronghorn disappeared that fall, we figured some hunter drove a white pickup through our pastures without permission, and got close enough to shoot him.

In another pasture, burrowing owls ruffled their feathers and crouched in old prairie dog holes as we passed. Later in the spring, owlets would gather at the burrow entrance, climbing on each other's shoulders to see out. We let the prairie dogs alone until they destroyed most of a hay bottom. Then we obtained "bombs" that asphyxiated them in their burrows. We chose bombs so as to kill the rodents with less risk to the surrounding population of coyotes, owls, and other predators; we never bombed a hole with owl scat outside it. We used the area to sort cattle before taking them to the home corrals, and often had to do tricky high-speed maneuvers there on horseback. While it's true that I've never personally seen a horse break a leg in a prairie dog hole, my horse has stuck a hoof in one and fallen with me several times, hurting me badly enough so it was difficult to ride a horse, or do the other work that constitutes my living. For several years after I decided to stop suffocating the prairie dogs, we kept cattle out of the area and let grass grow, hoping natural predation would cut their numbers. Finally, my lessee, frustrated by my cautious tactics, used his D-9 Caterpillar to bulldoze the mounds flat and fill in the holes. Grass has grown over the area.

When driving through the pasture, we stick to the trails we've used on this land for sixty years. Even driving over grass buried under snowdrifts leaves broken grass that will be visible next spring. And everywhere we can see the tire tracks of hunters who have somehow avoided our signs and warnings and driven all over the pasture. The route of a single drive over the grass remains visible for several seasons.

You'd find none of our garbage on our land, though hunters and railroad repair crews regularly toss out soda cans, tinfoil, and plastic bags. An amazing amount of junk thrown out the windows of cars on the highway blows fifteen miles through the pastures, including balloons and Styrofoam cartons from fast-food sandwiches. All of this junk could be fatal to any ruminant that eats it, whether it's a cow or wildlife. Passersby often use the broad entrance to our private road to empty their bladders and wastebaskets. We don't mind the former, but we make them pick up the latter, if we catch them. We dream of finding an address in the piles of garbage we gather every year, so we could drop by to return the trash.

In the 1980s, I often rode into our neighbor's pasture to collect our cattle when they trespassed. One day when I found no cattle, I counted ten deer, seven antelope, two coyotes, and dozens of smaller animals including a great horned owl. The grass was knee-high on my horse, and the bottoms of draws overflowed with water from the last snowstorm. Riding in the same pasture when I was a child, I once saw two turtles larger than washtubs mating or fighting in one of the ponds.

Counting the animals set me thinking that this pasture, and others like it in this area, is really "wilderness" by the *American Heritage Dictionary* definition: "Any unsettled, uncultivated region left in its natural condition." Of course, the pasture is fenced, but so are most parks. Our neighbor turned his cattle into the grass in late June and removed them in October or November. Later, passing through to check our own pastures, we always startled deer or antelope bedded in grass so deep they didn't hear us coming. In early spring, the grass had time to grow strong before it was grazed again. The little streams had some manure in them, but supported an abundance of water life. The edges remained grassy because the number of cattle was never high enough to trample them down. Grouse dropped by in late fall to gobble buffaloberries and wild grapes.

If the public could enter this land to enjoy its beauty, the two-track trail would be worn down to dust. The streams would be clogged with beer cans and toilet paper. Someone would have to build toilets and set up trash cans on concrete pads, with asphalt paths leading to the parking lots. Signs would read, "Give a hoot. Don't pollute." Unless the parking lots were surrounded by stout barriers, some folks would drive straight up the ridge to prove their four-wheeler was "truck tough," ripping sod and starting erosion. People walking along the fragile limestone cliffs would startle the owls. The young and athletic would climb the limestone ledges, crumbling them into the creek, and rolling boulders down.

Eventually, my neighbor died, and his land was sold at auction in 1999. A man from a nearby town came to look over the "wildlife pasture" for a home site. Conscious of the high fire danger at the time, he parked his pickup just inside the gate, and used an all-terrain vehicle to inspect the land, leaving tracks where the tall, dry grass broke off. While he was looking, his pickup burst into flames; he'd parked in tall grass, and a tailpipe can get hot enough to start a fire. The local volunteer fire department put out the grass fire, but the pickup burned. The land-seeker was surprised when they presented him with a hefty bill for their services. He may have been more amazed when my lessee, whose land he had to cross to reach the pasture, billed him for his fire-fighting time as well, and I billed him for loss of grass and a storage shed. He was perplexed when I explained to him, as he was leaving with his burned-out pickup, that he had trespassed by crossing my land without permission. He seemed to regard our actions as hostile, and not to realize how lucky he was that the fire had not been larger.

The man's bid was not nearly high enough to buy the land, and it remains in private hands—though the price a neighboring rancher paid for it represents far more than the cattle he can pasture there will pay. Posted against hunting and trespassing, the land will remain, for now, nearly as wild as it was when the first homesteader built a little house and corral and dug a dam. Carefully managed, the land is in better shape now than it was when the homesteader gave up and left. Further, it's healthier than it would be as either a public park or a home site.

Not every rancher is so careful with his land. But anyone concerned about the effects of grazing on prairie and its wildlife should look over local ranch lands before commenting, and should never accept broad generalizations about "grazing in the West" without examining them in the light of local conditions. Be brave; drive in and talk to a rancher. Ask how long the family has been there. Investigate before you condemn. You may discover more interests in common than you can imagine.

Unfortunately, some land owned either by individual or corporate ranchers is not open to the public, because some of us have suffered damage from hunters or other trespassers. Still, if you ask permission, you may be allowed access if you promise not to be careless. This won't help everyone, of course, because if we let in everyone who promised to be kind to the land, the thundering herds would trample it by their sheer numbers.

Still, perhaps some who care about prairie can be content knowing that someone is watching over it.

Why Giving Up Meat Won't Save the Planet

To be memorable, a good slogan should be short and simple. That's probably why "Save the Planet! Stop eating meat!" has made it onto the bumpers of cars, even in my agricultural corner of the West. Unfortunately, a good slogan doesn't have to make sense.

I'm a rancher, so when I want beef, I pick out a likely heifer from the hillside and encourage her to stroll calmly into a small corral containing feed. I kill her without scaring her, with one bullet in the center of her forehead, and cut her throat. I hang her body by the ankles from a tractor loader to skin and gut her, hauling her head and innards to a hillside where the coyotes will feast for several nights. I cut and wrap the meat for my own freezer and serve it to my guests as organic beef. I know—because I was present every day of that cow's life—that all she ever consumed was grass, hay raised without herbicides or chemicals, pure water, and salt.

Most urban Americans buy beef wrapped in plastic from a well-lighted supermarket. Relish that steak while you consider the life of the animal who furnished it. The calf may have been born on a ranch like mine, where someone helped the cow if necessary, and watched the calf for signs of sickness until it was six months old. Quietly, we herded the cows into the corral and separated them from their calves. Within an hour, we'd loaded the calves into a truck—we don't allow our truckers to use prod poles, electric tools that administer a shock. Unloaded at the sale ring, the calf hardly had time to miss its mother before it entered the ring with fifty other calves and was sold to the highest bidder.

Then a trucker crowded as many calves as possible into his truck and sped east several hundred miles to a feedlot in Iowa or Nebraska. There the calf was dumped into a lot where it may not even have had space to lie down. Shoulder to shoulder, hundreds of calves struggled to a feed bunk to eat corn protected by the latest agricultural herbicides, guaranteed, according to their advertising, "to kill everything." The biggest calves, like schoolyard bullies, always ate the most. Some of the weakest may have been injured, or died. When it wasn't eating, the calf stood idle, often knee-deep in mud for six months or more, until it was killed for your dinner.

Environmentalists, vegetarians, and other folks who advocate giving up beef to "save the earth" quote statistics showing that sixty million people a year could eat the grain fed to cows, a fallacy that distracts us from its lack of logic by playing on our sympathies for starving people. First, cows don't need to eat grain to be healthy, edible, or even delicious. Second, some grain fed to cattle can't be fed to humans except as filler, because our bodies can't absorb it. And these days, feedlots are experimenting with feeding cattle wood shavings, along with bones and offal from butchered cattle.

When your feet are under my table, the meat on the menu was formed from grass and hay produced by old-fashioned sun and rain in our pastures. In the winter, we feed the cattle a nourishing cake composed of grains, vitamins, and minerals, stuck together with molasses. Most of the cows I've eaten lived the way cattle did for centuries before humans started interfering: largely undisturbed on prairie grass.

Two or three companies own not only most of the cattle fed for slaughter in this country, but most of the nation's grain, flour, pork, eggs, and chickens. Once my cattle fall into the clutches of these companies, they are crowded together with cattle from other regions in small pens. Knee-deep in mud and their own wastes, they are vulnerable to disease as they never would be on the prairie, and exposed to germs carried by cattle from other areas, even from other countries. Runoff from these feedlots will pollute streams and even underground water, not only with the contents of the cow manure, but with the chemicals used to grow the grains. Cattle previously raised on a diet of grass suffer diarrhea until their systems adjust to eating only grain while their flesh inflates with fat.

In other words, much of our food production industry is dependent on monopolistic companies, not individual ranchers. Driving ranchers off public lands and out of business won't stop either the unhealthy feedlots or the pollution. When family ranchers sell out, their holdings are often bought by corporations, giving big business tighter control over food production, and thus over the price you pay to eat. Land owned by such corporations is likely to be managed by a formula devised without any particular knowledge of the landscape.

Feisty individual ranchers who object to centralized commerce may be called "un-American" or worse. But without them, your dinner would be more costly, and you would have less influence over what it contains. Major companies often ignore or subvert pollution laws, arguing that food is necessary for national security. And close alliances with government agencies may give them more control over public lands than ranchers have ever had.

None of this is necessary. The whole complicated scheme is an elaborate edifice built to create profits. Range-fed beef is lean, organic, healthy. If meat-eaters bought beef directly from a local rancher, both parties would profit, and both would be helping to preserve their right to independent action. The buyer might supervise his or her cow's daily life, monitoring the amount of fat in the eventual steaks. The buyer might choose to do the butchering, earning dinner up close and personal. If ranchers had a ready market for beef raised without chemicals, they could operate more cheaply. Both buyer and seller would strike a blow against both monopoly and pollution, and more surplus grain would be available for those sixty million hungry people. Maybe some of them could even afford birth control.

If you eat supermarket beef, you might also want to research Department of Agriculture inspection regulations; within the last few years the agency has reclassified a frightening collection of animal diseases as being "defects that rarely or never present a direct public health risk," and allowed "unaffected carcass portions" to be passed on to consumers. In other words, meat workers are supposed to simply cut out cancer, lymphomas and tumors, sores, and intestinal worms, among other things, and send the carcass down the line to be wrapped and sold to you. Some feedlots are experimenting with feeding the waste, including the diseased parts, to other cattle, though fear of foot-and-mouth disease may stop that nasty trend.

Feedlots where range-bred cattle fatten are often owned by the same companies that hold the farms where the corn is produced, the meatpacking plants where animals are slaughtered, and the grocery chain stores where the price is affixed. None of the steps by which the beef on your plate is produced compares to the risks and labor the family rancher puts into his herd.

On my ranch, calves range over miles of pastures, free to romp, grazing on native grass. Their wastes are deposited on the ground and scattered by bugs and birds. Rains wash a little manure into stock dams, but none of our cattle waste reaches water used for human consumption. Feedlot operators are regularly granted "permits to pollute" rivers and streams by county or state governments, who hope to bring jobs to impoverished rural residents. The average feedlot dumps tons of cattle waste into rivers in the nation's heart every week, corrupting more water than I've ever seen.

Want to save the planet, but you like meat? If you live where grass grows, take a spring drive and locate cows with calves at their sides. They won't be far from the ranch house. One of our problems in recent years is impromptu rustling, where someone stops on the highway, slings a calf into the trunk of his car, and sells it at the nearest sale ring. So don't stroll around in the pasture or sit looking at it too long, or you may be mistaken for a rustler.

Instead, locate the ranch house, drive in, and introduce yourself. Explain that you don't want to eat meat with chemicals in it, so you want to buy directly from the man who raises the animal. Likely the rancher may be a little hesitant. We've all heard stories of militant animal rights activists. But if you're willing to learn, most ranchers will be happy to explain to you how their operation works. You might be able to pick out your calf the day it's born, name it, watch it grow, and specify what it eats.

Take a leisurely drive into the country every couple of weeks to visit your future dinner. Wear old clothes and waterproof boots, and be prepared to take your time. You might be able to observe the operation and visit with the rancher if you offer to lend a hand with his work. If the rancher believed the slogan "time is money," he probably wouldn't be ranching. Bring up local issues and ask how he feels about them. In an exchange of views, both of you will probably learn.

A few years ago, I read a manifesto of "Green" political proposals that sounded as if it had been written by my rancher father. I was dumbfounded when the accompanying commentary suggested the concepts were idealized and politically unrealistic. Self-reliance, one of the core ideas, is a way of life on the ranch. We don't buy more than we spend, and we acquire only the equipment we need for our "small is beautiful" operation. We work to make our cattle-raising operation blend with the harmony nature has already established on our ranch. We practice nonviolence, handling our cattle with horses and on foot much of the time, never striking any with a whip. We never shoot coyotes, though we shoot over their heads if they venture into the yard where children and pets play. We don't shoot deer that supplement their diet with our haystacks and salt.

I found only one Green desire we didn't already practice in its fullest sense: diversity. Still, when I first moved to the ranch, we raised chickens for meat and eggs to use and sell; I planted and harvested a large garden until my husband died and I got too busy. We sometimes harvested seed from a late alfalfa crop, to sell if the price was high, or to use in replanting exhausted fields. We bought black bulls to breed our Hereford heifers because my father noted that the first cross was always full of vigor. "Works that way in people, too," he said reflectively.

Defining the Sustainable Ranch

Every week someone somewhere mentions creating a "new paradigm for western environmental policy," probably in a meeting where experts declare the need to remove cattle from public lands. Environmental leaders hint darkly that cows exist only because "powerful ranching interests control Congress."

People who advise rural folks on economic strategies seldom live in the West or have the foggiest notion of how and why ranchers survive here. Public figures offering counsel on the West's problems appear not to grasp the reality every ranch kid knows at ten years old: resources—especially the soil and water imperative for life—are scarce. If shortsighted people govern the West in ignorance, ranchers in worn boots will jostle each other on every city street corner while public lands become dusty zoos full of starving elk.

Only grass keeps most of the West's thin soil from blowing east in swirling clouds to fall into the Atlantic Ocean. Evolved over millions of years, grasses utilize unique combinations of nutrients and water in specific ways unique to each prairie region. Grass is the main product of Western rangelands. Disturbing the surface of the earth—plowing and bulldozing space for houses, highways, and parking lots—destroys grass and encourages weeds. Even ardent vegetarians don't eat "creeping jenny" (field bindweed). Every farming method tried on arid prairies has been less successful than Nature's. Few crops could thrive under these tough conditions as well as grass does.

The most sensible way to sell grass—or "realize its market potential" if you think in economic language—is inside a grazing animal. If, as Aldo Leopold commands, we make the land's needs basic to planning in the West, we must consider two resources—water and grass—first. By Leopold's gauge, sustainable ranching may be the most logical and practical profession on the plains. If a ranch has been in business for a hundred years, its owners or managers are working to maintain its water, grass, and even wildlife.

Of course, my rancher father didn't teach me how to "sustain a naturally functioning ecosystem." He said, "This land will take care of us if we take care of it." I learned by watching his actions that he considered antelope, deer, badgers, and coyotes important to our ranch. He didn't call it an ecosystem, but it is. Much of our land lies on either side of a long, normally dry draw that drops out of the Black Hills on the west and stretches to the Badlands on the east. The antelope and deer graze among the willows, helping keep them in check; badgers and coyotes helped us keep the prairie dogs and moles under control.

Folks who live in town rarely consider predation relevant to their lifestyle unless they meet a mugger. Visiting Yellowstone Park, they expect to gawk at elk and geysers, but be protected from grizzlies and forest fires. Managing the park for those isolated elements has nearly eliminated everything else in the park—the animals and vegetation that create the variations of a healthy environment. As a rancher, I battle predatory blizzards, bankers, and environmentalists, but I try to remember that Nature thrives on conflict, and that I may survive through skill rather than power.

Undoubtedly, the West was settled by a rugged tribe chasing profits in cattle and grass. Gradually, though, they deduced why too many cows or too many people destroyed their livelihood. Ranchers who came west in the 1800s knew nothing of ecosystems, but if their descendants are still here, they know that any sustainable economy proposed for western prairies must start with consideration for grass and water.

Environmentalists who give ranchers an opportunity to prove cattle raising can be sustainable may be surprised at the ecological health of a well-managed ranch. Most alternatives are more destructive. Before banning cattle from public lands, we should examine the consequences.

Slouched in my saddle following cows, I've spent hours considering the possibilities of domesticating other grazing animals. Recent immigrants to my neighborhood, for example, raise bison, touting their lean flesh and ability to survive plains winters without human help. Disadvantages are less obvious unless you share a fence line with the herd, as I do. Bison go everywhere together, pounding trails to dust. Tired of their range, they march through the tightest, tallest fences. They're quick-tempered and hard to herd.

Deer and elk? Too fast to catch with a horse or the average pickup, they can jump most fences. Pronghorn? I recall once reading a letter from an eastern woman to an environmental magazine. She'd noticed that wool growers did a lot of complaining about coyotes, and suggested that they should stop being so lazy and do the sensible thing: build fences to keep the coyotes away from the sheep. Maybe she would think we should raise antelope, but I doubt I could confine or harvest an animal able to run sixty miles an hour and duck under a barbed wire fence four inches high without slowing down. It would be even harder to sell my "product"—grass—if it was packaged in a wilder critter than a cow. Horses? Like bison, they gallop in groups, destroying plants, and though the meat is relished in some countries, it is unlikely to be added to the American menu because we have made cowboys, and their horses, into mythical heroes. A cow is a sensible compromise.

Cooperation between ranchers and their critics is the way to find an answer to the challenge of land use in the West. Antagonism arises because neither faction knows enough about the other's position. Ranch publications make environmentalists' issues sound like an invading horde, while folks in favor of preservation portray ranchers as barbarians. Simple minds and one-dimensional thought processes are an advantage to an army, but residents of the West ought to know better. As an environmentalist born and raised on a ranch, I don't like to visit national parks or cities. Both resemble zoos too much for my taste—noisy, crowded, artificial environments that drive their inhabitants insane—in strong contrast with the well-managed ecosystem where I live.

Ranching Is Going, Going—But Not Quite Gone

Do you hear fiddle music as the last rancher rides off into the sunset? Many people think ranching is doomed, if not already dead and buried. I'm not ready to concede defeat, but if ranchers want to avoid extinction, they need to make some tough choices.

Already, the traditional rusty pickup with a dog drooling over the tailgate is being displaced by shiny double-cab jobs with dual tires lugging clipped dogs in cages. And no one wants to talk about water, the silent partner in any speculation about the future. The value of agricultural land is debatable, altered each time ranches are diced into subdivisions.

I remember the first rancher in the neighborhood who sold his ranch for double what the tax assessor said it was worth. He related the news with the self-satisfied air of someone who's just sold the Golden Gate Bridge. Loitering in the aisles of our local grocery store while the owner tallied the cost of our purchases in her old gray head, shoppers muttered to one another. "Did ya see that house them new people are building?"

"Hard to miss. If it don't blow off the top of that hill in the first blizzard, it's gonna be bigger than the town hall."

One chuckled wisely while the other repeated the old saying that we'd all make more money if we sold the land, put the money in the bank, and lived off the interest.

Gossip turned to bellyaching once we realized how much our neighbor's windfall was going to raise our taxes. Livestock raisers said they didn't know how they could hang on if the taxes went much higher and cattle prices didn't keep up. Each time another ranch sold, the selling price rose, making all the surrounding ranches "worth more"—but only if they were for sale. We congratulated all those canny former ranchers as they packed for the move to Arizona. No one mentioned that making money without working went against everything we believed.

Meanwhile, rumors flew: the newest buyer owns an island, and is going to use this place for hunting. Is he putting in gold plumbing? We groused at speeding construction vehicles on the dirt road, and a few of us lamented the number of deer, rabbits, badgers, and coyotes run over, happy none of our kids got in their way. Shrugging, we repeated clichés: "Got to get bigger to get better. It's progress; what can you do?"

Nowadays we don't stand around chatting. We toss remarks at one another as we fill our go-cups in the new combination gas station/bar/café out by the highway. Those newcomers from California occupy every hilltop in sight—apparently don't know how the winter wind tugs at the roof and piles snowdrifts in front of garage doors. Maybe they don't care because they won't be here in the winter. Property taxes are so high our grandfathers are spinning in their graves, but the new highway makes trips to town easy, a good thing since most of us have jobs there. Instead of stocking up on groceries once a month, we pick up something for dinner at the deli on the way home. We don't buy anything but our daily coffee fix at the station on the highway, but it's sure nice to have those tourist dollars in the little town's treasury now that we need more deputies and a town marshal to catch the speeders, and isn't that regular trash pickup handy? Shame old Anna died before she had a chance to enjoy her retirement after she closed the grocery store. Gotta run!

Some cynics suggest that once all the recalcitrant old ranchers are replaced by politically correct tofu eaters, the West will be knee-deep in garbage shipped from the East Coast. Now that tourism has moved ahead of agriculture as the primary business in many states, some folks might welcome garbage. We could pave it, providing jobs, and creating ever-growing parking lots for convenience stories and tourist destinations like Mount Rushmore.

A few activists predict an open range will stretch from the Canadian border to the southern tip of Texas, unfenced and untenanted except by wild bison, wolves, and other native animals. One group even wants to bring back the woolly mammoth but would settle for elephants.

I can visualize that future: Angry bison chase bicyclists along the paved roads and parking lots of suburbs covering the prairie as far as the eye can see. Folks on ATVs and SRVs and other alphabetical recreational transport aim their movie cameras at a couple of lean wolves trying to get a little privacy behind the last sagebrush. Joggers in bright orange elastic underwear pause to scrape elephant dung off their Nikes.

By contrast, in my ideal future, ranching would remain the backbone of the arid shortgrass plains for simple economic reasons that affect both meat-eaters and those who prefer tofu. Millions of years of evolution have developed plants best suited to the western landscape. The best way to harvest their bounty is—so far—inside a grazing animal.

Ranchers and newcomers might work together to keep ranching alive. For starters, we might teach people who move into ranching communities how to get the most from their new homes. Just as we instruct new residents on the dangers of weather and wildfire, let's educate them on the meaning of community, something they came here to find. Properly trained, new residents might provide a means to revitalize ranching country economically and philosophically while appreciating the history, personalities, and conservation work of longtime ranchers.

The rural western Dakota ranching community where I grew up still enjoys qualities cherished by the pioneers who settled there in the 1800s. Many of us still don't lock our doors or take keys out of our pickups—a friend might need a phone or a ride. Agreements can be sealed with a handshake, and spring branding is a traveling potluck as families help one another. "The check is in the mail" usually means someone put it in your mailbox without a stamp. Because everyone knows everything, a hospitalized friend came home to find neighbors had cleaned her house. She didn't dare get sick again after they gossiped about the dust balls under the beds. Still, contributing to local legend was a small price to pay for the kinship. As my friend Margaret always said, "neighbor" is a verb.

Rural communities might adopt an idea from Driggs, Idaho, where a handbook provided to prospective residents of the Teton Valley offers detailed information on soil, wildlife, water rights, and weeds. The chapter on grazing, for example, provides specific tips on native vegetation, riparian management, livestock rotation, and fencing methods and customs. Suggesting ways to be a responsible horse or dog owner, to burn trash safely, is a friendly way to help strangers become informed residents.

As for ranchers, they need to start saving their own skins by figuring out how to make money, legally, without having to do any more work. One solution might be to devise ways to charge for labor they already do in the course of running sustainable ranches wisely: preserving wildlife, native grasses, and open space.

Beyond that, they might have to change some long-held beliefs, consider learning new ways to preserve prairie life. Forty miles south of my ranch, NO ZONING signs decorate fences through a pretty valley where new houses spring up every week as ranchers exercise their right "to do what I want with my own land."

Those ranchers would probably agree that rights require responsibility. They may even realize that other western communities have chosen to prohibit development in terrain best suited to grazing. If western ranchers decide not to decide, they will give up their right to choose their future. They may sacrifice the "right" to ranch.

They'll be like that rancher who came into the bar and started downing whiskey after whiskey. When a sympathetic friend asked him what was wrong, he shook his head in despair. "Some blankety-blank Californian took my ranch away from me."

"That's terrible. But how could that happen?"

The old rancher gulped and said, "The so-and-so met my price."

If ranchers want to avoid exiting the western stage—to the sweet strains of that fiddle, of course—they need to be their own best friends. That means taking a hard look at reality and making some tough choices. "The only thing necessary for the triumph of evil," as Edmund Burke said, "is for good men to do nothing."

THE COW IS
MY TOTEM

...

Humans who choose to identify with animals have almost always chosen carnivores, the winners in the great eating lottery. In prehistoric times, shamans and their followers selected critters at the top of the food chain for totems. Today, people seeking self-confidence may adopt a "power animal." Just as a warrior once emulated a bear, wolf, or tiger, wearing its fangs and claws to symbolically transfer its power to himself, some folks now wear animal images in jewelry, amulets, or on T-shirts. Again, only a select group of animals qualify for this honor. No self-respecting, self-proclaimed shaman would expect to sell a million copies of a hardbound how-to guide to personal enlightenment with a frog or a cockroach on the cover.

Totems take other forms in modern society, as well. Traditionally, cars and sports teams are Cougars, Tigers, Panthers, Grizzlies, Lions. The only herbivores included in this nationwide name game are those with lethal strength or at least dignity, like Buffaloes or Rams. I doubt if any sports team was ever named the Sheep, or even the Elephants.

We also use animals to symbolize human traits we consider less than admirable: "You're chicken!" we scream on the playground. Over coffee, we nod sagely and observe, "Rats desert a sinking ship." In more imposing surroundings, such as a congressional chamber, we may remark, "He's sly as a

fox and filthy as a pig." Behind a presidential podium, any of us might pro-
claim, "Let slip the dogs of war."

Perhaps this verbal familiarity is one reason some folks have trouble taking any animal seriously, but we are equally adept at prolonging animal
myth. Since most of us were raised on *Little Red Riding Hood,* wolf experts
have a hard time convincing us that wolves mate for life, practice baby-sitting within an extended family group, and rarely attack humans. Conversely,
humans raised with cuddly stuffed animals and television shows featuring
tigers on leashes may not realize how dangerous a real animal, a buffalo, for
example, can be. Rangers in Yellowstone Park were once horrified to see a
man place his small daughter on the back of a buffalo and step back for a
photograph. After he'd retrieved her and was a safe distance away, they tried
to explain that the animal could disembowel another buffalo with one swipe
of those picturesque horns. The doting papa probably didn't believe them,
but occasionally buffalo make dead believers out of folks who think nature is
"sweet."

Most of us now know we can learn a great deal from animals simply by
observing the way they are, without picturing them either as furry humans
or as savage brutes with nothing in common with us. But even vegetarians,
members of the Sierra Club, and other politically correct modern thinkers
tender more respect to meat-eating animals than to, say, cows. Those of us
who make our living from cows and joyfully eat them are not invited to the
chic cocktail parties held to benefit whales. Yet, with the exception of those
who wear plastic shoes (recognizable by their limping gait), most of us benefit from cows every day.

I think more folks should begin to view cows as part of nature, and I suggest some of us might even consider adopting cows as totems. They possess
certain admirable traits, and might come to symbolize a benign way of living
on the earth. This idea isn't likely to be popular at first glance, since cows are
seldom featured on TV wildlife shows, but stay with me a minute.

Many of us have adopted our opinions about animals from the strong
views of others. Some environmental groups— Earth First! for example—de-
test cows and recommend destroying even the windmills that bring them
water in the arid Southwest. The king of angry environmentalism, Edward
Abbey, speaking in May 1985 at the University of Montana, said public lands
were "infested with domestic cattle," and called them "ugly, clumsy, sham-

bling, stupid, bawling, bellowing, stinking, fly-covered, smeared, disease-spreading brutes," and "a pest and a plague."

Ugly? Hard to say what Ed's standard of beauty might have been; perhaps he loved moose. Clumsy? Shambling? Clearly, he never tried to head off a young cow—afoot or on horseback—when she wanted to go through a gate. Stupid? He never had to find a herd of cows in a blizzard. If a cow bawls and bellows, she's in distress—her calf is lost, or she's hungry. Perhaps the human responsible for her isn't watching closely enough; a happy cow is too busy eating to moo. Stinking, fly-covered? Smeared? These adjectives suggest Ed did his cow observation in feedlots. Healthy cattle on open range clean themselves until their hides gleam, and are far enough apart that their parasites rarely carry or spread disease.

I think Abbey knew all this, but enjoyed causing controversy. Strong statements may be a good way to get people's attention, as PETA (People for the Ethical Treatment of Animals) proves with its in-your-face advertising. The danger is that drama may rest on misinformation, as Abbey has just demonstrated. Environmentalists who admire Abbey without having his intelligence, guts, or knowledge have been cursing and attacking cows since his talk. They ought to take a good look at the human species before they do anything drastic. Abbey's description could apply as well to most of us.

Abbey suggested that anything with four legs and horns on public lands should be regarded as a game animal and shot, ignoring laws governing hunting seasons. He didn't say the game should be eaten, although elsewhere he extolled the virtues of a good steak. He abhorred the bovine practice of making deep trails to locations visited regularly—to water, feed, along fence lines—and the resulting erosion. He deplored the cow's habits of defecating in its own water supply and eating the best grass, leaving noxious and sticky weeds to overpopulate.

In assessing Abbey's comments, let's be honest. Many humans do the same things. Open a wilderness area to hikers, and you'll soon have deep trails to everything interesting. It is possible to erect a fence that will turn cows, especially since they prefer not to walk straight down hills, but humans have nifty brains and opposable thumbs. No matter what kind of barrier authorities construct, people get through it. Humans, not cows, cause brutal erosion as they crash straight down slopes.

Humans also think it's fun to roll rocks, something no cow ever did on purpose. Once I parked my car along the road in Spearfish Canyon, in the Black Hills of South Dakota, and strolled up-canyon, enjoying the warbling of water and canyon wrens. I heard a crash and discovered some fun-loving lads were above me on the cliffs, enjoying themselves by flinging rocks down on top of my 1954 Chevrolet, still wearing its original paint after twenty-five years. The boys weren't good representatives of the intelligence of the species, I hope, because they made two mistakes. First, as I strode angrily up the road, they screeched threats when I approached another car, revealing it belonged to them—or one of their fathers. Second, they forgot about the regrettable human tendency toward vengeance. They howled with dismay as I sliced the air valves from a couple of their tires. I could still hear the echoes bouncing off the canyon walls as I drove away.

But I digress. I was speaking of cows, who would never commit either of those destructive acts. Cows leave trails that cause erosion; so do humans. Cows defecate in their own water supply. Have you heard what generations of humans have put in your water? Not only sewage, but chemicals that will literally curl your hair and dissolve your bones, not to mention those of your unborn children. The worst an animal can do to a water supply is defecate or die in it. Cows may do both, but so do other animals, and the contamination can be corrected by boiling. Humans are the only species that poison their own water, know they shouldn't, and still can't stop themselves. Cows don't neatly cover their manure piles the way a fastidious feline does, but neither do most humans. I've seen backcountry campgrounds surrounded by mounds of human excrement festooned with toilet paper—a human product that's not even necessary for clean defecation, and something cows never leave dangling from the scenery.

And what about cows' eating habits? Yes, they can overgraze an area, but they're hampered by the lack of that opposable thumb, although some can open gates without it. It's the rancher's responsibility to open the gate and put the cattle in a new pasture with more grass. Maybe he borrowed so much money from the banker to buy the piece of land to keep it from being developed that he can't afford more pasture. Show a rancher a buffet table and he'll do just as you will: eat the things he likes first. The point is, humans are supposed to be smart enough to understand these things. If cattle are damaging the ecological balance, it's a *human's* fault, and opponents should reason with the human, searching for alternatives, not shoot the cow.

Considerable opposition to the presence of cows in the natural world is based on misinformation, as is the case in so many disagreements. Volume of delivery plays a part as well. If an environmentalist screams that I'm immoral for raising cows, I may, of course, be tempted to shout at the poor blockhead, instead of sympathizing with his or her ignorance.

Why should you know anything about cows, you ask? Because hardly a day passes that you don't consume parts of one, that's why. Cow blood provides compounds necessary for in-vitro growth of cells in medical research, and is used in plywood adhesives, fertilizer, and foam fire extinguishers. Edible tallow is used in vegetable oils, shortening, and chewing gum; fatty acids derived from tallow appear in tires, candles, crayons, cosmetics, soaps, fabric softeners, linoleum, jet engine lubricants, as well as in synthetic motor oil, food packaging, fishing line, acne medication, and furniture, among other uses. Glycerin, derived from tallow, is used in pharmaceuticals including cough syrups, tranquilizers, eye washes, contraceptive jellies, and poison ivy solutions; in dynamite, liqueurs, shaving cream, toothpaste, sunscreens, and hair dressings. Many medications are supplied in capsules formed of glycerin from cow fat. Bones from cows are used in charcoal ash for refining products such as sugar, in ceramics, and in dental implants; gall is an ingredient in a cleaning agent for leather; the strings on tennis rackets and musical instruments are made of cow intestines; a cow's heart may be ground for use in pet food, but also furnishes materials used in cardiovascular surgery and to repair hernias. Very few people lead a life free from the influence of cows.

A shopper who insists on organic produce may not know the difference between range-fed beef and the beef in the supermarket that was fattened on feedlot corn. Yet if we are what we eat, shouldn't we know as much about meat production as we know about recycling, or those chemicals some folks use to make lawns green and weed-free?

We all live in a society that has learned enough to voice concern about what's in our water, and how long our garbage stays in a landfill. Beef is an important part of many diets, and yet most eaters couldn't tell you where their dinner was born, or what happens to it between its last gambol on the hillside and their plate. We owe it to ourselves to learn the facts before we condemn cows.

What about cattle on public lands? If you believe cows have fewer rights to be on public land than elk and snowmobiles, study bovine habits before writing the slogans. Certainly the ecology of some high mountain regions may be so fragile that any traffic will damage it. But in the nation's great grasslands, well-managed grazing could be balanced with the needs of the public, and our pet wildlife. Some ranchers are experimenting on private or public lands with resting heavily used areas in an attempt to restore grass. Other authorities, including wildlife biologists, now believe that since grazing animals developed simultaneously with the plant communities of the West, they may be essential to a healthy ecosystem, improving it even with their hooves.

Many experts now agree that the risk of losing wildlife habitat to development is of greater concern than the damage that might be done even by poor grazing practices. Driving ranchers off land they have occupied for a hundred years removes from the land the people who have been most attentive to it for the longest time. A society that values open space and wildlife habitat should realize that ranching can provide these things. Perhaps we need to alter public policy so as to enable ranchers to improve their management practices, and remain on the land they know better than anyone else.

Again, I seem to have strayed like a cow hunting green grass in April from the idea of humans adopting cows as totems. I've allowed myself to be trapped in answering charges leveled against cattle, when I'm really more interested in providing information on their good qualities. Without wishing to reopen an old debate about whether behavior is instinctive or intelligent, I can testify, having observed cattle closely for fifty years, that they possess uncanny judgment. When a blizzard strikes, no matter what pasture the cows are in, they will find the best spot to shelter themselves and their calves *from that particular blizzard.* If the wind is in the north and carrying heavy snow, they choose a sheltered spot with room on the south so they won't be covered as the snow builds up in front of them. If the storm comes from the east, they'll take refuge in a different area of the pasture. Like us, they don't control the weather. Sometimes when the wind changes, cattle get caught in a place they can't escape when the storm is over. Then I have to exercise my intelligence to figure out where they are, and break a trail to them with either a truck or a horse. Maybe they know I'll rescue them.

While I'm shoveling a path to the garage, starting the truck, driving to the barn, and shoveling the drift away from the barn door, the cows stand broadside to the sun, warming up. While I load sacks of cake in the truck, drive into the pasture, and start hunting for them, they absorb free solar energy. While I am getting stuck in another drift, the cows may exhibit humanlike behavior, the white ones making rude remarks to the black ones, but I doubt it. By the time I arrive at their blizzard hideout, they are ready to follow me to a pasture closer to home.

Cows are also liberated, in their fashion. Unlike most modern businesses, they've had cooperative baby-sitting since the days when saber-toothed tigers threatened their offspring. In spring, when calves are young, cows prefer not to make them walk all the way to the corral each time Mama wants a drink, or leave them bawling and confused when she runs to the lunch wagon. So each day a certain open area of the pasture, away from rocks or brush that could conceal a creeping predator, becomes the nursery. Most of the cows move away to graze and drink while their calves stay in one spot, like fawns, until their mothers return to let them suck. Attended by several cows at all times, the calves don't move even when we drive into the pasture with sacks of cattle cake or a hayrack full of feed. The baby-sitters stick steadfastly with the calves until relieved of duty, grazing, feeding their own calves, and acting as lookouts. During one fire in our neighborhood, several calves were run over by fire trucks. Even the engine noise and the smell of smoke didn't break through their training, though apparently the baby-sitters had abandoned their posts.

One summer evening, contemplating the myth of placid cows, I sat on my deck and watched a coyote hunting mice in the field below. When she was full, she ducked under the fence and started up the slope. Back at her den, she would regurgitate a few tasty morsels for her pups. Perhaps deluded by the evening calm, or tired, she lowered her tail, keeping a low profile as she trotted along the trail—straight into the center of a herd of grazing cows.

My first clue of trouble was a bellow that might have come from a wounded elephant, a high-pitched scream of fear and wrath. I grabbed the binoculars and found the coyote. She'd strolled over a little knoll directly into the nursery. The two or three baby-sitting cows sounded the alarm. The coyote looked back over her shoulder, assessing her predicament. Not ten feet away, a cow was pawing dirt up over her back, bawling and tossing her horns. From every direction, cows were running toward the nursery. Bags swinging, heads raised, they all bellowed in outrage, assuring their calves that rescue was on the way. Most of the calves were still lying down, maybe trying to decide if Mother's instructions to keep still applied in this situation. One or two leaped up bleating in terror, convincing the oncoming cows that blood had been shed. A moment before, three bulls had been placidly drinking at the water hole. Rumbling threats, they galloped up the slope, persuaded some magnificent stranger was seducing their harem.

I estimate that at that moment, fifty thousand pounds of fury was stampeding toward one forty-pound coyote.

The coyote's next minor lapse might have been fatal. She chose to run straight up the hill. Instinct stood on her side: cows abhor a steep, direct climb. Even with a horse and rider behind them, they move upslope reluctantly, preferring to angle and climb slowly. The coyote bet her ability to accelerate against the heavy, heat-sodden cows in a sprint to safety.

Pay attention; ignorance can be deadly. The coyote didn't know cows on the other side of the hill had heard the sounds of panic. As she lunged up the hill, cattle appeared on the horizon the way the Indians always appear ahead of the wagon train in a Hollywood Western. Storming to the rescue, the cows galloped down the hill howling murder. In seconds, the coyote was surrounded. Dust boiled up from the grassy hillside as the whole galloping mass converged on her.

The cows crashed and collided, pawed the ground, slung snot in the air. After a few moments, the dust began to settle. A few cows ran out of the mob, murmuring anxiously, found their calves, and started away. A dozen or so remained, throwing clumps of grass in the air with their horns, still threatening mayhem. Two of the bulls squared off and slammed their heads together. Confused about the nature of the threat, they fell back on masculine custom: if in doubt, fight.

Glassing the scene, I wondered if they'd stomped the coyote to furry scraps. Then I glimpsed a trace of movement at the hilltop and focused on the coyote just as she flopped down a hundred yards beyond the nursery, panting hard and facing the cows. When she hunted the field below me after that, she always left it by a narrow fold in the hill that hid her from most of the cows most of the time.

Cows don't devote all their energy and instincts to predator control. Perhaps their hobby is finding holes in a fence, or a gate left open "just a minute" while a rancher checks a water hole. Cows can materialize from empty prairie just in time to dash through the gate before the pickup can reach it. If I'm riding a horse, trying to put a particular cow through a gate, her companions can calculate precisely—to the inch—the distance at which I can't stop them before they escape. If I'm on my younger horse, they wait until I'm farther away.

Despite my liking for them, I must admit that cows use their abilities to deceive humans fairly often. When city people ask ranchers how to tell when a cow is going to calve, we look wise and talk sagely about physical details that announce the event. Challenged, we may admit to a sixth sense developed by experience. To hear us tell it, we are never wrong.

Among ourselves, however, we joke about our errors. When calving season begins, nearly every rancher sorts into a particular corral or pasture close to the barn the cows most likely to calve first. Cows that won't calve for several weeks are pastured farther away. Storms tend to bring on calves, so if a blizzard is coming, we cut the heavies again, putting those closest to calving into a corral or shed. The scientific explanation for this involves the effects of air pressure on the cow's womb, and depends on good old reliable logic. But all honest ranchers have spent hours getting heavy cows to safety only to find new calves in the most distant pasture after the storm. We shrug and say you can't always tell what a cow will do. I think the cows may be making the decisions. Often, a cow looks ready to calve when she's shut in the gate at night. In the morning, she'll march out the gate and go as far as possible from people and buildings—and then calve. I believe cows simply prefer privacy, and can sometimes control the urge to calve until they get it.

Nothing convinced me I was right more than an experience in early 1989 when a photographer for *Life* magazine visited the family ranch to photograph me during calving season. Anxious to do his job well, he carried three cameras and slogged through snow and mud with me day and night, taking pictures of every major event in my daily life. But he particularly wanted to photograph a cow giving birth.

After the first few days of failure, we sorted ten cows most likely to calve into a corral right beside the barn. When I spotted the signs of birth from the house, he accompanied me to the corral, no matter what the hour. As his stay lengthened, we checked the cows every half hour during daylight, and every hour at night. The cows in the corral had grown so used to his presence the photographer could scratch most of them behind the ears. First he named them, and then he started pleading with them. For an entire week, not a single cow calved when he was present.

The day he raced to town for an hour to shoot another assignment, two cows calved. On another day, we looked at the cows on the way to the house for coffee. Five minutes later, from my kitchen window, we saw through binoculars a cow licking a newborn calf in the corral. When we left them, cows must have shot out calves like seeds in a watermelon-seed-spitting contest. Finally, we decided the cows had simply made a collective decision that this intimate moment should not be exposed for a national magazine. The critters acted in a way contrary to everything I know about biology, every rule of calving season. They won. When the story appeared, it contained no photograph of a cow calving.

Unlike most humans, cows are sensible in their work habits. Their job is to eat grass, processing it into bone, flesh, and milk their calves will transform into meat. They are dependable in their work, but not fanatical; workaholics are unknown in their world. On a day when the thermometer and the blood in their veins register temperatures above a hundred degrees, cows don't run back and forth in the valleys trying to make a living, or to do better than their mothers did. They graze in the cool morning, drinking deep of whatever water is available, muddy or clear. Then they spend the afternoon lying on the highest hill available, chewing their cud where any prairie breeze can find them. After sunset, when the air cools, they stroll down for another drink before grazing through part of the night, gracefully becoming nocturnal as the best way of adjusting to heat. They appear to sleep well, with no apparent nightmares about the job.

Humans behave slightly differently when the thermometer reaches the century mark. We punch air conditioner buttons, shiver in offices, curse traffic, swelter as we dash outside to eat cardboard food in noisy crowds. At night, shut inside boxes insulated against cold, we don't realize we've also effectively trapped heat. We tumble restlessly in hot beds or grumble at the air conditioner's roar while cool breezes blow across spacious, empty decks and lawns. After working like slaves to afford unnatural cooling, we pass up the natural variety. Cows don't.

Few humans have explored bovine artistry, although Xenophanes touched on its possibilities when he wrote in Fragment 15: "If cattle and horses, or lions, had hands, or were able to draw with their feet and produce the works which men do, horses would draw the forms of gods like horses, and cattle like cattle, and they would make the gods' bodies the same shape as their own." Cows do create beauty, albeit unconsciously, particularly at salt licks. Since each bovine seeks salt daily as a dietary supplement, their hooves wear off the grass and create depressions around the lick. If a rancher always dumped the fifty-pound blocks on the ground in the same spot, they'd dissolve in puddles during rains, and the cattle would trample and waste the expensive stuff. Ranchers used to build wooden salt boxes, open at the top and built so they drain, yet solid enough to withstand hundreds of hooves. Adroitly, cattle sculpt both salt and its container. As they lick, the salt blocks are slowly carved into abstract white shapes that change daily.

Modern ranchers who use old rubber tires as salt boxes miss the second medium in the sculptures: wood carving. Holding salt for years, the boards in an oak or pine salt box absorb some of the flavor; when the salt is running low, the cows lick the boards with their big rough tongues to get the last morsels out of the crevices. Several boxes on my ranch have been sanded into rounded shapes smooth as fine furniture, with a gleaming golden patina and no splinters.

If possible, cows scratch almost as much as they lick, removing winter hair, or relieving fly bites. When one cow finds a post with a projection placed to reach those hard-to-scratch spots between the shoulder blades, under the hip bone, or in the center of the flank, every other cow in the herd is soon rubbing on the same post. Some of our oldest posts are twisted cedar, cut in the Black Hills during the early days of settlement. Where they have been polished by cowhide for forty or sixty years, they glow with dull, variegated red light. A master woodworker might admire the finish, created with natural suede, oil, and hours of labor by the cows wearing the polishing cloth.

Perhaps folks who want cattle off public lands have temporarily forgotten one of their most familiar abilities, that of producing a pure white liquid that nourishes our precious—although too numerous—children. All cows produce milk, not just the Holsteins and Jerseys in the television ads. We judge how rich a cow's milk is by looking at her calf: the fatter it is, the better the milk. All female mammals are accorded respectful admiration for this ability, as long as they do it in private. Perhaps we don't wish to be embarrassed by reminders of our origins or our greedy natures; a woman who attempts to breast-feed in public may be banished to a smelly toilet. Like human women, the cow has been portrayed by advertising and cartoons as a silly creature, in ignorance of her noble suffering. Perhaps women should reserve the cow totem for themselves, in defiance of such attitudes.

A cow's stomach is remarkable, too, not only for being one of the darkest places in the universe, but for its double construction and its ability to digest almost anything but metal. Some cows must survive with awful indigestion caused by careless humans. A local packing plant once displayed wrenches and other tools, beer cans, parts of cars, and nails found in cows' stomachs. Occasionally, when a cow dies for no apparent cause, the rancher may assume she died of "hardware disease," another illness she didn't face before she started hanging around with sloppy people. Society honors football players and jockeys because they compete with broken bones and pulled ligaments, but the cow gets little respect for her toughness.

When I was a child and less fastidious than I am today, if I forgot my handkerchief I would blow my nose on my shirttail; so I admire cows' ability to clean their nostrils with their tongues. The same tongue bathes her calf from ears to hooves, as well as cleaning all accessible parts of her own hide including spots I wouldn't believe it could reach if I hadn't seen it. A cow can wrap her tongue around a tall stand of grass and reel it in to her teeth, then tuck that bite inside her jaw while she sends the tongue back for more. With the aid of their tongues and a flexible neck and hind leg, cows have been known to sample their own milk, though perhaps it would be more polite not to mention that. A mother who would take food from her child is an aberration, not appropriate for the benign image I have painted here, but she's certainly agile.

I also envy cows their hooves, nicely sharpened and pointed but seldom used as weapons. Instead, cows use them to scratch behind their ears. When a fly settles between her shoulder blades, a cow can dispatch it with a flyswatter at the end of her spine. In cases when a hoof or tail won't reach the desired spot, and the scratching post is miles away, some cows can fall back on a handy horn, nicely detailed for reaching tiny itches. Meanwhile, humans buy self-defense weapons, and search endlessly for a compatible person to scratch our itches.

Bovine horns poke holes in the cow's placid reputation, too. Probably developed as a logical and necessary defense, horns are hardly necessary since humans killed most of the predators. Most ranchers use hornless breeds, or dehorn their cows to protect other members of the herd from injury. A horned cow in a herd of hornless ones will always be boss, and her horns grow pointed and polished to a high gloss as she uses them to enforce her will. The cow we nicknamed Can Opener because she'd broken one horn kept the other sharpened like a razor and became adept at poking any creature in her way. Once in a while she drew blood. I think there's a lesson here about pacifism versus armed preparedness, but I'll let someone else spell it out. Still, maybe ranchers need to reconsider raising horned breeds. Maybe restoring to cows their natural armament would cut down on calf rustling. A few horned cows might also prove a deterrent to folks who think cutting fences is activism.

A cow's most amazing organ, however, is the largest: her skin. It enables her to spend most of her life outside. Unless a range cow has difficulty calving, she may never enter a barn. A small herd, like ours, includes at least a hundred animals. We can't afford a winter shelter that big. Besides, crowded cattle are less healthy than those free to find their own protection from storms. When it's forty degrees below zero with a thirty-mile-an-hour wind, the cows are outside. Now that some officious weatherperson has invented the windchill factor, people aren't supposed to go outdoors when it's that cold, even in their miracle, space-age fabrics. But no one has told the cows. They lie in snow that melts around their bodies, chewing their cud and surviving on dry grass and cattle cake. On days when the thermometer reaches 110 degrees, they're still outside, lying on a hilltop in the breeze, protected by a hide that functions in both extremes.

Remembering that the average American once ate the equivalent of fourteen cows in a lifetime, it seems only right that cows should be accorded more respect that we've given them. I've seen cows on T-shirts, socks, cups, lawn chairs, and posters, for example, but they're always black-and-white dairy cattle, never the chunky beef cattle I've known and loved. Even the occasional statue, like the huge one along an interstate in North Dakota, memorializes the Holstein, an animal no longer truly bovine but refined by human interference into a machine for creating milk, one step away from computerization. A poet I know tried to inject interest into a long trip by telling a busload of tourists that the cow statue was a North Dakota fertility goddess, and watched them scribble that in their diaries without questioning. I admire her attitude. But the poet may also have been tuning in to an ancient truth.

The cow I want for my symbol, my power animal, is a Hereford-Angus cross, familiarly known as a black whiteface. Her heritage is impeccable. On the Hereford side, her red whiteface ancestors originated in Herefordshire, England, as rugged draft animals. Imported to the United States in 1817, the horned version managed to look both beautiful and dignified, and proved her hardiness by replacing the longhorn on the western ranges. On the Angus side, she is descended from Scottish breeds noted for small, lively calves, imported in 1873 to be crossed with longhorns. Independent Angus bulls have been known to leave a pasture full of loving cows and swim a river to lie in bachelor paradise on a nearly inaccessible island. Autonomy and vigor are attributes most humans could cultivate to our benefit.

The calf these two bloodlines produce gets up within minutes after birth, and grows vigorously on a diet of sparse grass, without chemicals. If it's a female, she raises a calf when she's two years old, even in the leanest of dry years, and has a sensible, fair disposition: She'll kick you if you hurt her and are in range, but she won't chase you very far if you leave her calf alone. The crossbred steer is the wonder of the bovine world; he gains weight quickly and efficiently, is tractable enough to put up with feedlots that resemble concentration camps, and gives his life to become lean, tasty meat.

In many early societies, a mark of respect for vanquished enemies, human or animal, was to eat their hearts. In that way, the victor partook of the courage and strength the other had shown, and honored the loser for putting up such a good fight. Considering that tradition, and the number of beef hearts I've eaten, and all the admirable, underexposed qualities of cows, I hereby record that cows are my passion, as well as my living.

WADDLING OVER

THE DAM

. . .

"Get comfortable," George whispered. "This will take a while."

My moccasins were already soaked from trudging through the swamp to the edge of a series of beaver ponds. I found a hummock of grass rising a few inches above the muck, and sat on it while water rose slowly around my feet. George settled on a slightly thicker clump of grass a few feet away, and leaned forward, parting the cattails to look toward the pond. The water's surface was utterly still. Out on the plains, the sun was rising, but the edges of the high cliffs above us were just beginning to glow gold.

George and I had been getting acquainted since late winter. I was becoming engrossed in proving myself a good friend, and beginning to wonder if he had potential as a mate. We were both living in Spearfish, where I taught and George attended classes. For weeks, the sky had been clear over the northern Black Hills of South Dakota; fire danger was high, and the air clogged with dust and pollen. When George remarked on how much trouble he was having breathing, and proposed a camping trip, I didn't realize he was subjecting me to one of his compatibility tests.

On the Fourth of July, we loaded his backpacking tent and a kerosene stove and lantern into the old blue van already half-filled with other survival gear he considered essential, and followed gravel roads and logging trails into a secluded area leased to ranchers for summer grazing. Tourists who resent rough roads and cow manure never find such places, and the terrain was too rugged and stony to attract casual hikers.

We'd left the van parked tidily in a concealing aspen grove a mile down the canyon, and established a dry camp—with no natural water—on a shaded hillside above a clump of chokecherry bushes. George always behaved as if he was in potentially hostile territory. He explained that we'd avoid mosquitoes by camping on the incline. Pressed, he admitted he wasn't sure it was legal to camp there. We knew we wouldn't be setting fires or leaving garbage, but forest officials are notoriously skeptical. From our vantage point, George pointed out, we'd spot anyone looking for us in time to pack up and slip away.

George had brought a five-gallon jug of water, and I welcomed the opportunity to test some homemade dry mixes of soup and stew that could be prepared with a minimum of pans and cooking. We both hoped they'd taste better than the gruesome mixtures sold as backpacking food. We cooked on the camp stove, heated water to wash dishes, and packed trash to haul home.

As a celebration of the national holiday, we'd driven and hiked up Cement Ridge, one of the northernmost fire lookouts in the Black Hills, where we visited with a lonely ranger. Around us lay miles of blue ridges and peaks, rippling unevenly to the surrounding plains. Civilization seemed to have reached the edge of the hills and stopped. A haze lay over the state's second largest city, south of us, and wisps of smoke rose from sawmills in Spearfish, on the north. Cars glittered, spinning along webs of road anchoring the prairie in all directions, but we could see no movement in the nearer hills. Aspen, oak, pine, spruce, and birch blended into a navy blue blanket softening the granite and limestone slopes.

Eventually, brains filled with distance, we'd looked closer. Below us lay a narrow green valley unmarked by roads. A lean stream glinted, looking no bigger than a trickle, but George made me look until I could see beaver dams creating a chain of ponds like sheets of stained glass.

"Have you ever spent much time watching beaver?" George had asked.

I told him about a family camping trip when I was a child. My sleeping bag was so flimsy that by dawn I was too cold to lie still any longer. Waiting for the grownups to wake, I walked to a creek, and squatted down to wash my face. Fog hung low over the water. I heard a sharp slap! and saw my first beaver. For two hours, I huddled in the willows, watching, until the worried calls of my mother finally penetrated my chilly brain and I stumbled back to breakfast.

George nodded at the dams below. "I spotted these when I was looking for places to trap. We'll get up early and go down there."

"When you trap them, do you just throw the bodies away, or do you eat them?"

"Both; fed some to the dog. The mountain men always talked about how good beaver tail was, so I boiled one up once; pure fat. Would have tasted good after a starving winter living on jerky."

Years later, I confirmed his opinion. A beaver tail, cooked, is a single paddle-shaped chunk of fat. The scaly skin peels off easily, and the flavor is sweet, more like butter than lard or cooking oil.

Once, my rancher father reported that beaver had moved into the creek running through our hayfields. Reluctantly, he called Game, Fish, and Parks officials who trapped and removed them. When I protested that he was eliminating wildlife in favor of cattle, he said, "I like beaver, but they're cutting down the willows." Their dams would create ponds too deep for the cows to cross safely in winter. "And if the willows are gone," my father said, "the cattle will do more damage to the banks going to water and grazing." Now that I own the ranch, and better understand the multiple responsibilities of managing land, I think of that incident whenever I hit on what seems like an easy solution to a problem.

My revulsion for beaver trapping was replaced by lust the instant I saw George's tanned beaver hides, called plews. The outer guard hairs were rich, creamy gold, arranged in smoothly interlocking tufts all over the pelt. Below lay the tawny, chocolate layer of dense underfur—*muffon*—which insulates the animal from wet and cold despite its watery lifestyle. The thick lower fur, perfect for felt hats, made the beaver's life dangerous in the 1800s, until fashionable folk switched to silk just in time to save the charming rodents from extinction. George supplemented his air force retirement pay by trapping for several winters, and kept a dozen fine hides for himself. Whenever I got the chance, I stroked them. I could have gone on fondling them for hours. One day I held two hides at my waist and showed him how they would make a knee-length skirt. Please, I begged him. "No," he said. "Everybody'd want to pet it."

After we left the fire lookout in late afternoon, we took a long nap, and ended the day by climbing to the flat top of a nearby hill to watch fireworks in the surrounding communities. Nestled into sun-warmed rocks, we could see eruptions in all four directions, including a few flashes from Custer, more than forty miles distant. We slept folded in deep forest silence. Miles away from cars and motorcycles, we heard branches creak and pinecones drop softly into duff. Stones rolled as night hunters—coyotes? cougars?—prowled the rocky heights.

Crows woke us at dawn more effectively than any alarm clock. Even when he was trying to impress me, George was not congenial company without his morning coffee. He didn't speak until we'd emptied our coffee cups and eaten homemade pemmican. Then he led the way through the tangled woods for an hour, directly to the first beaver pond.

"How did you manage to walk straight here if you've never been here before?" I asked. He looked at me as if I'd just fallen out of a spaceship. "Well, we saw them from the ridge yesterday. I just walked that direction."

Once we'd adjusted to our grassy seats, natural sounds flowed into our ears. Water trickled softly from the beaver dam just ahead of us. Squirrels chittered somewhere to the east, and underbrush crackled, perhaps an elk coming to water. A distant scream made me tip my head back to see a patch of clear sky where a winged shape circled, coasting on wind currents. Hard to tell at that distance, I was thinking, when George whispered, "Golden eagle." Closer, something skittered along a fallen aspen and jumped noisily into last year's leaves, and a frog trilled almost under my left foot.

Soon, a smooth brown head rose near the dome of the beaver lodge, and a huge beaver swam to the dam and climbed awkwardly out. He waddled back and forth on the dam for a while, peering as if nearsighted, reaching out with fat paws to wobble a stick as if testing its strength. Then George pointed with his chin to call my attention to another beaver, leaving a wake as it swam toward us. This one pulled itself up on the bank, stared hard at our concealing cattails for a moment, then turned its head sideways. Curved teeth the color of tea flashed briefly, and a slender willow dropped. The beaver shoved it into the water, followed with a cautious splash, and nudged the willow ahead until it reached the lodge. The beaver dived, and the willow tipped upright and disappeared. A few minutes later the beaver surfaced, and repeated the whole process.

Meanwhile, the larger beaver, which we now guessed was the male, had finished his dam inspection tour. Sitting in a shifting patch of sunlight, he licked a front paw. A construction foreman would have recognized his manner: satisfaction, mingled with vigilance.

Suddenly his stout body stiffened and he leaned forward, then slid down into his pond. His tail smacked the water so loud I jumped. The smaller beaver on the bank near us left a willow half-severed and disappeared without a ripple.

The big beaver sped toward our hiding place, then paused, apparently treading water, and stared straight at us. His little round ears stood erect over flashing black eyes, and his long brown teeth clicked. His tail rose. *Slap! Slap!*

Just then a smaller beaver scrambled over the front of the dam. The one confronting us turned to look, then sped that way, leaving a deep V in the water. Looking awkward, he climbed the bank and catapulted into the other beaver with an audible thump. The two wrestled, chattering and squalling. When the intruder tumbled into the pond, our male slid after, and the two chased each other in circles. Then they wrestled again and sank. A minute passed, two.

A sleek brown head popped up, and the small beaver swam rapidly toward the dam, zipped over it, and disappeared downstream. The larger beaver surfaced and followed, making a noise like a whale spouting water through its blowhole. For ten minutes after the other beaver had galloped out of sight, the big male paced back and forth on the dam, snorting and snapping, occasionally sliding down the inner bank to swim in circles, whacking water with his tail.

Abruptly, he turned away from the dam and swam toward our hiding place again, staring as if he could see us. A mosquito chose that moment to plunge a sizable cylinder into my cheek, and begin pumping blood at approximately the rate of the Alaska pipeline. I held still while the beaver slapped the water repeatedly, swimming in circles but always returning to stare into the reeds at us.

When he returned to the top of the dam and began pacing its length, George said, "He knows we're here, but he's not sure what we are," and gently mashed the mosquito. Blood squirted over my glasses, and I let it dry there, knowing very well my indifference to such details increased George's respect for me. Gradually, the beaver's shuffle along the top of the dam slowed as he calmed down. Finally he swam to the lodge, climbed onto its broad hump, and moved over it, sniffling and looking closely at every detail. Every now and then he'd gaze toward us again.

Meanwhile, the female reappeared, chopped loose the willow she'd left hanging, and dragged it under the surface. When she emerged, she climbed up on the lodge and warbled gently. In a moment, three smaller heads rose, and followed her to the bank. She climbed out, followed by a slightly smaller version of herself. Both began gnawing purposefully on willows. Two smaller beaver, the kits, round and bouncy as beach balls, scrambled up the bank.

At once, the male humped across the dam, and swam to his spot directly in front of us and climbed out on the bank. Stationing himself between us and the kits, he paced the bank for several minutes, then rushed back to the dam and looked downstream, huffing and blowing water.

The kits tumbled over one another on the ground for a few minutes, then moved to the right, almost out of sight. One flopped, and sailed out on the pond's surface as if shot from a cannon. Almost at once the other followed. They swam back to shore, and repeated the show as George whispered, "Slide." Occasionally they'd pause to nibble at grass or cattail, and several times dropped down in the sun to nap or groom each other.

It was nearly noon when the entire beaver family swam to the lodge and ducked inside, leaving the water still. George sat up straight, took a deep breath, and looked at me. Six or seven hours had elapsed since we found the pond. Water stood at ankle level around my moccasins, and my legs were numb from the knees down. Both our faces were splotched with blood from mosquitoes we'd murdered in slow motion. When I tried to lift my foot, my thigh muscles locked. I bit my lip to keep from groaning. George extended an arm to heave me up, and supported me while I found balance again.

Walking slowly along the beaver pond while the blood returned to our feet and legs, we saw dozens of aspen, birch, and willow stumps with broad teeth marks, and found the muddy slide the kits had used. Ten feet from the bank we also found a round hole with damp edges, a concealed entrance to the pond.

In later years, when one of us said, "Remember the beaver?" we'd both smile, recalling that long, chilly morning of silent companionship. The last time we remembered the beaver together, George was lying in the hospital bed where he died. He smiled and closed his eyes. I like to believe his breathing slowed as he relived that morning. He'd lost his huge pelts, "blanket beaver," in a tipi fire a few years later, too busy rescuing his trapping partner, Jerry, to worry about possessions. He'd left one small pelt at home. It's the only one I have now. Sometimes I open its hiding place and place it on my knees while I write, stroking the fur.

Twenty years later, I went back to Cement Ridge. The view had changed. Gold mining companies have removed entire mountains, literally scouring to bedrock for gold fragments too puny to be worth hard-rock mining. "Modern" mining methods require tons of rock to be piled up, then sprayed with cyanide to release the ore. The waste rock is dumped in heaps, the cyanide leachate contained in ponds. Out-of-state hikers I met asked me what was in the water. They'd seen dead birds floating on the surface.

I glanced only once at the beaver dams, as if looking might draw deadly attention to them. They remained.

But a flood in 1991 sent frothy water that smelled like bitter almonds boiling down nearby creeks. Fearing contamination of their shallow drinking wells, citizens filed a lawsuit against Brohm Mining, with help from the Atlantic States Legal Foundation (ASLF) and Technical Information Project (TIP). Late in 1993, the suit was settled out of court after the Environmental Protection Agency agreed to enforce the Clean Water Act in heap leach mine operations. In 1994, TIP, a grass-roots research organization I'd served any way I could for more than ten years, ceased operations. We were too far in debt ever to escape, tired of living in poverty while developers, sleek as beaver in the fall, fattened on South Dakota's riches.

RISING FROM

THE CONDOS

...

Near my ranch in the Black Hills of South Dakota, development is way ahead of residents' understanding of its consequences. Few of my neighbors are ready to discuss how we might control the events unfolding among us. Most of us are still at an early stage: whining about how we're going to lose the things we imagine we treasure. Clean air and open spaces, wildlife and hunting, small towns where a handshake seals a bargain. We haven't begun to admit that besides the romance of ranching, which provides much of our state's wealth in cash and environmental benefits, we also stand to lose income from our number one industry, tourism. In fact, anyone who suggests such a thing, as I regularly do in essays and speeches, may be invited to "go back where you came from" by tourism officials and ranchers both.

So when I heard that my friends J. David and Jane Love had donated land in Jackson to help create affordable housing there, I wanted to know more. Like many nonresidents who enjoy visiting Jackson, I'd lamented the town's changes. I'd easily assumed its residents were unconcerned about the ordinary people who must live and work in a community where costs of living are higher than average.

In addition, I am a ranch-owning widow with no natural children and a deep commitment to preserving ecology. Western tradition would dictate I leave the ranch to members of my extended family. All firmly established in nonranching professions, they'd probably sell it to the highest bidder—who could blame them? So I'm exploring ways the family ranch might remain just that: a small rural business that will sustain not only a family but wildlife and native grass. A land trust offers one possible solution, and the Love story a way to learn more.

Most Americans regularly see headlines like this: "NEW SUBDIVISION PLANNED—EXPLOSIVE GROWTH PREDICTED." The language of expansion is becoming familiar everywhere even though many westerners think it's all happening in their hometown. "COST OF LIVING GOING UP—WAGES LAG BEHIND INFLATION RATE." The reports have become so routine we may yawn and turn the page. But the announcement that inevitably follows gets our attention: "PROPERTY TAX RATE WILL RISE."

All over the West, the name "Jackson, Wyoming" is invoked in community discussions as a graven image of the "evils of development." To many of us, the Wyoming resort stands for the "cancer of change." But thirty years ago Jackson residents who loved their valley's beauty and atmosphere said, "We don't want to be another Denver," or maybe "Las Vegas," or "Vail, Colorado." A writer for the *Wilderness Report* of December 1977 defined the conflict in Teton County, Wyoming, with the headline: "BEAUTY OR THE BEAST OF DEVELOPMENT?"

Among westerners, militant language is common in talk of change. We speak of being "under siege" as we "fight" to preserve our way of life, repeating the same arguments—though the name of the city cast as the living symbol of "what is wrong with growth" may change from year to year.

Jackson already had a housing shortage in 1948 when J. David Love and his wife, Jane, moved their four children into an unfinished basement on Clark Street. On the shoulder of Snow King Mountain, their home was so far out of town no one would deliver milk. They couldn't afford to hire a carpenter, so they began improving the house themselves. "A window a year," says Jane.

"I was very keenly aware of contemporaries who didn't have a place to live," David adds, explaining that they lived in the basement five years before they could afford to move upstairs.

The family wintered in Laramie where David, adjunct professor of geology, established and supervised the U.S. Geological Survey's research office. Jane had been a housemother at Bryn Mawr and taught science at Brearley, a girls' prep school in New York. Besides raising their children, she edited David's frequent writings, insisting that was not unusual. "All wives are supportive." David reiterates firmly that Jane "has always been my best critic and supporter," since she holds two degrees in geology.

Every summer, the Loves met new citizens of Jackson who loved the place and had found a job—but couldn't afford a decent house. As costs of land and construction rose along with living expenses, these newcomers often paid high prices for inadequate housing, or moved to a nearby town, driving dangerous highways all winter. So the Loves began renting their cabin during the winters, often at a lower cost than Jackson's average. Some renters worked to maintain or improve the house in lieu of rent.

"These people were essential citizens," Jane reminds me, "people who were charged with the education and well-being of the townspeople and their children." With a sly smile, David adds, "In fact, some of the most illustrious students in the Jackson schools were conceived in our house."

Like the modern settlers, the French-Canadian trappers who came to Jackson Hole in the 1820s were looking for a good life. Heading west, they probably mumbled about crowds in the eastern valleys. Later, whites christened the narrow valley for trapper Davy Jackson. Of course, the Crow, Blackfoot, Gros Ventre, and Shoshone had been hunting amid its warm springs and the adjacent Yellowstone geysers for centuries before.

In 1977, when the "beast of development" story appeared, Jackson Hole was still "the most intact ecosystem remaining in the lower 48 states," providing winter habitat for many species of wildlife, including the nation's largest elk herd. The Tetons towered over eighteen million acres of national parks, forests, wildlife refuges, and wilderness areas encircling 75,000 acres of private lands. Five thousand people lived in the county seat, another 4,000 in the county. Nearly four million other folks visited in 1976. Naturally, some wanted to stay, so county officials approved 1,054 subdivision lots between 1970 and 1976, expressing concern about the area's future.

During the 1970s, some Jackson residents talked of creating a coherent plan to keep growth from destroying its most attractive qualities. "We're all in this Hole together," said members of a steering committee, warning that the town faced "runaway boom and bust expansion which will hurt every one, grocer, motel owner, retailer and carpenter." When the population rose 11 percent in a single year, some residents predicted the valley would become "every man's tinsel town," with "a Kmart on every corner."

Other residents feared antidevelopment sentiment would curtail growth and reduce their earnings. One day three hundred Building Trades and Associates members drove every piece of heavy equipment they could find—including cement mixers and front-end loaders—to the street in front of the county courthouse. Protesters' signs read: "Karl Marx is alive and well; ask the County commissioners."

Still, commissioners approved a housing project on the former Rafter J ranch during the late 1970s, publicized as providing affordable housing lots for working people. However, no price restrictions were established. Such controls might guarantee a particular house remain perpetually affordable, but banks weren't anxious to loan money for building projects with price ceilings. Today, a Rafter J home trades for more than $250,000, too expensive for essential Jackson citizens like law enforcement officers or utility and telephone personnel.

Most Jackson residents embraced the theory of planning and zoning as a way of directing growth, but learned that putting the ideas into practice raised knotty problems. In 1977, after three years of deliberation, Jackson's first comprehensive development plan was approved. The momentum of change built so fast that Jackson officials had a hard time keeping up. In 1986, only 38 building permits were issued in Teton County. In 1989 the total was 180, and it rose to 200 by November of 1993. Before 1986, land prices averaged around $15,000 an acre, rising to $25,000 by 1993. In scenic areas, an acre cost $50,000. Home-buyers could expect to pay from $150,000 "up to the multimillions," said a county commissioner.

By 1986, J. David Love was widely known as "the grand old man of Rocky Mountain geology," and achieved more modest celebrity as the source for John McPhee's *Rising from the Plains*. While McPhee's topic was western geology, he was so charmed by David's love of his subject and his state, as well as by his family's intriguing history, that the book strayed miles from its apparent topic, even including selections from the unpublished manuscripts and diaries of Ethel Waxham Love, who wrote of her life on the isolated Love ranch in the middle of Wyoming. J. David Love was born there in 1913 and educated mostly by his mother for his first eight years. He received his B.A. and M.A. from the University of Wyoming and his Ph.D. from Yale. Working for energy companies, he explored for oil in the southern Appalachians and elsewhere before coming home to Wyoming.

As the years passed, the list of people who had rented the Loves' house during the winter grew with the town. Moving on, those renters often asked if they could buy some of the Loves' six acres in Jackson. But, says Jane, "as values skyrocketed, none of them could afford it."

"So you need a place to live?" asked a 1993 headline in the *Jackson Hole Guide*. "Chances are, you're out of luck." Rental operations reported 100 percent occupancy at the beginning of the summer. The good news: Teton County's unemployment rate was only 1 percent, the lowest in the state, with an average of nearly one job for every man, woman, and child in the county.

The bad news? Most of the jobs were in service industries where minimum wages didn't keep up with inflation. The county couldn't hire a planner until it boosted the salary from $45,000 to $51,000 a year.

County commissioners investigating other housing plans learned that no single formula guarantees success. Each plan, including federal subsidies, offered new complications. For example, federal Minimum Property Standards, applied by both the Farmers Home Administration and the Department of Housing and Urban Development, effectively prohibit small, basic houses. Other financing plans created new obstacles. In Aspen, Colorado, the average cost of a house soared above $1.5 million in 1994; even doctors lived in government-subsidized housing. The Colorado ski resort started its affordable housing scheme with a $6 million bond sale and used a special sales tax and a 1 percent real estate transfer tax to provide $2 million a year in housing subsidies. But in Teton County, where real estate sales were $286 million in 1994, commissioners lacked the authority to initiate transfer taxes on real estate revenues.

Jackson newspapers regularly reported housing needs. In May of 1992, the *Jackson Hole News* observed that "hundreds of seasonal workers are needed to make beds, cook meals, and wash dishes, but there are never enough accommodations to go around." Once the summer workforce filled apartments, motel rooms, and campgrounds, some camped in the woods around Jackson. If federal land managers tried to enforce restrictions limiting length of stay in one spot, workers moved their camps. Temporary camping trailers and pickups with toppers filled every alley in Jackson. As town planner Bruce Bowman put it, "If you had anything—a chicken coop—you could rent it in the summer."

Local governments were having difficulty "hiring entry-level employees like policemen and teachers," said the News, because they couldn't find housing. "Teachers are discovering they cannot afford to move here because modest starter homes cost $120,000."

In 1993, a population survey for the Alliance for Responsible Planning and Jackson Hole Chamber of Commerce estimated the peak summer population at 52,000 people. Three out of four were tourists, second-home owners, and seasonal workers. The business consultant who did the survey predicted that if tourist numbers increased in proportion to the anticipated increase in residents, more than 100,000 people would squeeze into the valley each summer—a prospect he called "alarming."

Meanwhile, in a 1992 cost-of-living survey, Jackson topped the list of Wyoming towns in every category: housing, medical care, clothing, food, transportation, and a combination described as "recreation and personal care." With the state's average cost of living expressed as 100 points, Jackson hit 133.7. During the fourth quarter of 1992, average rent for an unfurnished two-bedroom apartment in Jackson was $659, up 11.7 percent from the year before and more than twice the state average. A mobile home, including lot, rented for $475, up 17.3 percent from the year before. The state average was $318.

As land prices rose, Jackson gained and lost population at the same time. While new business and high-class developments spread, the workforce kept moving "over the hill," commuting more than a hundred miles to work and back from villages and towns in Wyoming and Idaho. While some residents wrote letters to the editor, others just grumbled into their beer about capitalism and the American Way. Predictably, neighboring towns began to protest collecting fallout from Jackson's growth.

"Victor, Driggs and Alpine get our service workers. Sublette County gets our garbage. And Dubois gets our gravel pit," said a news story in October of

1993. "Our neighbors aren't going to take care of Jackson's growth problems much longer." Worried that Bondurant would become a bedroom community for Jackson, Sublette County commissioners adopted a zoning plan requiring each home to be situated on thirty-five acres. County Clerk Mary Lankford said, "I think that people here want to preserve the quality of life we have now. They don't want to see us turn into another Jackson."

On the other side of Togwotee Pass, Fremont County residents declared that they paid the price for Jackson citizens' desire to preserve their vistas and watersheds. A gravel pit three hundred yards from a subdivision ran day and night, creating dust and noise, chasing wildlife from the Du Noir drainage.

"Teton County buying gravel from Fremont is fossil-fuel environmentalism," said Anna Moscicki, a former Jackson councilwoman who had moved to Dubois, explaining the prevailing attitude. "Your own back yard is very precious, but it's OK to burn millions of gallons of fuel to get gravel from someone else's back yard."

After years of watching Jackson struggle with planning issues, citizens of the nearby towns realized how much they'd learned from observation. They were more determined than ever to preserve, in their towns, the atmosphere that attracted all those people to Jackson. Residents of Driggs and Victor, Idaho, used to refer to planning and zoning as "the P and Z words," equating them with other profanities. Attitudes have changed. Teton Valley, Idaho, for example, is creating a district zoned for commercial use, and has formed a land trust to preserve open space. Newcomers receive *A Homeowner's Handbook for Living in Teton Valley*, a nifty guide providing information about local planning law as well as basic information about the local ecosystem—history, a soil map, facts about local water, wildlife, grazing, fencing, storm preparations, laws about horses and dogs—intended to help them make informed choices about living there.

Dave Martin, owner of the Aspen Meadows Subdivision—the one next to the gravel pit—summed up the change in thinking. "We have to get smart like Teton County." Suddenly, many groups were working on some aspect of preservation. South of Dubois, for example, the Nature Conservancy was given part of the 4,738-acre Red Canyon Ranch, considered important big-game winter range. The group bought more of the property to keep it from vanishing under developments called "ranchettes."

Meanwhile, in 1990, a handful of Jackson citizens established the Jackson Hole Community Housing Trust as a private, nonprofit organization dedicated to creating affordable housing. In a typical Trust home sale, the land under the house is leased and the resale price is permanently restricted. Trust officials have often persuaded businesses to make particular donations. The Jackson Hole Ski Resort, for example, twice donated half its "pre-opening day" lift-ticket sales to community organizations, including the Trust.

In July 1993, the Housing Trust, in partnership with the Teton County Housing Authority, broke ground for its first project, Mountain View Meadows, a total of thirty-six homes on 4.5 acres. By the spring of 1994, thirteen families chosen from more than seventy applicants owned their first homes. The new homeowners, who'd lived in the valley an average of eleven years, drew household incomes ranging from $17,000 to $32,800. They included a bookkeeper, a bar manager, waitress, bus driver, mechanic, a photo editor and assistant, computer software technician, a couple of fishing guides, a school custodian, purchasing manager, secretary, sales director, and an emergency medical technician.

Prices of the one- to three-bedroom homes varied from $62,300 to $87,900, with monthly mortgage payments from $460 to $636. In addition to a lease fee for the ground on which the home stood, homeowners paid dues of around sixty dollars a month for upkeep of the development. One new owner, Karla Swiggum, said she'd moved twelve times in ten years, doing the "typical Jackson Hole shuffle," before she was able to settle down.

Late that year, the U.S. Department of Housing and Urban Development (HUD) called the Mountain View Meadows project "the most successful project of its kind in Wyoming" and commended the project's builders—Teton County Housing Authority and Jackson Hole Community Housing Trust—for their persistence. Many similar agencies had become disillusioned by the difficulty of creating such projects in a boom atmosphere, said acting state HUD coordinator Bill Garrett, but "these guys stuck with it." Bill Knight, director of the Housing Authority, noted that "in an era of serious government bashing, I have to say that my experience with state and federal governmental agencies has been nothing but satisfying."

In the middle of Jackson's unrest over planning and development, J. David Love and his wife, Jane, were pondering what to do with land they owned in Jackson. They said later, "If we had sold our six acres on the hillside to the first developer who approached us about six years ago, it would have been covered with condos."

For example, Manuel Lopez, owner of Snow King Resort, wanted to build another ski run. Jane's reply? "Manuel, you're part of the problem. You bring people in to ski and for summer recreation and of course they want to stay."

The couple examined their alternatives and consulted their four children, who agreed with their decision. Always practical, Jane says, "It just seemed to me no one wanted to do anything about the housing shortage. We thought it was time to put our money where our mouth was. Since we never had any money ourselves and therefore wouldn't miss it, we said, 'Why don't we just give it to them?'"

The couple approached the Jackson Hole Community Housing Trust and offered to help create affordable housing in Jackson by donating slightly more than an acre of their six. "We didn't know a thing about trusts when we made the decision," say the Loves.

Jane added, "We'd received a few surprise gifts and helping hands in our lives and thought it would be nice to pass them along to other young people struggling to get a leg up." She smiles. "It's nice to surprise someone else."

The idea of the community land trust (CLT) has ancient roots in the view that the earth is naturally given, or God-given, to all people in common. The principle that people cannot own land absolutely is deeply embedded in the Judeo-Christian tradition, though Americans have altered the way we look at property. In India, a successor to Mahatma Gandhi initiated a voluntary land-gift program that eventually centered on villages. The Jewish National Fund of Israel is a countrywide land trust. In Mexico and Tanzania, government land reform policies have given trusteeship of local land to village communities.

In America, the CLT was conceived in the 1960s as a democratically controlled nonprofit institution designed to hold land for the common good of any neighborhood, while making it available to individuals through long-term leases. A typical CLT acquires land through purchase or donation, retaining title and thus removing the land permanently from the speculative market. Trust members determine what is appropriate use for the property, and the land can be leased to individuals, families, cooperatives, community organizations, businesses, or for public purposes. No seller can profit from unearned increases in market value, and no buyer can be priced out of the market.

Nationally, CLTs are often combined with other methods of controlling land use, such as conservancy trusts and limited equity cooperatives. Different models serve the needs of various communities. The most important element seems to be people of goodwill who talk honestly about their community, its needs, and the threats to those qualities. As the former president of the Jackson Hole Community Housing Trust, Loring Woodman, observed in 1994, "There are good people at all levels of the economy. They contribute in necessary and meaningful ways. If we value their work, we should be able to find them a place at the table."

During 1995, the Jackson Hole Community Housing Trust developed a partial solution to financing its current work. Jess Lederman, its new director, had been a private investor on Wall Street. In his book *Housing America,* Lederman documented the most successful affordable housing programs in the country. The most successful communities, Lederman believed, "the ones with the highest quality of life," are those that found ways to help residents of all income levels to own homes, communities "where as many people as possible had an equity stake in their neighborhood."

Lederman announced that the Trust was "selling the ground lease fees" from housing projects as a low-risk, high-yield investment. Investors would be repaid over a thirty-year period from homeowners' monthly lease payments. He also devised a "double-barreled donation" program whereby an individual could exchange a gift to the Trust for their selected charity's chance to receive a portion of future ground lease fees.

In the meantime, people continued to surge into Jackson Hole. A local consulting firm, Summit Perspectives, said the average price of a home reached $561,485 during the first half of 1994, up 46 percent over the year before. More than a hundred residential lots sold, averaging $339,403 each. Officials estimated that four hundred people still didn't have affordable housing, and predicted another tax increase. They warned homeowners to expect at least $650 in taxes for every $100,000 in property value.

Middle-class Jackson residents joked that the town's rich suffer from a disorder known as "square foot envy": everybody wanted a house bigger than his neighbor's. While longtime residents crooned lullabies about "accrued market value," few volunteered to share the wealth.

"Our land has gained in value," Jane said, "not due to anything we have done to improve it, but as a result of changes in the community. We'd like to give some of that accrued value back to the community." In private, her voice rises a bit, "When you have so much, how can you not *share?*"

David interprets the gift as a simple extension of the traditional western neighborliness. Besides, he added in 1994, "I'm eighty-one. We're not going to be able to live forever, and we're not going to be able to take it with us." He chuckles, picturing their property "trundling along behind a hearse."

Loring Woodman, former president of the Housing Trust, says, "They did it because it's the right thing to do to maintain the community." Few people knew of the Love gift until 1994, when the issue of affordable housing in Jackson became considerably more complicated.

An October 1992 editorial in the *Jackson Hole News* expressed a familiar cynicism about benefactors, saying the family's gift was unique because of "their financial profile—hardly rich." In the next breath, the writer hinted at the acrimony surrounding the affordable housing movement, saying the gift was also unique because "the donation is a true gift, not something wrested from them through a planning process or given as a condition of approval for some development."

As the Loves worked with the Housing Trust, they also talked with developer Manuel Lopez, finding a way to continue, as Jane says, "having our cake and eating it, too." Giving an acre to the Housing Trust dedicated it immediately and perpetually to affordable housing while providing a generous tax break for the Loves. Jane notes with satisfaction that they saved the view for Jackson residents as well.

Snow King Resort eventually won approval to build forty condominiums and expand its ski run on Love Ridge, uphill from the Housing Trust development. The rest of the skiing operation stands on land leased from the Forest Service.

In September 1996, a bulldozer dropped its blade at the base of Snow King Mountain, breaking ground for fifteen affordable homes on land the Loves had given to the Jackson Hole Community Trust. Called Flat Iron Townhomes, the development was named for the livestock brand registered by David's father about 1905, still owned by the family, and one of the oldest brands in Wyoming. The original Love house had been sold and moved, though the nearby spring is still used for irrigation.

Most of the guests gathered for the ceremony turned their backs to crudely painted billboards along the property line. "J.H.C.H.T. IS A HOAX—A LONG-TERM TIME-SHARE JOKE—NOT FOR WORKING FOLKS—AFFORDABLE HOUSING THIS IS NOT!" The signs were one part of a protest to the Flat Iron housing development organized by neighbors who owned adjacent property. The organizer was a native son who had recently returned to Jackson after years in Alaska as a deep-sea diver and was shocked at the changes.

"This is where I grew up," he said, gesturing to the grassy hillside at the base of the mountain. He disagreed with the Trust's approach to affordable housing. "If these people met the codes," he said, "we'd welcome them as good neighbors." Another neighbor, who owns adjoining property zoned for greater density than the Flat Iron, added, "We need rent and loan assistance, not condos in competition with currently available housing." The two opponents, contending that the Flat Iron's high density and tall buildings were out of place in their locale, collected fifty signatures from neighbors who agreed.

Opponents also pointed out that Jackson's planning director had recommended against approval of the Flat Iron and filed an appeal when the town council approved the development anyway. Trust officials met with some of the protestors, and the Trust revised Flat Iron plans in response to their concerns. Eliminating one planned unit made Flat Iron's density equal to that of the adjacent Pitchfork Townhouses. Trust planners shifted and lowered other buildings, agreed to leave hedges along a property line, and said opponents had helped improve the development.

In September the two opponents, one by then running for a seat on the town council, asked for a temporary injunction to halt construction of the Flat Iron development. Trust officials, stunned, estimated an interruption in building would cause the organization to lose an estimated $2.9 million. A construction supervisor said his company would have to lay off sixty employees if the job was stopped, and that a delay until the next spring would add $700,000 to building costs. Judge Nancy Guthrie of the Ninth District Court refused to grant the injunction unless the opponents posted a $200,000 bond to cover costs of putting construction on hold. When opponents failed to post the bond, the Housing Trust continued to screen buyers for the Love homes.

David and Jane Love maintained public silence about the controversy until December 31, 1996, when they wrote a guest editorial for the *Jackson Hole News*. "We sympathize," they said, with the leading opponent's "dismay at the many changes that have taken place in the community in the almost twenty years of his absence," adding that they often felt overwhelmed by the "tide of humanity that has arrived and needs accommodation in housing, traffic patterns, fire and police protection, human services."

They invited those who challenged the development to look through back issues of local newspapers and read the minutes of town meetings as a way of understanding that many people in Jackson were trying to meet the same goals: keeping the town livable for everyone.

"We are sorry," the Loves continued, "that our former neighbors are upset by our decision to donate land to the Housing Trust," and noted that they'd invited neighbors to their home to discuss the plan. "We appreciate their reluctance to lose the hillside, just as we regretted the building of over thirty townhouses across from our front door and the snuffing out of our view of the Tetons by a two-story apartment building next door."

Acknowledging their neighbors' objections and their own reservations about the town's transformation, they reminded readers of the forces that alter our countryside: "Though we would have preferred not to be part of changing forever the area so many of us have enjoyed for years, escalating taxes and other trends in the neighborhood made us feel it was time to leave. . . . It's true," they concluded, "that the quality of living—the old-time feeling—is no longer what it was, but that is the price all must pay."

Challenges to the Flat Iron documents have continued for several years. Legal documents filed by each side, and court actions taken on those documents, totaled 104 by January of 2002. The *Jackson Hole News* later commented editorially that "the sense of community we grew up with or moved here to share has been shredded in pitched battles regarding our future," leaving a "bitter aftertaste." In fact, the tangle of events surrounding the Flat Iron development is proof that no matter how seriously upset we may all be about change in our neighborhoods, we are ultimately powerless against a new reality.

Still, other Jackson residents were learning about the aims of the Housing Trust and beginning to inquire about other gifts that might ease the housing shortage. One longtime resident has willed her home to the Trust. David Love says he has spoken with several large landowners who want to explore ways they might contribute money or land to the general welfare of Jackson. Stanley Resor, whose family had owned one of the valley's largest ranches since the 1930s, donated to the Housing Trust 3.4 acres in his posh Granite Ridge subdivision, saying he'd like teachers to receive first preference.

During the summer of 1997, homeowners moved into the Flat Iron project, enabling the Loves to observe the solid results of their donation. The average householder in the Love development had an income of $37,860 and had lived in Jackson more than ten years. The new residents included three bookkeepers, a nurse, a carpenter, two heavy machine operators, one teacher, one counselor, five retail managers, one escrow officer, three retail clerks or assistants, two bank employees, a legal assistant, and a utility lineman. There were three newlywed couples and a total of three children.

"My parents moved to Jackson when I was eight years old," said one of the brides. "I loved growing up here." She and her husband had looked at houses for a year before choosing the Flat Iron development. "Now we just need some furniture."

Another homeowner teaches elementary music at several schools in Jackson Hole. His wife is a therapist in the community counseling center. For two years, with their nine-year-old son, they'd rented a home while looking for property they could afford. He wrote to the Loves to express appreciation and respect for their generosity, a letter that can symbolize the best results to be expected from such a gift.

Jackson was "the perfect place for us to call home," he wrote, recalling how his grandfather hunted and fished on horseback in the nearby Wind River Mountains, swapping stories with other sportsmen in the Silver Dollar, a classic Jackson bar. "My parents were raised on farms near Pavillion, Wyoming, and I tell people (with a certain amount of pride) that when I was born my parents lived at Home On The Range, WY (now called Jeffrey City)."

Following a typical pattern for young people in sparsely settled states like Wyoming, the writer left the state when he was twenty-five. But "no matter how hard I tried, I could never shake that deep, ever-present pull to come back." His wife, however, was skeptical. She'd grown up in New York and the San Francisco Bay Area and "was not at all comfortable with the general setting here in Wyoming," though she agreed to consider Jackson. Her husband was dubious about the chances for both partners to find jobs, but they did so with "perseverance, prayer, and a bit of luck!" adding, "It is difficult to express the feeling of peace and contentment that I have felt since we moved back." Standing on the ridge top where David and Jane Love moved into a basement home and scrimped to add a window a year, the new homeowner tells how he loves to gaze at the surrounding beauty, to breathe clean mountain air. "I am finally in a place where I feel that I can make a difference," he writes, "and enjoy what the community has to offer, and where I can begin to contribute to the community and truly be 'at home.'"

Besides recounting his own journey and his pleasure in his new home, this townsman considered how other residents of Jackson have been affected by their city's growth. "It seems to me that it is good to try to maintain a balance between tradition and change," he remarks. "I feel that this is the essence of Jackson Hole and of many of the people who live here. Your gift of land to the Housing Trust exemplifies this seemingly contradictory yet complementary balance."

Apparently the letter writer, like the Love family, and like the members of the Housing Trust and other citizen groups working to save what is best about their community, would agree with classicist Edith Hamilton about the duty that residents of a place have to others. Hamilton said, "When the freedom they wished for most was freedom from responsibility, then Athens ceased to be free and was never free again."

CODA

WALKING BURIAL GROUNDS

"Prairie Rest" reads the sign at the cemetery gates. My notion of rest differs from my dog's, but we're both anxious to pause after several hours of bouncing over narrow plains roads.

These prairie rests are one reason I drive to most of the readings or workshops I present. Travel by car offers hours of uninterrupted thought, pleasure in silence and scenery on the way to agreeable labor. My perversity in avoiding airplanes may be one reason I'm almost unknown more than two states away from home. Publicity experts advise me to promote myself more. They don't say I'd be publicizing my work, but my *self,* as if the body, not the words, was important. Wandering among the ranks of the dead reduces my worry over the value of such advertising to its proper measure.

Below this knoll, a couple of cumbersome locomotives are swapping places on entwined tracks. On chalky cliffs rising south of the two-street town, thousands of immigrants cut their names, waiting for the oxen to rest on the overland journey. Thousands more, coming through in the century since those first travelers passed, carved their names as well, and are now scorned for defacing the history we recognize in the earlier names. Steadily, the wind etches its own history, perpetually erasing the human testimony.

I park in the shade of a spruce tree planted by someone who decided to stay here, rather than pass by, and fill Frodo's water dish from my bottle. He scrambles over the backseat and tumbles out, and we drink together in the shade. Zigzagging, he maneuvers to pass every carefully tended tree, connecting the dots in yellow along his route. His behavior is never improper. He centers his attention on trees and larger bushes, sniffing at tombstones only if he finds evidence of mice.

I walk fast, swinging my arms and legs, bending and stretching to work the stiffness out of my shoulders. Comfortable in cemeteries, I don't whistle to frighten ghosts, even after dark. The worst dangers on the prairie are above-ground, and noise is no protection. On the contrary, in graveyards, I sense a friendly crowd making their presence known in quiet whispers that might be the sound of grass.

Sprinklers count cadence for my exercise, whispering news bulletins about shrinking aquifers beneath my feet. Irrigated grass is clipped short and fabulously green, disavowing its location. Pioneer settlers of this gaunt prairie would stare in wonder if they rose up through the sham sod on this hot June day.

A shoulder-high metal shaft, now empty, once provided a faucet for passersby. I read the Spanish surname on the green bronze plate aloud, thanking them for the thought. The modern watering system has no provision for thirsty strangers, human or canine.

Stones above these dead affirm their plains setting. Among the familiar uprights of commercially polished marble stand homemade concrete slabs. "Let's put pretty rocks in Grandma's stone," someone said, pressing into the damp mortar bits of quartz and granite, mica and agate, feldspar and chert. A sparkling geode stands on top, nearest heaven.

For a little while, in earth's time frame, these headstones will offer terse clues to the unwritten accounts dispersed under the sod.

In a city cemetery I visit often, one concrete stone is plastered smooth and white, with a design outlined on it in whiter shells. No name, no date. Another stone bears a carving of a man on a motorcycle, leaning to speed around one final curve. Japanese stones stand only a modest foot or two high, with a single line of characters I cannot read. Rows of ribbony agates march down the vertical stalk of a concrete cross; those embedded on the horizontal arm spell "Mother." Did she walk the prairie collecting them, peering among grasses and sagebrush, arranging her favorites on the windowsill above the sink? I hope she's pleased her family used them to decorate her modest marker.

My favorite grave in that cemetery is marked only by a scarred anvil fixed to a plain granite base. The message is clear. The man whose name does not matter to me was a hard worker, a blacksmith. Birds may splash his badge with manure; vandals may try in vain to knock it over or steal it. Eventually, rust may pare it down. But the anvil may endure after polished marble has been overcome by weather. It will speak its judgment as long as its shape can be understood—and I cannot help wondering how long that will be.

These days, few professions can be so deftly and durably portrayed. A personal computer wouldn't last long.

In old burial grounds, I sometimes find a sunken site without a stone, as carefully watered and clipped as the other graves. With no emblem to guide my speculation, I usually stop to wonder what sort of life ended here. Why was no time or money spent on the final symbolic gesture? Was the survivors' love, and perhaps their cash, spent instead on the living?

An hour down the twisty Wyoming road, I pause at another cemetery lying on a flat shelf above a creek. Rounded hills dotted with sagebrush overlook the valley. A few lilac bushes survive among the graves, but sandburs are more common. Here are no trees for Frodo to water, but he investigates the spindly bushes. The grass is deep, and several rusty spigots lead to lengths of black plastic pipe trickling into green stripes among the graves. Slim crosses tower hot and stark above beds of crushed white quartz. Some plots are entirely caged in black wrought iron, vibrating against the breeze. Names like Severini, Corrigan, Lopez, and Pantzapoulos croon a tale of miners with picks and shovels, the dust of the far countries of their origin mingling with the loam of this valley.

Set into some of the stones are delicately colored oval portraits, their paint as fresh as yesterday's bouquet. I study the faces, looking for the tenacity or desperation that brought them to this desert gulch. A recent stone is etched with figures wearing helmets and numbered football jerseys, below notes from a song I cannot hum. Close by stands a glass-enclosed football.

Frodo flushes a rabbit and gallops down an aisle between the stones, yipping in frenzy. Turning to keep him in sight, I see a man standing on a nearby hill, shovel in hand, watching me. I wave and walk down the path after the dog, calling loudly to show I am no vandal, that I do not allow my dog to behave like a Visigoth.

Near my car, parked on the shoulder of the gravel road, is the black silhouette of a riding boot announcing a separate plot, graves fenced in rough, weathered boards and rusty barbed wire. Several sunken burial spots are corralled by pickets weathered to splinters. Only when I walk between the two rows of graves do I realize they are tiny. Over one, quartz pebbles in a rough concrete slab with worn horseshoes embedded in its base spell out "Baby Pinkerton 1897." A pink quartz heart reads "Little Benny Trahan, d. 1909." Graying boards, face down in long grass, recall another baby, anonymous now, returning to cracked earth. The grass here is crisp and shattered, sunburned.

T. S. Eliot said, "No honest poet can ever feel quite sure of the permanent value of what he has written; he may have wasted his time and messed up his life for nothing." I've never delivered a child, but my hours scribbling words on paper have spawned volumes tucked into a narrow space on my shelves. Yet despite the esteem given to people who create, our only value as humans may be our eventual descent into earth. My worth may exceed Baby Pinkerton's only because I weigh more, have more to give back to the ground. Like these children, I will nourish the grass in one tiny spot for generations of antelope, and perhaps cows.

As I open the car door, my eye fastens on a cruciform line where none should be, at the foot of a limestone outcropping on the other side of a field. Squinting, I can see several weathered crosses leaning against a modest cliff, surrounded by berry bushes and a few tall elms.

Sensing my hesitation, Frodo jumps out again, tail wagging and ears erect, and races off. I'm halfway to the little group of markers when a jackrabbit springs from a clump of sagebrush. Averaging five feet a jump, he is in no danger from the short-legged dog yipping and sprinting in his wake. Jackrabbits have become rare on the prairie. Maybe fear of dogs will help him survive.

Reaching the cliff, I find the crosses are small, pushed into mounds of earth no larger than the dog. I hope this is where children in the nearby town bury their pets, but I'm not sure. Some of the crosses are fragile with age, bearing names once deeply carved. The creek running below the cemetery may have altered its course, as mining by the Severini, Corrigan, and Lopez menfolk changed the contour of the valley. The elms are tall and old. Perhaps death and burials occurred before the citizens chose a cemetery site. Maybe bereaved mothers buried their children in this shaded cluster, pretending they were temporarily away on a picnic.

Pets or children? I sit in the shade watching the dog sniff the rabbit's spoor. We are so proud of the great memorial monuments we leave behind us, but the dog can find no satisfaction in them. Even his sensitive nose will find no trace of the humanity beneath the largest stone. The rabbit's single brief sprint writes a more meticulous story on the earth and wind than a slab of marble ten feet tall, carved with a lifetime's accomplishments.

Two hours farther along the road, in South Dakota, I impulsively turn into a well-known trail leading to a gumbo hill where familiar flesh lies, my grandmother, beside the step-grandfather I never knew. Her first husband died under the wheels of a logging train in Oregon and is buried with his family in Wyoming. At twenty-two, she became a widow with two children.

From this particular cemetery hill, the Cheyenne River is a muddy trickle, but a month ago I drove across the massive highway bridge and felt it shiver with the weight of a flood swirling beyond the channel past the ancient cottonwoods at its edge. During several long nights one summer, I lay in my tipi listening to those cottonwood leaves murmur stories, tales of those who camped there before us.

A new highway passes over the railroad tracks that brought fortunes to a few, skirting a town so eager for growth it volunteered to store the radioactive waste no other city in the nation wanted. On the eastern horizon stands the novel profile of a hill named for a frontiersman and rancher who snatched thousands of acres surrounding the town. He and most of his descendants now occupy smaller plots of land close by.

Burial fashions differ from one community to another. On this hill, tons of gravel and concrete imprison the grave earth. Perhaps their heirs expect the dead to bubble up through the tough grass and walk the night. Low walls surround some family plots, the great gray slabs smooth and unbroken. Elsewhere the shabby expanse is cracked and weed-covered. Perhaps the family has died out or moved. Or maybe concrete offers no opportunity for repair, only replacement. On newer sites, a thin green mat, plastic posing as grass, covers the conglomerate. At least it requires no water. A blue storage tank for the town stands ominously at the crest of the burial hill.

In the far bare corner of the exposed hillside, I find myself again surrounded by babies. Someone once cut sandstone squares, carving names and dates into the face of each stone. The shapeless lumps melt into gumbo where wild iris barely survive. A triangular nugget of deep pink quartz is veined with glittering mica. I'm surprised someone hasn't dug it up for a lawn ornament, until I think where I am. The folks who stayed on this prairie understood that keeping a fence meant setting anchor posts deep. Like an iceberg, the invisible part of the stone may be larger than its tapered point.

Back in the car I pour water for the panting dog, and pick ticks off his ears while he gulps. The air is stale. I roll the windows down and cautiously drive a lane built for buggies to the road out.

Through the swirling dust from my tires, a white Madonna inside an upended bathtub waves a benediction. These odd creations are a phenomenon so strange they defy humor. I suppose they are practical. The fragile statues are doubtless expensive and might weather badly. Thrifty, we dislike waste—but how many uses can the average person find for a discarded bathtub? Some ranchers use them to water horses or calves. In my neighborhood, these are the same folks who line old machinery up on the hillside to rust, and dump their trash in a gully next to someone else's fence. A few people park old bathtubs on the lawn, filled with geraniums, but even with recycling in vogue I don't expect to see a Recycle Your Bathtub campaign. When we have finished the spendthrift phase of our development and must begin mining waste dumps for precious metals, will folks find a way to salvage these tons of metal? Will they be so desperate they'll even search the cemeteries, leaving the ladies in blue homeless?

Crossing a corner of Nebraska, I once stopped beside a log church built in the late 1800s by Bohemian immigrants. A mile ahead on the flat prairie I could see a farm. The one I'd passed two miles before was still visible. The churchyard was overgrown with grass, its fence drooping. As I began to walk among the prairie shafts, kneeling to pull the grass away so I could read epitaphs, a pickup left the farm ahead and cruised slowly toward me. I stood and waved at the farmer staring from behind the wheel. Touching his cap, he looked carefully at my Dakota license plates and turned back toward home. Ten minutes later, a car drove slowly by. I stood and waved again. The driver made a U-turn, heading back to the other farm. The dead may seem to lie alone here, far from civilization, but their neighbors still stand sentry.

One rough-cut granite boulder dominated, looming ten feet over the grass, one side beautifully carved into a columned portico emerging from the stone's natural surface. Perhaps the stone symbolized a well-established family leaving its ancestral holdings to transpose itself to a new land. Beside this stone stood a narrow pillar of the same dark gray granite. Both bore the same name. One of the men died at forty-eight in 1914; the other was twenty-four at his death in 1918.

Surrounding the father and son's shafts were nine small markers, two rows of white stones. Eight of the stones were crowned with the figure of a resting lamb; on the ninth, two lambs lay together.

For a half hour, I crawled along those tombstones, pulling grass away and scratching dirt from the incised letters with my fingernails before sitting back on my heels to stare. Each stone bore a girl's name with dates to show she lived no more than a week. All were buried here before the father and son.

I found no tombstone for a woman, no sunken unmarked rectangle. The mother is not buried with her flock of dead lambs, or beside her shepherd and her son.

When I climbed back into the car with the exhausted dog, the horizon was more distant than before, the route more hazardous. All afternoon, driving past neat farms, and for years since then, I have wondered about that wife and mother. Adding and subtracting, reflecting on the homesteaders' tendency to marry young women who could birth strong farmworkers, I realize she may still live. Perhaps she is an honored guest in the home of another child who inherited the family farm. Perhaps she moved away. Perhaps she simply crumpled and vanished in the eternal wind.

Don't ask me the family name, or tell me to search the county records. Official ledgers, their blanks filled by crisp black type on clean white paper, could not tell that woman's story. If I knew all the facts, wrote and rewrote until my words vibrated with truth and power, her story would not be mine. Her epic can never be whole unless she writes it herself.

Kneeling among her lambs, I breathed the dust of her dead, wept my own tears into sod that surely absorbed hers. Then the gusty silence. Then the grass.